SACRED TREASURE,
SECRET POWER

Also by Robin Mackness

ORADOUR:
Massacre and Aftermath

Guy Patton
and Robin Mackness

SACRED TREASURE, SECRET POWER

The True Story of the
Web of Gold

PAN BOOKS

First published 2000 by Sidgwick & Jackson

This edition published 2001 by Pan Books
an imprint of Macmillan Publishers Ltd
25 Eccleston Place, London SW1W 9NF
Basingstoke and Oxford
Associated companies throughout the world
www.macmillan.com

ISBN 0 330 37351 X

A CIP catalogue record for this book is available from
the British Library.

Typeset by SetSystems Ltd, Saffron Walden, Essex
Printed and bound in Great Britain by
Mackays of Chatham plc, Chatham, Kent

Acknowledgements

We would like to thank the following, among the many others who have helped in their own ways: Howard Barkway; Jon Boulter; Ian Campbell; Celia Brooke-Captier; Marcel Captier; Roger-René, Marie-Noelle and Tristan Dagobert; Luana Davie; Nicole Dawe; Madeleine Desmoulin; André Douzet; Barry Dunford; Alain Feral; Michael Gauffman; Nigel Graddon; Georges Keiss; James McGrath; Cecilia Merody; Alan and Frances Pearson; Jennifer Priestly; Gay Roberts; Jean-Luc Robin; Matthew Scanlon; the staff of Mill Hill Library; Derek and Dawn Stoller; Simon Trewin; Col. Barry Turner; Gordon Scott Wise; the members of the Rennes-le-Château Research Group; and our respective families for their tolerance and support during the preparation of this book.

G.P. & R.M.

Contents

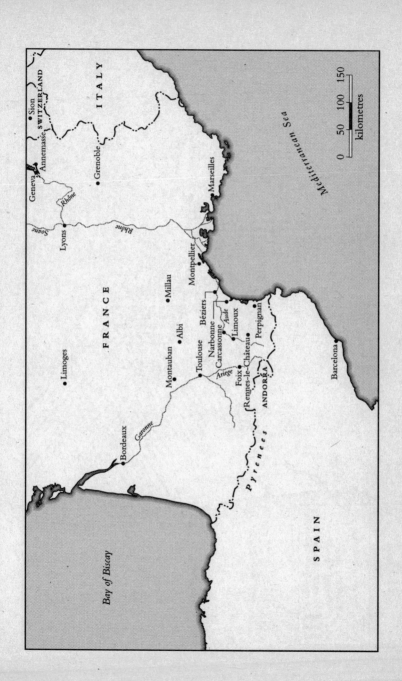

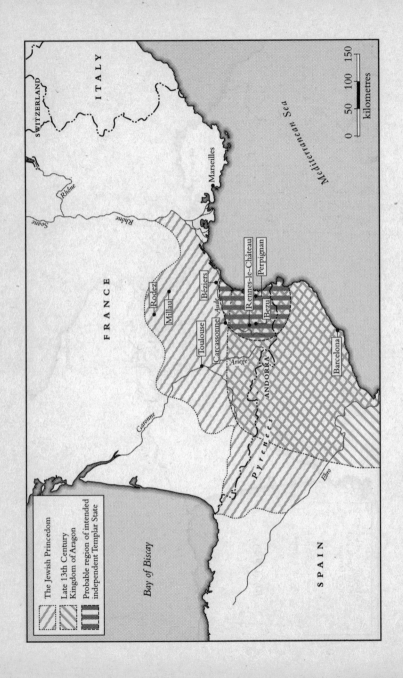

SWITZERLAND

ITALY

FRANCE

Rhône

Soane

Rhône

Garonne

Rodez

Millau

Toulouse

Carcassonne

Ariege

Aude

Béziers

Rennes-le-Château

Perpignan

Bézu

Marseilles

Mediterranean Sea

Pyrenees

ANDORRA

Ebro

Barcelona

SPAIN

Bay of Biscay

The Jewish Princedom

Late 13th Century
Kingdom of Aragon

Probable region of intended
independent Templar State

0   50   100   150
kilometres

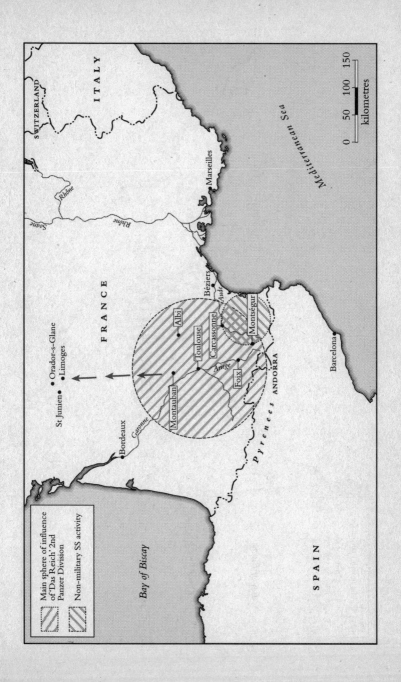

SWITZERLAND

ITALY

FRANCE

Rhône

Saône

Rhône

Marseilles

Mediterranean Sea

0   50   100 150
kilometres

St Junien•
• Limoges
• Orador-s-Glane

Béziers

Albi

Aude

Toulouse

Carcassonne

Montségur

Garonne

Montauban

Ariège

Foix

Bordeaux

Pyrenees

ANDORRA

Barcelona

Bay of Biscay

SPAIN

Main sphere of influence
of 'Das Reich' 2nd
Panzer Division

Non-military SS activity

Introduction by Robin Mackness

I FIRST MET Guy Patton because he wrote to me, having read my book *Oradour: Massacre and Aftermath* published in 1988. I had received quite a few letters at that time from other people, and I had learnt to treat them with caution. Some had been overtly hostile, accusing me of being anti-Semitic, anti-French, and a few other things besides. Some had purported to ask questions about the story, only to degenerate into open hostility when I endeavoured to answer them. A French telephone campaign against my wife and myself suggested we were on some sort of French hit-list, to the extent that we felt it prudent to change address.

I mention this partly to explain why I initially treated Guy with some circumspection, and partly to introduce the quite extraordinary fuss provoked in France by the book, the relevance of which was about to be revealed to me.

After a few exchanges of letters and telephone calls, I arranged to meet Guy. It seemed he had been engaged for a number of years in the historical research of an intriguing sequence of events and situations, which he was convinced, among many other things, explained the disagreeable lengths to which the French authorities had gone when investigating my own adventures. I had been stopped on the *autoroute* near

Lyon by French customs (although about 150 miles from the border) and accused of trying to smuggle twenty kilos of gold, some of it of Nazi provenance. What should have been a relatively simple matter, in the heart of France, became a twenty-one month nightmare of imprisonment and interrogation. Guy suspected that he knew the reason for this treatment, and the ideas he produced at our first meeting were quite staggering. It was not very long before I saw that some areas of his historical research that ended in question marks were explained (if not answered) by my own first-hand experiences.

Guy's research had been original and, as such, much of it was inevitably contentious. He was not merely serving up a rehash of well-established history, but was attempting to re-think much of what we all took for granted, and to establish some strands in an interpretation that was both new and frightening. There was clearly a case for cooperating to bring together our different parts of the same story.

The book that follows is our attempt to draw together some less obvious strands of European and Middle Eastern history which have emerged and developed over the past one thousand years to affect to a quite terrifying degree a number of events happening today.

The central theme of the book starts with the well-documented theft by the Romans of the Jewish treasure from the Temple in Jerusalem in AD70. Looted again, this time from Rome a few hundred years later, the treasure disappeared into the Pyrenees, since which time it has never been reliably seen again. Nevertheless we believe we can identify points in time when it has surely been bubbling just beneath the surface, given the activities of various individuals. Quite apart from the myths that have surrounded the treasure (and a few other treasures that seem to have become amassed with it), history has revealed such incidents as the French noblemen in medieval times, accused of counterfeiting currency. It was discovered that the counterfeit coins contained more gold than the official currency! At another time, an alchemist claimed to have perfected the secret of transforming base metals into gold, a feat that has eluded more sophisticated scientists. In more recent times, we have the impossible task of accounting for the wholly disproportionate activity on the part of Germans, including the SS, who spent years before World War II prospecting and digging in this part of the Pyrenees. During the war there continued to be much unexplained SS activity in the area. It has never been explained why such units should have been deployed so far from the front line, especially in time of crisis.

The strength of these local legends attracted serious attention long before the days of the SS. In 1244, the Crusaders cornered the heretic Cathars on the impressive mountaintop of Montségur in the name of defending 'orthodox' Christianity but probably more likely in an attempt to locate their alleged fabulous treasure. The Cathars submitted to being burnt alive, rather than reveal any details. It might seem unlikely that they would have willingly gone to such an agonizing death if they had had nothing to conceal. Again, in 1307, the French King Philip IV was envious of the vast wealth inexplicably amassed by the Knights Templar and, in an attempt to purloin it, he had as many Knights Templar as he could find arrested, tortured and put to death in a fruitless attempt to discover the source and whereabouts of their wealth.

More recently, it seems highly probable from the connections we have uncovered that Francois Mitterrand's presidential campaign was helped by the French secret society, the Priory of Sion, whose Grand Master claims to be the custodian of the treasure, and, indeed, admitted transfering a vast quantity of unexplained gold to a Swiss bank in the years after World War II. That same Grand Master has been quoted as saying that the Jerusalem treasure will be returned to Israel and the Jews 'when the time is right' – although the criteria for that condition have not been specified. All French secret societies are obliged to register and lodge their statutes and objectives with a local police headquarters, a condition required by a central government paranoid about secret societies since the experiences of the Revolution. The Priory of Sion chose to lodge its statutes at Annemasse, near Geneva, on the Swiss border (although the statutes were actually registered at nearby St Julien en Genevoise). This choice of location was to have unfortunate consequences for me, for that is where I had told the French customs officials where I was headed, and possibly contributed to my harsh treatment, although it added enormously to the relevance of much of what follows in this book.

Our story necessarily falls into two quite distinct parts: before and after 1914. They centre on the breakdown of European order brought about by the Great War. The indiscriminate and largely pointless slaughter in that conflict heralded the breakdown and eventual destruction of confidence in anything of permanence or predictability. That confidence had been the cornerstone of the former old order. The United Nations, and the League of Nations before it, were established in part as an attempt to fill the vacuum left by the collapse of the old order, which had been in terminal decline since 1914. Gone were the days when a Queen Victoria, the 'Grandmother of Europe', could wag a reproving finger at some errant cousin – perhaps a tsar or a kaiser – thereby restoring international harmony and compliance.

With the collapse of the old order, we also see the decline of faith and, more importantly, a rising scepticism in the true motives behind faith. The previous unassailability of the Vatican, for example, is now seen by many as very open to question. From its stance in World War II, the Vatican probably saw Communism as a greater ongoing threat than Nazism. This was inevitably but a small jump from the appearance of favouring Nazis over the Jews. In the context of the twentieth century, political alignments of this sort have brought into hostile question the true motives for many of the Vatican's historical actions, hostility that the Vatican has done little to quell. It remains tight-lipped about the more contentious parts of its history, on which it could certainly shed new light. It has been adamant in keeping its wartime records closed even to the extent of refusing to participate in the 1997 London conference on the so-called Jewish heirless assets (although it sent silent observers to that conference). Political expediency and faith are uneasy bedfellows; it has not gone unnoticed that with the effective demise of Communism as a world force, the Vatican appears to have regrouped to face what it probably sees as the new threat to its dominance: the rising tide of Islam. This regrouping may even involve a fragile *rapprochement* with the Jews; consider the declaration that Christians are no longer to hold the Jews responsible for the death of Christ. There is even the suggestion that the next pope might be of Jewish origins.

The assumed existence of this vast treasure, still hidden somewhere in the Pyrenees, has been a constant factor in the shadowier areas of European politics, particularly in those areas where the influence of secret societies is felt. But the covert level of politics has always been enormously influential, and probably never more so than in the twentieth century. Mass communications and the consequent insatiable demand for information has encouraged the growth of covert organizations, whose work can only be conducted outside the glare of public attention and accountability.

The last century saw a proliferation of secret or semi-secret societies, each with their own agendas and objectives. The Freemasons and the Knights Templar date back to antiquity, and some branches today wield awesome power. It has been claimed – with much justification – that the P2 Masonic Lodge could have brought down the Italian government, providing as it did a government-in-waiting, in the event of a Communist takeover. It certainly shook the Vatican to its roots, almost bankrupting the Vatican's own bank.

France is riddled with such secret societies, backing a range of activities, including the restoration of the monarchy (for which there is surprising support in France). It is not for nothing that France's rulers have sought to centralize everything of substance in Paris, keeping real power under their control and away from the provinces. For 200 years, France's rulers have been able to resist the spectre of overmighty provincial subjects taking to the barricades. This dread is also no doubt the reason behind the French penchant for political intervention – often blatant – in the judicial process. And since the Revolution also dispossessed the Church of Rome, clandestine forces have been able to occupy the vacuum.

At a more personal level, it is perhaps not surprising that the *cognoscenti* in Paris were driven to such excitement when they learnt that I had been stopped in my Swiss car on the *autoroute* near Lyon, having driven from Toulouse in the Pyrenees with twenty kilos of gold. My initial interrogation by customs centred on their wish for me to reveal where the gold had come from and to admit that I was taking it to Switzerland – a not unreasonable assumption since I lived in Lausanne at the time. In fact, I was delivering the gold to a contact in Evian, on the French southern shore of Lake Geneva, but I realized that to have admitted this would have had disagreeable consequences for my contact there. I therefore invented the destination of Annemasse to give my contact an opportunity to make himself scarce when I failed to arrive. This arbitrary choice of declared destination prompted a run of telephone calls and a great deal of excitement among my inquisitors.

When I met Guy ten years later he was able to suggest a possible reason for this. All I knew at the time was that the whole manner of my interrogation changed from that point on. The violence and menaces of one of my interrogators immediately abated, and there was a wholly disproportionate emphasis placed on the significance of Annemasse and why I was going there. Of course, the relevance of this escaped me at the time; I was just relieved that they were now concentrating on Annemasse rather than anywhere else and, to be frank, my very real relief that they now ceased their physical and distasteful attempts to have me admit all manner of other things. I noted all of this in the relative peace and quiet of Bonneville Prison during the following weeks, where I was able to write some 250,000 words of a diary, without appreciating more than a tiny iota the true significance of the events I was living through. This diary was posted out in instalments, under the guise of letters to my wife in Lausanne. All letters (apart from letters to lawyers) went through a censor, but since I had no idea of the significance of Annemasse, those letters contained nothing that could have done anything to raise the temperature of any excitement or nervousness in Paris. Each letter reached my wife in Lausanne within two days of my posting it.

François Mitterrand was the French president at the time, and it might not be too fanciful to imagine that his very personal interest in the gold myths in the Pyrenees, which we discuss, was not unconnected with any of this. He was still president in 1988, six years later, when all the major Paris publishers were told that they would receive a tax audit the next day, if they published the French edition of my book. Shortly after the publication of my book in Britain, I was invited with a very eminent British historian to take part in a Radio France programme concerning Oradour. On being consulted, the French customs told Radio France (who told me) that I would be arrested if I set foot in France. The threat evaporated when their bluff was called, and they were told (with something rather less than the whole truth) that we were coming anyway, surrounded by a phalanx of well-known international journalists who knew of the threat and smelt a story in it. I do not know who triggered that threat, but maybe we can guess.

As my eighteen-month sentence progressed, I was subjected to mounting demands that I reveal the information that French authorities were seeking from me. This was: who had given me the gold? and why was I taking it to Annemasse? There were promises of restitution of what I had lost (however they would have quantified that), and the more sinister threat that I might not be released if I continued to refuse them. However melodramatic this might sound almost twenty years later, the chilling fact was that the eighteen months of my sentence came and went without any sign of my being released (let alone after nine months, the halfway point which is normal in France). I was in fact released after twenty-one months, but only after some reciprocal chicanery through a journalist in Paris threatened to bring considerable embarrassment down on the French authorities.

Rennes-le-Château, a charming little hilltop village in the Cathar country of the Aude, between Carcassonne and the Pyrenees, has become a symbol for the covert activities of the Priory of Sion (whose statutes had been lodged in Annemasse). This most beautiful part of France has had a chequered history, having been dominated over the past 2000 years variously by the Visigoths, the Merovingians, the Moors, the Franks, the Cathars, the Inquisition, the Jews and even the SS.

The trigger for an upsurge of interest in this region in more modern times and what it might contain was the sudden expenditure of unexplained wealth by the parish priest of Rennes-le-Château, about a century ago. Nobody has been able to prove what he actually discovered, but his activities for the remainder of his life suggest quite persuasively that he must have discovered something of great value. The rekindled myths have been enough to sustain generations of frustrated treasure hunters, who are now banned, allegedly because of the damage they caused. It also sustained the otherwise disproportionate interest of the SS from 1933. I know from my meetings in more recent years with the widow of Raoul, the man who had helped me with his version of events leading to the massacre at Oradour, that German activity in this part of the Pyrenees became more frantic in 1944. The advance north by the allies in Italy and the certainty of invasion in the West, can only have rung out the unwelcome message to the Germans that their time in the Pyrenees was running out, and whatever they were going to find there had to be found very quickly before the opportunity was lost to them for ever.

Another factor that Guy and I discussed was the unlikely posting of SS General Heinz Lammerding and his Second SS Panzer Division to Montauban, near Toulouse. Conventional history suggests that this was to regroup and retrain the division, which had had a very tough time on the Eastern Front. The same conventional history suggests that this posting placed them midway between the Atlantic and the Mediterranean, well-positioned in the event of an invasion on either of those coasts. This is not very persuasive. An invasion of the south of France would have been rather pointless when such excellent progress was already being made in Italy. There would have been horrendous logistical difficulties in invading from the Bay of Biscay. Even if successful, this would have then resulted in a prolonged fight through France, before reaching the real goal of Germany.

It does seem much more likely that, at a time when Germany was clearly running out of money as targets for looting dried up, the Pyrenees might have offered a last-stand answer. Lammerding was very close to the Nazi inner sanctum, and he would have been trusted absolutely for a mission of such sensitivity.

When the merest possibility of such a vast cumulative treasure is at stake, there are inevitably many agendas at work. This book tries to pull together some of these strands. It is a bizarre and sometimes frightening story. This is its beginning; we have not yet seen its end.

Robin Mackness
Compton, Berkshire, 1999

Introduction by Guy Patton

IN 1989, I WAS living on Malta – the island home of the Hospitaller Knights of St John, from 1530 to 1789. The imposing fortifications, palaces and other buildings constructed by the Knights fascinated me, and I undertook some basic research into the Order's history, and that of their main rival, the Knights Templar. I already had an interest in comparative religion, especially Christianity, Judaism, and Islam, and had also read a number of books on politics, psychology, and the esoteric. The addition of the history of the medieval Knights to my previous interests aroused some interesting lines of thought.

Knowing of my interests, a friend recommended that I should read *The Holy Blood and the Holy Grail*. I found the book compelling, especially the story of Abbé Saunière, priest of Rennes-le-Château in the late nineteenth century. The main thesis of the book, that Jesus may have married Mary Magdalene, and that possibly, after the crucifixion, they (or at least the Magdalene) escaped from Palestine to the south of France, is a long-held tradition in that part of the country. Rather more contentious is the suggestion that Jesus' bloodline, having continued through his children, resurfaced in the dynasty of the fifth-century Frankish kings, the Merovingians.

Furthermore, the book proposes that a secret society, closely associated with the Knights Templar, was established to act as guardian of this Merovingian bloodline, the Merovingian dynasty having been toppled from power in the seventh century by the Carolingians – with the approval of the Roman Catholic Church.

But despite my reservations, I found the many strands of research within the book enthralling, and was determined to visit the village of Rennes-le-Château as soon as circumstances allowed. This I was finally able to do in September 1991, when returning from London to Malta by car. Impressed by Saunière's church renovation and his other building, I was very pleased to learn more of the Rennes-le-Château mysteries from some local people – both French and English. I was particularly struck by the profusion of symbolism in the church, and by the geometrical layout of Saunière's domain. Without doubt there appeared to be some hidden meaning in all this.

Before leaving the village, I joined the Terre de Rhedae Association, a French organization that produces a first-class annual bulletin dedicated to researching, protecting, and promoting the village. I also met local Templar historian George Keiss, and subscribed to his research society CERT (Centre d'Études et de Recherches Templières). Both these associations have provided a wealth of research and more importantly, personal contact with very knowledgeable locals.

On my eventual return to England, in 1992, I continued to research the subject by reading whatever English or French books I could gain access to. The reliability of the information contained in these books varies enormously, but there are valuable insights to be gleaned from them all. I then discovered a group of English researchers known as the Rennes Group (now the Rennes-le-Château Research Group), whose chairman, Jonothan Boulter, lives in London. I joined them in active research and debate on the various aspects of the mystery. Many of its members have great expertise in the diverse fields encountered in Rennes research, and have greatly contributed to my own acquisition of knowledge. The Group publishes the *Rennes Observer*, a quarterly magazine which contains details of members' findings. I have since become the group's secretary.

I first contacted Roger-René Dagobert after reading a series of three articles he had contributed to the Terre de Rhedae bulletins. These articles raised some interesting points, not least his assertion of the continual involvement of the Dagobert family since the early seventh century in the mystery of the lost treasure of the Temple of Jerusalem. Subsequent meetings in England and France, access to Roger-René's archives, and regular correspondence with him, has revealed a most remarkable story. This story extends over nearly 1400 years, from the assassination of Dagobert II, through the activities of General Dagobert in the 1780s, to the actions of Nazi SS, and others, in Limoges in 1944, that lead to the massacre at Oradour.

In November 1995, Roger-René advised me to read *Oradour: Massacre and Aftermath*, by Robin Mackness. This book deals with the tragic events of June 1944 of which Roger-René was acutely aware, having been a fourteen-year-old living in Limoges at the time of the Oradour massacre. Furthermore, his father had been closely involved with key people and events of that time. Robin Mackness had also uncovered, through bitter experience, the ongoing repercussions of the Oradour incident. Robin's revelations, and the researches of Roger-René, coupled with my previous researches, revealed the existence of a web of secrecy and deception. What had begun as a fascinating tale about a simple country priest had now grown into a most extraordinary re-evaluation of European politics, expecially the role played by secret societies. I was soon to form a mental picture that could at least in part explain the so-called mysteries of Rennes-le-Château.

Having put together a chronological outline of events, and the activities of various groups and individuals, I contacted Robin Mackness through his publisher. I was interested to learn whether he had any information, not revealed in his book, that might confirm some of Roger-René's assertions. I was also interested to know what he thought of the scenario that I had constructed. This initial contact with Robin was cautious but, after a couple of phone calls and letters, we finally met in September 1996. However, it was not until a year later that we formed a collaboration to get this extraordinary story into print.

In the course of writing, I have endeavoured to take into consideration further developments pertinent to the story. Recently published books and current events in French politics, such as the resignation of Roland Dumas (a key figure in the story), have added confirmation to the conclusion of this work.

This book cannot offer concrete proof of the continuing existence of the treasure that is its theme, but it does provide extensive evidence of a powerful belief in it. Throughout the centuries this belief has drawn diverse people to the Corbières in search of the treasure. This belief has also motivated various groups to work under the cover of secret societies or to work conspiratorially and disguise their actions. Unwittingly, many innocent and sometimes prominent individuals have become involved in these conspiracies or secret societies, supporting them in the first instance in good faith.

This book also highlights the dangers of extremism in its many forms. Whether in politics, religion, commerce, or the world of finance, there exist those who, driven by an extreme passion that makes them lose sight of 'moral values', can endanger their own cause, not to mention society at large.

There are, of course, those who will not accept some of the interpretations and speculations made in this book. However, to my knowledge they have failed so far to offer a convincing alternative. All the research has been gathered in good faith – every effort has been taken to avoid betraying any confidences – and I readily acknowledge the help given by all those whom I have been privileged to meet in the course of this quest. I hope that they will not be disappointed by what I suggest, even if it is at times controversial. What I hope is that it will open up the debate on the Rennes mysteries to a wider forum. This is certainly not the last word on the subject and, as research reveals more pieces of the puzzle, the web in which the thread of gold is woven will become even clearer.

Guy Patton
London, 1999

PART ONE

FATE OF THE
HOLY TREASURE

The Jerusalem Treasure · Romans and Visigoths
A Pyrenean Kingdom · Rhedae

A LITTLE LESS than forty years after the brutal crucifixion of
Jesus of Nazareth, the Jewish Messiah, the streets of Jerusalem
echoed to the insistent tramp of legions of the Roman army.
Exasperated by the continuous guerilla warfare waged by the
Zealots (Jewish militants dedicated to the liberation of their
ancient homeland) the Roman general, Titus, led his troops in
a wholesale attack on the city.

The former governor, Pontius Pilate, arguably the man
responsible for the crucifixion of Jesus, had long since been
replaced. According to some reports he was sent back in
disgrace to his family lands in the south of France; he had not
handled the political situation competently. From AD66, the
Romans had been effectively at war with the Jews, and by
AD70 the Emperor Vespasian and his Roman hierarchy had
had enough.

The principal focus of this attack was the magnificent
temple that dominated Jerusalem from its position straddling
the hill of Mount Moriya, to the south of which is Mount
Sion. The Temple of Jerusalem was less of a military target
than a symbolic one: it represented the heart of the Jewish
nation itself. The building under siege had been erected on the
command of King Herod, who had reigned over Judaea

immediately before the birth of Jesus. But it had been constructed on the foundations of a much older temple, which in
turn is alleged to have replaced the legendary Temple of
Solomon, built to house the Ark of the Covenant. The power
of the symbolism of the ancient Temple is still in evidence
today, as thousands of orthodox Jews pray in front of the
Wailing Wall, its oldest surviving part.

Yet there is some confusion over the reality of what actually
was Solomon's Temple. Out of what remains today the only
account of its construction comes from the Old Testament.
But in addition even from that, it is clear that the story of the
building is intertwined with something else. For the account
of 2 Chronicles ch. 9 also mentions the presence of the most
incredible treasures of gold, silver and precious gems, much of
which was supposed to be a gift from the Queen of Sheba.
However, like the stones and mortar, most of this was to
disappear in the sackings of Jerusalem by the Egyptian pharoah
Rameses in about 930BC and later, in 586BC, by the Babylonian king, Nebuchadnezzar. 2 Chronicles ch. 36 also reports
that at that time all the city's residents were taken into captivity
in Babylon. Great empahasis is placed on the fate of the
treasure, and in verse 18 it is recounted that, 'all the vessels of
the house of God, great and small, and the treasures of the
house of the Lord, and the treasures of the king, and of his
princes; all these he brought to Babylon'. Before leaving the
city, the Babylonians broke down its walls, and set fire to the
Temple and all the royal palaces.

'Three score and ten' years later, however, the Jews were
to return to Jerusalem. In Ezra, chapters 1, 2 and 3, it is
reported that under the direction of Cyrus, King of Persia, not
only was the Temple reconstructed, but also an enormous
quantity of treasure was returned to its precincts.

Around 35BC, dissatisfied with the existing temple, Herod,
on his accession, decided to build a more splendid replacement
intended to rival Solomon's Temple of legend. Though little
now remains, the dimensions of Herod's Temple are impres-

sive; the temple buildings were built on a platform approximately 470m long and 300m wide, about nine and a half times the area of St Peter's Basilica in Rome. But Herod's Temple no longer housed, in its Holy of Holies, the Ark of the Covenant, that most symbolic of all the ancient Jewish artefacts. This disappears from all accounts sometime between 750BC and 650BC. Nevertheless the temple did, as expected, contain the sacred and priceless treasure that had been amassed by the Jews over the previous centuries. This included what is now a well-known symbol of the Jewish faith, the seven-branched candlestick called the menorah, as well as other sacred articles, together with a large quantity of gold and silver.

The archaeology of the Temple itself aside, however, confirmation of the existence of a huge treasure, deposited in and around it, was found in 1952 during the excavations of an important religious settlement by the Dead Sea. In a cave at Qumran, researchers discovered a scroll of rolled copper upon which had been engraved an inventory of the nature and locations of this treasure. The exact sites were not easily identifiable to modern researchers, but a considered estimate of the actual quantity of treasure revealed some sixty-five tons of silver and twenty-six of gold. These were secreted within and around the precincts of the Temple, just prior to the Roman invasion.

With ruthless efficiency, Titus and his legions devastated and pillaged the Temple. The holy treasure was duly transported back to Rome. A record of this survives to this day in Rome, in the form of the Arch of Titus, built in AD81 by the Senate in pride of place at the top of the Via Sacra near the Forum and the Colosseum. On the right-hand vault of the Arch is a bas-relief depicting the return of the triumphant General Titus, his troops bearing this symbolic and priceless treasure. Clearly shown is the massive seven-branched candlestick, carried on the shoulders of Jewish prisoners.

The sacking of Jerusalem, and the removal of the sacred treasure from the Temple, tore the heart from the Jewish nation. All organized conflict with the Roman Empire finally collapsed three years later, with the destruction of the mountain fortress of Masada near the Dead Sea, and the mass suicide of its heroic defenders. This tragedy was to find a parallel with another religious sect, nearly 1200 years later, in the mountainous region of south-western France.

The most important source of information about this early period comes from the writings of Josephus, a former Jewish commander who had been arrested in Galilee in AD67. A shrewd and persuasive man, he managed to gain the confidence of the Emperor Vespasian and even became a military adviser to the Roman commanders given the task of overseeing the destruction of Jerusalem. Taken to Rome after the fall of Masada, he spent his days compiling detailed histories of the times. In his *Jewish Wars Against the Romans*, Josephus confirms the pillaging of the Temple treasure: 'Among the great quantity of spoils, the most remarkable being those that had been taken from the Temple of Jerusalem, the Table of Gold that weighed several talents and the golden Chandelier made with such skill to make it worthy of the use to which it was destined'.

For the next 350 years this treasure remained (along with wealth looted from all over the Roman Empire) in the Imperial Treasury. But as it lay there, the might of Rome moved into decline. By this time, the burden of defending its vast borders was immense and costly; it was becoming vulnerable to the powerful forces emerging from the east. Finally, in AD410, Rome fell to the might of the Visigothic king, Alaric, heralding the disintegration of the Roman Empire.

The Visigoths (West Goths), one of two divisions of a group of Germanic peoples, had separated from their cousins the Ostrogoths (East Goths) in the fourth century. Becoming agriculturists, they had settled in what is now Romania, until attacked by the Huns and driven across the Danube river into the Roman Empire. At first living harmoniously within the Empire, the increasing demands of taxation from their Roman overlords was to provoke a violent reaction. From minor revolts and skirmishes, tension escalated into outright war, and on 9 August 378 they utterly defeated the army of Emperor Valens on the plains outside Adrianople. Valens himself was killed. The Visigoths wandered the region for four years until settling at Moesia in the Balkans, entering into an accord with the new Roman emperor, Theodosius I, who charged them with defending the frontier. During this time it also appears that the Visigoths converted to Christianity, although to the Arian sect, the doctrine of which did not accept that Jesus was the actual son of God.

Within a short time the Roman army included barbarian generals who were wielding considerable political power, and seeking to expand their own lands. They moved south into Greece, and thence, after an initial failure, into Italy. It was thus that Alaric was to arrive at the gates of the city of Rome itself.

The sack of Rome was mild, and almost respectful. The Visigoths admired the civilization achieved by the Romans although this respect did not prevent Alaric from plundering the treasure. However, his death within the same year, 410, was to prevent him from enjoying the spoils. It was to be under the command of his successor, Ataulphus, that the Visigoths set off further west, through a virtually defenceless Gaul, eventually establishing a Visigothic kingdom that occupied most of modern Spain and the south-west of France. They continued to maintain a fragile *détente* with the Romans, at times supporting them and at other times attacking them.

Visigothic artefacts clearly show their admiration for the advanced cultures they encountered: they had absorbed Roman and Grecian-Byzantine influences and, combined with Germanic metal-working skills, created exquisite jewellery and ornamentation; a magnificent collection of jewelled crowns and crosses, known as the Treasure of Guarrazar, can be seen in Madrid's National Archaeological Museum. Visigothic architecture also demonstrates a sophistication with excellent masonry and stone vaulting. These people were far from being 'uncivilized' barbarians; perhaps this popular image arose largely as a reaction to their adoption of Arian Christianity, which had been declared heretical by the Roman Catholic Church.

Having settled in their new kingdom, straddling the Pyrenees, the Visigoths established their capital at Toulouse, and created well-fortified centres of power at Toledo, Carcassonne and Rhedae, now the little hilltop village of Rennes-le-Château. Evidence that the Visigoths had possession of an immense treasure is borne out not only by the Guarrazar artefacts, but from commentators and historians including Procopius, El Macin, Fredegaire, and the Englishman, Gibbon. That this included the spoils of Rome is confirmed by their references made to the Missorium, a magnificent jewel-encrusted golden plate weighing about 100 pounds, and also to the Emerald Table with its gold stands and pearl inlay.

Meanwhile, the Frankish tribes, having crossed the Rhine border (from their homeland in what is now Belgium and Germany), were pushing into northern France (then called Gaul). Within 100 years, united under the rule of Clovis, the first Frankish king, they had established their own kingdom in northern and central France. The Visigoths were thus contained from expanding much further north than the Pyrenees; the northernmost territory of the Visigoth kingdom now occupied an area known as the Languedoc. This status quo existed for the best part of 200 years until an unwanted and aggressive intrusion appeared in the south of Spain.

By 650, Islam, the religion created by the prophet Mohammed, had swept throughout the Middle East and Egypt, and was converting the Berber tribes of North Africa. It was only a matter of time before the eyes of the Islamic Berbers of Morocco turned towards the nearby Iberian peninsula. Led by the Moorish commander, Jabel-al-Tariq, from whom Gibraltar takes its Anglicized name, they invaded Spain in 711, rapidly expanding throughout the whole peninsula. In the face of this relentless tide, the Visigothic king and his nobles were forced to leave their fortress town of Toledo and to retreat northwards with their possessions, until they arrived at their fortified city of Carcassonne. When Tariq arrived at Toledo, it is recounted that he demanded the legendary treasure of the Temple of Jerusalem, of which he had full knowledge; but by this time the Visigoths had fled north taking it with them.

The Arabs appreciated the symbolic value of the lost treasure as well as its material worth, because Islam considers itself to be the half-brother of Judaism. According to the Bible, the Arab nations are descended from Ismael, the exiled son of Abraham and his Egyptian hand-maiden Hagar; he is therefore the half-brother of Isaac, the Israelite patriarch. Within the Islamic faith, Abraham, Moses, Jesus, and other biblical leaders are highly revered as prophets. To Tariq, this shared heritage can be seen to have extended to the treasure of the Temple of Jerusalem.

It was the Franks, led by the able Charles Martel, grand-father of Charlemagne, who pushed the Islamic tide back into Spain. The Franks then turned their attention to the Visigothic fortress of Carcassonne. According to the Greek historian, Procopius of Caesarea, in his *De Bello Gothico*, the Franks too were fully aware of the treasure, which they also believed to have come from the ancient Temple of Jerusalem. While at this point physical documentary record of the fate of the treasure becomes obscured, the prevailing legend supported with the historian Firmin Jaffus and the archaeologist Cros-Mayrevieille, affirms that the treasure was now removed from Carcassonne. Further, persistent local legend claims that, faced by the threat of attack, it was taken to the last Visigothic stronghold of Rennes-le-Château, to be carefully concealed in a number of locations nearby. And it is here, in the remote high valley of the Aude, that deposits of the ancient Temple treasure appear to have remained, largely undisturbed, for the past 1200 years.

But the spoils of the Temple may not be the only treasure to be concealed in the region. Although differing in their details, a handful of local stories share at their core a Queen Blanche, or Blanche of Castille, and a royal treasure. Perhaps these are inspired by the presence of a local fortress called Blanchefort, and by the linguistic coincidence between Rennes-les-Bains (or Reynes-les-Bains, as it was known by 1406) and Reine-les-Bains, which associates a Queen (*reine*) and the baths (*bains*) for which the valley is famous. But Blanche of Castille, the mother of St Louis IX, King of France, did become regent in the mid-thirteenth century, while her son was away on crusade, and as such, was in charge of the royal treasury. Concerned by the power and rebellious nature of some of her nobles, she decided to leave Paris and is said to have transported the royal treasure to Rennes (a fief which at the time belonged to the crown), before confronting the growing threat. Though she succeeded in defusing the situation, she died a little time after. Thus we have a second cache of hidden treasure.

The secret of its location could have been passed on through King Louis, who was to die in Tunis, to his son, Philippe the Hardy, who, it is said, improved the defences of Rennes. But the secret appears to have died with him. His son and heir to the throne, Philippe the Fair, took drastic steps in an attempt to gain control of the wider region, by then in the grip of the Knights Templar. Yet despite his success at crushing Templar control, he was unable to recover the treasure.

So did the Templars become the guardians, not only of the treasure of the Temple of Jerusalem, but also that of Queen Blanche? This would have been to add to their own enormous wealth, amassed over nearly two centuries. What's more, Claire Corbu and Antoine Captier, local Rennes-le-Château researchers with old family ties to the village, state in their book *L'Héritage de l'Abbé Saunière*, that they believe this treasure of the Templars was buried in the region too.

Another long-time Rennes researcher, Tatiana Kletzky-Pradere, notes that the nineteenth-century priest of Rennes-le-Château, Abbé Saunière, named his dog, 'Pomponnet', and his monkey, 'Mela'. Could it be mere coincidence that a first-century Spanish geographer and writer, called Pomponius Mela, refers to an ancient treasure deposited in the mines of Pyrene, located exactly south of Carcassonne? Could Saunière have known of both these writings and have had access to the treasure? The researches of Rennes writer Gérard de Sède do state that a Mme. Baron, a villager who knew Saunière, told him that there were in fact two dogs, Pomponnet and Faust, and two monkeys, Capri and Mora. Yet as with the other aspects of this story that are to become linked with Saunière, these are perhaps clues not to be discarded lightly.

Visitors to Rennes-le-Château, now with only a few dozen permanent residents, will find it difficult to appreciate that this is the site of the ancient Visigothic stronghold of Rhedae. The diminutive medieval château at the heart of the village is built on Visigothic foundations, as is the church adjacent to it, dedicated to St Mary Magdalene. It is this building which has become the centre of the so-called mystery of Rennes-le-Château, with which Saunière is so intimately associated. Archaeological excavations in the village and the neighbouring fields have revealed extensive Visigothic remains and artefacts. Only about 2.5km north of Rennes, behind the village of Coustaussa, in a place called the Grand Camp, are the remains of some substantial dry-stone walls 2m–3m high and over 2m wide. In the neighbouring valley of Rennes-les-Bains are extensive stone walls buried within the undergrowth that have more in common with defensive structures than agricultural terracing. Yet astonishingly, in view of the rich history and visible remains, neither the village of Rennes nor its surrounding area has been properly excavated by archaeologists. Indeed, excavations of any kind have been vigorously opposed. What is it that the authorities wish to remain undiscovered?

Languedoc, the area which forms the backcloth to this unfolding story, extends from the valley of the River Arriège in the west to the Mediterranean coast in the east, and from the towns of Albi, Millau and Nîmes in the north to the mountains of the Pyrenees in the south. For administrative reasons, the French government has joined the Catalonian area, Roussillon, to the Languedoc to form a region which has as much Spanish cultural influence as French. The name Languedoc derives from 'language of the Oc', which refers to Occitan or Provençal, a dialect with Spanish connections. This unique mix of French and Spanish culture, and its geographical isolation from centres of political power, has helped to form its distinctive and remarkable history.

The Languedoc is further divided into smaller departments, one of which, the Aude, encompasses the dramatic Corbières with its craggy peaks, vineyards, and river valleys with densely wooded slopes and rocky outcrops. Here is to be found the village of Rennes-le-Château and its surrounding countryside, the Razès. Lying at the north-west corner, on the River Aude itself, is the fairytale city of Carcassonne, with its high turreted walls and sturdy towers.

Modern geophysical maps reveal the presence of a diversity and abundance of metal ores, including significant deposits of gold and silver. The Romans appear to have been the first to have fully appreciated, and exploited, these extensive mineral deposits, and evidence of their mining activities are known. The restored Roman baths at Rennes-les-Bains, utilizing the natural hot springs, and the existence of original Roman roads, gives some indication of the esteem in which this valley was held. With such evidence of significant Roman occupation in the area and its strategic and easily defendable position, it is quite easy to understand why the Visigoths, admirers of Roman culture and their military ability, should have chosen Rennes-le-Château to establish the major stronghold which was to become their final refuge in the face of Frankish dominance.

Among the region's extensive cave networks, two in particular are worthy of mention. Right in the heart of the Hautes-Corbières is to be found the tiny village of Auriac, a name that recalls its association with ancient goldmines (the French for gold being *or*, coming from the Latin *aurum*) as does the hamlet L'Auradieu, and the little stream the Aurio. Close to the village is another stream, the Rec de L'Érmita, which emerges from a cave network around which are ancient mines, one of which is called L'Hérmita (possibly derived from L'Ermite), 'the Hermit'. The church at Rennes-le-Château, renovated in the late nineteenth century, is decorated with many symbols that refer to both caves and hermits. Just south of Rennes-le-Château is a cave network called the Grotte du Carla.

Like many of the other cave networks both of these have proved difficult, dangerous, or even impossible, to explore fully from their known access points. It may well be that some of these caves are more safely accessible from other ways yet to be popularly discovered. Interestingly, the words *carla* and *aven* (cave) appear in a message decoded from a cryptogram found at Rennes-le-Château after the death of its priest in 1917. It is a curious message containing direct references to the Hautpoul family, the Visigoths, the Templars, treasure, and a dead king. These are all to appear as motifs throughout this story.

So, as our starting point, we have a remote area encrusted in history and legend, and probably containing the secret of a great hidden treasure. Over the course of history it has witnessed and possibly inspired the naked aggression of forces both temporal and spiritual, in an insatiable quest for power and wealth.

STRUGGLE FOR
RELIGIOUS SUPREMACY

Arian and Roman Christianity · Islam and Judaism
Dagobert II · Septimania

WHILE TITUS WAS directing the destruction of Jerusalem and the removal of its treasure, adherents to the teachings of Jesus of Nazareth were sowing the seeds of a religion that was to come to dominate the Western world. Following the crucifixion of Jesus, groups of disciples set out from Jerusalem to spread the word of their master; some travelling east to Persia, some north-west to Greece, while others chose a life of reflection as hermits in the Egyptian desert. However, the most influential were those who crossed the Mediterranean to Rome, the heart of the Roman Empire. The most famous of these were Peter and Paul. Indeed, it was to be the interpretation of Jesus's teachings by Paul that would form the basis of what would become known as Christianity, and it was the Pauline version which produced the highly effective administration of the Roman Catholic Church.

This institution, originally set up to fulfil the spiritual needs of its many converts, was, of its very nature, in conflict with the region's already established religions – Judaism, Persian Zoroastrianism, Roman Mithraism, a host of pagan beliefs and, eventually, Islam. The resultant hostilities provided fertile ground for exploitation by less-principled adherents to these disparate religions; while outwardly acting to defend their beliefs, they were in a position to use their faith as an excuse or motivation for more covert activities. And as this story will reveal, this has become a long-standing tradition. It is under the cover of religion that some groups have secretly attempted to gain control of the Languedoc and its treasure, and to supress the parallel activities of their adversaries.

Although the Catholic Church came to dominate Christianity, in the first 250 years following Christ's death it was only one of a number of sects calling themselves 'Christian'. Since the original teachings were dispersed over a very wide area by disciples, some of whom would not have even seen Jesus in life, differences in interpretation inevitably arose, sparking controversy. The greatest controversy raged over the exact nature of Jesus: was he the actual son of God in human form? Or was he merely a divinely inspired human? And between these two extremes were varying degrees of belief in his divinity, or interpretation, differing from that of the orthodox Roman belief, such as the fifth-century Nestorian belief that he had a human body but the mind of God.

Established in Persia, from where it spread east as far as China, Nestorianism flourished alongside an even more influential 'heresy', Manichaeism – the dualistic belief that only the spiritual world was good and that all matter was intrinsically evil, thereby rendering it impossible for God to appear in human form. An offshoot of this belief played a dramatic role in the history of the Languedoc. Of course, the debate concerning the actual nature and teachings of Jesus continues to the present day, although not necessarily labelled heresy. The wide range of possible permutations of Christian belief has provided a platform for many claiming to offer spiritual sustenance.

The ultimate triumph of the Catholic Church over its rivals as the 'patent-holders' of the True Faith hinged on one decisive moment of history: the conversion to Christianity of the Emperor Constantine the Great. Constantine is said to have had a prophetic vision in which he saw a luminous cross in the sky, accompanied by the sentence *In Hoc Signo Vinces* ('In this sign you will conquer'), just prior to his victory in 313, over his rival Maxentius, at the Milvian Bridge, outside Rome. Tradition has it that this experience inspired him to adopt Christianity as the universal religion for the Roman Empire. In reality it could as much have been motivated by political expediency as a way of unifying all the disparate cults already practising within the Empire. Many traditions could be readily carried over: the Christian holy day, Sunday, was already devoted to the Sun by the cult of Sol Invictus, as was 25 December already a 'holy' day before it was adopted as the birth date of Jesus.

But it soon became apparent to Constantine that the Christian faith itself had many different sects, some of which were in outright conflict. To address this problem, in 325 he convened a council at Nicea where they were all to be represented. Even within his family there was a difference of opinion. His mother, Helena, was a devoted adherent of Pauline Christianity, whereas his wife supported Arius, the leader of the principal 'opposition'. The doctrine of Arius challenged the Roman view that Jesus was actually God, but considered him as the divine bridge between God and man. At Nicea, this and other fundamental issues were vigorously debated. Ultimately, Constantine, no doubt influenced by his mother's fervent belief, ruled in favour of the Pauline version and declared the Arians to be heretics. Thus it was on the foundation of Pauline Christianity that the institution of the Roman Catholic Church was built.

Yet the Arian teachings continued to attract converts. It was easier for many of the formerly pagan sects to accept a Jesus that was not actually God, and by the sixth century Arianism was the dominant belief in half of the Christian world. The centre of the Catholic Church at this time was Constantinople, the city rebuilt by Constantine as his new capital, whilst Rome itself came under Arian control once conquered by the Visigoths. And it was Arianism that they took with them as they migrated west across the south of France and into the Iberian peninsula. Possibly as a reaction to the successful expansion of the Visigoths, Clovis, king of the Franks, nominally adopted Catholicism, gaining him the support of the residual Roman hierarchy in Gaul. This enabled him to confront the Visigoths, winning a decisive victory at Soissons, in 486. But a spiritual legacy of the Visigoths remained, as well as a material one. Despite the best efforts of the Church of Rome and its military champions, the Languedoc, with its isolated communities and areas of hostile terrain, was never fully purged of its Arianism, and continued to be a fertile ground for heresy and resultant conflict.

There would likely have been another powerful motive for the Frankish conversion. It is unlikely that the ruthless Clovis, (who assassinated all his rivals to the throne) was not aware of the magnificent treasure of the Visigoths – the excuse of suppressing heresy was an excellent opportunity for launching an offensive which would have also offered a chance to get his hands on it. However, despite more than 200 years of conflict, the Franks were never totally successful. With the help of their ally Theodoric the Ostrogoth, the Visigoths were able to retain the area of Mediterranean France that is the Languedoc – then known as Septimania. The province of Septimania, which took its name from the veterans of the Roman VII Legion who had retired there during the reign of Augustus, will be seen to play a crucial role in the unfolding history of France – not least because it contains the last resting places of the treasure of Jerusalem.

All was not settled among the Franks, and following the death of Clovis the kingdom was divided among his sons. This weakened their power to continue the fight against the Visigoths – although that said, by 560 the Frankish kingdoms of Austrasia and Neustria encompassed most of France, southern Germany and Switzerland. The descendants of Clovis formed a ruling dynasty, the Merovingians – kings distinguished by their long hair which held a symbolic association with strength and power equivalent to that of the biblical Samson. Ruling for 250 years, the Merovingians achieved an almost Arthurian mythical reputation and became a powerful archetype of the 'divine monarch'.

Dagobert, a great-grandson of Clovis, became king of the reunified Franks in 630, and was the first of several illustrious personages to carry the name. By this time, however, a succession of court chancellors known as the 'Mayors of the Palace' had contrived to accumulate sufficient power to challenge that of their monarchs, and had virtual control of the kingdoms of Austrasia, Neustria, and Burgundy. In 656, following the death of Sigisbert III, his five-year-old son and natural heir, Dagobert II was kidnapped by the incumbent Mayor, Grimoald, and given into the hands of Dido, Bishop of Poitiers. Baulking at murdering the young heir as he was instructed, the bishop exiled him to the monastery of Slane, in Ireland, thought far enough away not to be a future threat. Meanwhile, Grimoald's own son was installed as king.

Having completed a comprehensive education and entered into the circles of Irish Celtic nobility, Dagobert married Mathilde, a Celtic princess. They moved to England, taking residence at York, where Dagobert formed a close friendship with Wilfred, the influential Bishop of York. He had played a key role at the Synod of Whitby, the dramatic confrontation between the Roman Catholic and Celtic Churches. The Celtic Church had evolved from the desert monastic tradition inspired by the teachings of the apostle Mark, and was spread north by missionaries who had travelled up the western seaboard of Europe to Ireland. Despite possibly being a more pure form of Christianity in spiritual terms, the Celtic Church was seen as an opposing force to the Roman Church and, like the Arian tradition, was branded heretical. Followers were given the choice of persecution or subjugation to the control of Rome. It was with the aim of consolidating and expanding this control that Wilfred sought to bolster the position of the rightful Christian king of the Franks.

Mathilde died giving birth to their third daughter and it is said that it was Wilfred who hurriedly arranged a second marriage for Dagobert to a Visigoth princess, Giselle de Razès. As daughter of Bera II, the Count of Razès, and niece of Wamba, king of the Visigoths, Giselle's marriage brought together the Visigoth bloodline with that of the Merovingians. The marriage reputedly took place in the original church at Rennes-le-Château, at that time the fortress of Rhedae, last bastion of the Visigothic empire in France. It was from here that Dagobert, enriched and confident, was able to launch his bid to recover the throne. By 674 he had managed to become king of Austrasia, and two years later Giselle gave birth to his son and heir, Sigisbert IV. Dagobert ruled with an iron hand, dealing competently with internal squabbles among his rebellious nobles; even bringing Aquitaine (to the west of the Languedoc) back into his kingdom. However, and surely to the disappointment of Wilfred, Dagobert lacked obvious commitment to the Catholic Church – indeed he leant more towards the Arianism of his Visigoth in-laws.

In 679, Dagobert was assassinated in the forest of Stennay, in the Ardennes, on the order of the Mayor of the Palace, Pepin the Fat, but with the tacit approval of the Roman Catholic Church, which felt able to support this act of political expediency in the name of suppressing heresy. The Church then endorsed the right of Pepin to assume control. According to tradition, Sigisbert, Dagobert's young son, was smuggled to the safety of his mother's family at Rennes-le-Château, where as Sigisbert IV he eventually assumed his uncle's title, the Count of Razès.

Indeed, the eighth century 'Knights' Stone' discovered during the restoration of the church at Rennes in 1891, appears to depict the young Sigisbert being carried to safety on horseback by an armed Knight. The tradition further maintains that this Knight, one of Sigisbert's father's trusted companions, was called Mérovée Levi; his name being of Jewish origin will prove to be significant. Henri Buthion, former owner of the

Abbé Saunière's domain, believes this sculpted stone once covered what was actually the wall tomb of Sigisbert, in the church. The chance discovery in the village, during the excavations along a road to lay a new water pipe, of other tombstones and artefacts from a Merovingian cemetery would seem to bear this possibility out.

It must be remembered that the birth of Sigisbert was the result of the dynastic alliance, through the marriage of Dagobert II, of the Merovingian kings and the Visigoth aristocracy; as such, Sigisbert would have been held in great esteem by his own people. Coming to Rennes, and assuming the title of the Count of Razès, he would also without doubt have been initiated into the secret of the fabulous Visigoth treasure. Further research will show that his genealogy may well have also included a Jewish element. This adds an intriguing new dimension to his and his descendants' attitude to the hidden treasure.

But there is also an alternative tradition concerning the genealogy of Sigisbert IV. Some sources claim that he was actually the son of Bera, the Count of Razès, whose own father was the Visigoth king, Wamba; Sigisbert later married Magdala, the daughter of Bridget, one of the three daughters of Dagobert II and his first wife, Mathilde. In this account, it is Magdala who was brought to the safety of Rennes-le-Château by the knight Mérovée Levi. If this version is correct, then Dagobert would have had no legitimate heir to the throne, since under Salic Law (adopted by the Merovingians) women were prevented from succeeding to the throne. Thus, while Sigisbert IV and his descendents would still have had a right to the title, Count of Razès, they could not have laid a claim to the Merovingian succession. Could it be that the Sigisbert story was manufactured in order to legitimize a claim to the throne – and the gold?

But there is other evidence which may clarify Sigisbert's relationship with Dagobert II. While probably not familiar to Britons today, there have been no less than four British kings of this name. Known by the more Anglicized spelling of Sigeberht, they reigned in the seventh and eighth centuries, in the kingdoms of Wessex, Essex, and East Anglia. This may give some support to the theory that Sigisbert was the son of Dagobert. Sigisbert would have been born shortly after Dagobert's return from Britain; the name would thus not have been an unlikely one for his own son.

The Merovingians continued to rule over the Frankish kingdoms in name only. The real power now resided in the hands of the descendents of Pepin the Fat, who were to form the Carolingian dynasty. Military champions of the Church of Rome, the first Carolingian was Pepin's own son, Charles Martel. Though never actually crowned king, it was the heroic Charles Martel who, as we have seen, achieved the subjugation of the Islamic Berbers (or Moors).

* * *

Meanwhile, Visigothic power became confined to the remote high valley of the Aude with its fortress capital of Rhedae, now Rennes. Yet while Visigothic power across the region may have waned, this concentration of activity in Rennes made something of a 'golden age' there. This is confirmed by a census report of towns of the Languedoc in the late eighth century by Bishop Theodulphe, commissioned by Charlemagne, the grandson and heir of Charles Martel, which shows Rhedae to be a city equal in importance to its neighbours, Carcassonne and Narbonne.

Charlemagne was crowned Holy Roman Emperor by Pope Leo III on Christmas Day, 800, in recognition of his extension of the influence of the Church throughout what were now Frankish domains. He granted Carcassonne to one of his commanders, in recognition of his military service, who adopted the title of Count of Carcassonne – Rhedae being one of his dependencies. A short while later Rhedae achieved its greatest glory when elevated to the status of a royal city with the marriage of Amalric, the son of a Visigoth king, to the

Frankish princess, Clothilde. Rhedae was now set to enjoy a period of culture and splendour that was to last about 200 years.

Preoccupied with the major conflicts between Christianity and Islam, and within the Christian faith itself, it is easy to overlook the presence of possibly the oldest surviving religious sect in the region. Living largely in close-knit communities, partly for security from the ever-present fear of persecution and partly because of their strong family ties and traditions, the Jews had established several flourishing communities outside the Holy Land, of which Marseille was one of the largest. Whilst first settling some centuries before, it was in Roman times that this Jewish community most expanded its influence and wealth, primarily through trade. In the neighbouring Camargue, a marshy island at the mouth of the Rhone, a local legend arose with some variations, which claimed that in AD44 Mary Magdalene, her brother Lazarus and several others, having fled to Alexandria then crossed the Mediterranean and arrived not far from the city of Marseilles, at the village of Ratis, now named Les Saintes Maries de la Mer. Shortly afterwards the party evidently split up and the Magdalene journeyed east some 50km to live out the rest of her life at the cave of St Baume. There she evidently died in AD60. (This account is actually accepted by the Catholic Church which has built a mausoleum for her remains at nearby St Maximin.)

Following the crucifixion, the followers of Jesus had been considered a political and religious threat by the elders of the Temple of Jerusalem. But since the Jewish communities throughout the Mediterranean were not under the centralized control of the Jerusalem faction, it is reasonable to believe that Mary and her close companions could have found a safe haven in the south of France. The legends surrounding the Magdalene and her arrival in France are investigated in depth by Margaret Starbird in her book *The Woman with the Alabaster Jar* (1993).

Mary Magdalene, the 'best loved disciple' of the Lord

(possibly even his wife according to the Gnostic Gospels), is believed to have been a Benjamite; Jesus was from the Benjamite's elder kinsmen the great House of Judah. Another tradition maintains that both Mary Magdalene and Jesus were of noble birth. If this is the case, her arrival in the south of France could have been even more significant for the Jewish community of the time than it was for the later Christian one.

At this point, from a synthesis of historical fact, biblical account and legend, an interesting scenario presents itself. On their return to Caanan after the Exodus, the land renamed Israel was divided up among its twelve tribes. It was on the border of the territories of the tribes of Judah and Benjamin that the city of Jerusalem was founded, in which Solomon was later to construct his Temple. It is reported in Judges 21 that the tribe of Benjamin came into conflict with the other tribes; a great battle ensued with many casualties on both sides resulting in the defeat of Benjaminites. There was subsequently a reconcilliation but not before, according to some traditions, a large number of the Benjamin tribe had fled to seek shelter under the Phoenicians at Tyre, with whom it appears they had already made contact. Through marriage, they would have become absorbed into Phoenician society. It is of course opportune to recall that it was Hiram, king of Tyre, who sent to Solomon the builders and materials needed for the construction of his great Temple.

A great sea-faring and trading nation, the Phoenicians colonized, from 600BC onwards, a substantial part of the Mediterranean coastline – including Marseilles and Narbonne on the southern French coast, and inland to Carcassonne, Toulouse and very possibly Rhedae. Some of the first Jewish communities in these cities could, therefore, have originated from Phoenician Benjaminites. Mary Magdalene could well have found there a community that welcomed her as one of their own. According to local researchers André Douzet and Antoine Bruzeau, descendants of the Magdalene could have also played a significant role in the secret of the treasure of the

Temple of Jerusalem. The biblical symbol adopted by the tribe of Benjamin was the wolf: an ancient Languedoc family which figures centrally in this story was called Luppe, a variation of *loup*, the French word for wolf.

A footnote to the Magdalene legend, unearthed by Douzet and Bruzeau, brings it even closer into the mysteries of Rennes-le-Château. They claim that Mary Magdalene's body was taken by a ninth-century nobleman, Gérard de Roussillon, to the abbey of Vézelay – which he had founded. Gérard de Roussillon was Count of Barcelona, Narbonne and Provence, in other words Provence and Septimania, which included the region of Roussillon which extends down to the Spanish border (now known as French Catalonia). They further claim that Mary Magdalene and company arrived not in the Camargue, but at Mas de la Magdalene on the Roussillon coast, near Narbonne, from where they say she could have travelled inland to Rennes-le-Château. Had Gérard discovered her body at Rennes and taken it to Vézelay? If so, this would help to explain why the later Magdalene cult should have taken such a strong hold at Rennes, and not least why the village church, originally the chapel of the château, should be dedicated to her.

With the eventual domination of the region by the inquisitorial Catholic Church, the significant role played by the Jews in the early history of France was very effectively concealed. It is often conveniently forgotten that early Christianity had grown out of Judaism; that Jesus, his family and all his disciples were Jews; and that the true mission of Jesus was the reformation of the Jewish religion, not the creation of a new one.

The Jewish communities flourished under the Roman administration, since the Romans were not unduly concerned about their subjects' theological beliefs provided they paid their taxes and remained subdued. And when the Romans were displaced by the Visigoths, the effect on the Jews would have been minimal. The doctrines of Arian Christianity did not conflict with Judaism in the way that those of the Catholic

Church did, so this allowed a more easy integration between the Jews and the Visigoths. There is evidence of inter-marriage between their respective aristocracies resulting in obvious Semitic names among non-Jews. For example, the name Bera occurs frequently in the extended family of Dagobert and his son, Sigisbert, the Count of Razès.

Two particular facts underline the positive relationship between both the Merovingians and the Visigoths and the Jews. First, the revised *Codex Euricus* of 681 (based on the codified law issued by the fifth-century Visigoth king, Euric), possibly the greatest legal achievement of the Visigoths in Spain, concerned itself with an examination of the existing anti-Jewish legislation and the behaviour of slaves. Jews were formerly subjected to harsh treatment by some influential sections of Visigothic society and in the second half of the seventh century were given the stark choice of conversion or enslavement. Why should the Visigoth administrators be concerned with Jewish rights sufficiently to create specific legislation? Second, both the Franks and their Merovingian rulers adhered to Salic Law as the basis of their legal framework. J. J. Rabinowitz, in *The Title De Migrantibus of the Lex Salica and the Jewish Herem Hayishub* (1947), reveals that a significant section of Salic Law, Title 45: 'De Migrantibus', is derived directly from the Talmud – that is, traditional Judaic Law. (Salic Law was derived from the legal code of the fourth-century Salian Franks who had settled in the Rhine region of the Netherlands.)

Thus the region of Septimania in the seventh–ninth centuries contained not only a very large Jewish population but a benignly ruled one, allowing it to exert considerable influence in society, and at the highest levels, permitting integration with the Visigoth, Merovingian, or Carolingian polity. These groups can be seen to have colluded with each other to safeguard their mutual interests. For instance, following their defeat by Charles Martel, the Islamic Moors were at first driven back to seek refuge in the heavily fortified city of Narbonne – already home to a large Jewish community. Though initially content to live in mutual cooperation with the Islamic invaders, Pepin III (or Pepin the Short, the son and successor of Charles Martel) wished to drive the Islamic Moors completely out of France and to have his claim to biblical succession (the divine right to rule) endorsed by the Jews, possibly also to lay a future legitimate claim to the treasure. In return for the creation of an independent Jewish principality, he persuaded the Jews to overthrow the Islamic defenders of Narbonne. So it was, that in 768, a formal Jewish enclave was established in Septimania which owed Pepin only nominal allegiance. Professor Arthur Zuckerman examines this fascinating historical development in his book *A Jewish Princedom in Feudal France* (1972).

Pepin also installed a king of the Jews of Septimania, whose name appears in its Frankish version as Theodoric or Thierry, and who was acknowledged by both Pepin and the Caliph of Baghdad as 'the seed of the royal house of David', a description that had also been inexplicably applied to the Merovingian kings. From his marriage to Pepin's sister Alda, Thierry fathered a son, Guillem de Gellone.

Guillem de Gellone acquired almost legendary status in his own lifetime, inspiring a number of epic poems to be written about him in the person of Guillaume d'Orange; even appearing in Dante's *Divine Comedy* and the earlier *Willehalm* by Wolfram von Eschenbach. Guillem was one of Charlemagne's premier commanders in the continual conflict against the Moors, eventually capturing Barcelona, thus extending Frankish influence across the Pyrenees. As King of the Jews of Septimania, Guillem also held the titles of Count of Barcelona, of Toulouse, of the Auvergne and – perhaps more significantly in this quest for treasure – of the Razès, the fiefdom which surrounds Rennes-le-Château.

A highly educated man, fluent in both Arabic and Hebrew, Guillem is said to have founded, in about 792, an academy of Judaic studies at Gellone, which attracted scholars to its renowned library. On retirement from his active military career, Guillem withdrew to the confines of his academy. Now the partially ruined monastery of St Guilhem-le-Désert, the former academy still houses a relic of the 'True Cross' given to him by Charlemagne (who in turn had been given it by the Patriarch of Jerusalem) in recognition of his military feats. Yet, his adoption as a champion of Christianity in consideration of his illustrious exploits in defence of the Catholic Franks against the Islamic Moors, and his canonization as St Guillem, has resulted in the relegation of his Judaic origins. But this dualism has its own intriguing legacies: it is reported by V. Saxer in *Le Culte de Marie Madeleine en Occident* that Gellone became one of Europe's first centres for the cult of the Magdalene during its term as a Judaic academy.

The crowning of Charlemagne in 800 as Holy Roman Emperor consolidated the position of the Roman Catholic Church over a vast region that included modern France, Switzerland, the northern half of Italy, and most of Germany and Austria. But the Languedoc, with its remote mountainous regions, continued to maintain a large measure of independence: heresies fermented; individual counts wielded great power and amassed great wealth; a liberal culture flourished in which knowledge, the arts, philosophy and ethics were held in high esteem. All these attributes, of course, offered sufficient reasons for avaricious northern barons and the paranoid Catholic Church to collaborate against this enlightened oasis of Dark Age Europe.

The successors of Charlemagne tended to be incompetent in their administrative skills; their lack of authority allowed others to make inroads into the kingdom: the Normans were able to colonize the north-western area of France now called Normandy. The Carolingians themselves finally gave way, in 987, to the Capetian dynasty; however, the title of Holy Roman Emperor passed to the German Saxon kings, most of whom belonged to the Hohenstaufen succession. Yet the Hohenstaufens were anti-Roman Catholic. With the complicity of the Church of Rome, they were soon to be replaced by the Swiss Habsburgs, who were to remain the Holy Roman Emperors for more than 500 years.

Meanwhile, in the remote foothills of the Pyrenees, the descendants of Dagobert II continued to hold the title of Count of Razès. And, together with a few other descendants of fellow-integrated Merovingian, Visigoth, and Jewish families, tenaciously kept the secret of the fabulous treasure of the Temple of Jerusalem. One of the most prominent of these families are the Hautpouls, who in the fifteenth century became the Lords of Rennes and Blanchefort, and occupied the château adjacent to the church in Rennes-le-Château. According to the researches of Lionel Fanthorpe, the Hautpoul family are descendants of the Visigoth king Atulph, an ally of Alaric, the sacker of Rome. They originally settled near Mazamet, the town north of Carcassonne, where today the actual village of Hautpoul clings precariously to the wall of a gorge, in the shadow of the Montagne Noire. Atulph was known locally as the King of the Black Mountain, and a little further south is the Montagne d'Alaric.

Jean Robin's *Rennes-le-Château – La Colline Envoutée* (1982) mentions other families of possible Merovingian descent. His findings are based on an ancient document, *Le Charte d'Alaon*, which though originating from 845, was only published in 1694. Lack of confirmation has permitted a lively debate on the authenticity of this charter, but seen together with the known antiquity of the families it mentions – the Grammonds, the Montesquiou, the Galard, the Luppe and the Comminges – Robin's conclusions would appear to be not unfounded.

Over time, historical fact and legend have certainly fused to create the powerful symbolism of an ancient bloodline, shared by the descendants of a Visigoth–Merovingian nobility, which in turn had a possible connection to the ancient biblical tribes of Benjamin and Judah. But fascinating as it is, the bloodline itself may not be what is important. Surely, of greater significance, politically, financially and historically is that the ancestors of these particular families of the Languedoc-Roussillon were those who shared in the secret of the treasure of the Temple of Jerusalem, believed to have been brought for safe-keeping to the mountains and valleys of the Corbières.

FOOTPRINTS OF
THE WARRIOR-MONKS

Alet and Blanchefort · The Knights Templar · Medieval Banking
A New Treasure · The Independent Kingdom

SITUATED ADJACENT TO the Roman road that extends south
from Toulouse to Carcassonne, and which passes through the
ancient market town of Limoux, is the pretty little village of
Alet-les-Bains. Approached over a medieval bridge across the
fast-flowing River Aude, the village still contains many vestiges
of its ancient past. Founded by the Romans, who named it
Pagus Electensis (meaning the 'favoured' or 'chosen place'), it
enjoys a naturally defensive position and hot mineral water
springs, used to the present day.

Surrounded by a twelfth-century rampart with four fortified
gateways, the village still contains many buildings of the
medieval period. But it is the ruins of the great cathedral that
dominate Alet. Originally an abbey, this magnificent structure
was founded in 813 by Bera, Count of Razès and Barcelona, a
testament to his wealth and power as lord or *seigneur*. Eventually elevated to the status of a cathedral – being the seat of a
bishop – its diocese extended over a vast territory, giving its
bishop great power. As with Rennes-le-Château, today's visitor will find it hard to believe that this sleepy little village was
once the centre of such influence and wealth. One wonders
why these apparently insignificant backwaters should have
attracted such a remarkable history.

A most curious highlight in the history of Alet occurred in the seventeenth century when the village, more or less in ruins following the brutal wars of religion between the Catholics and the Protestants, became a centre for activities the influence of which were to be felt throughout France. A leading light in the French Catholic Church, Nicolas Pavillon, specifically requested the position of Bishop of Alet, despite having been offered far more prestigious posts. Once established at Alet, he set about reconstructing the village and its ancient buildings. His extensive building programme included partial restoration of the great cathedral, a new bishop's palace, a school, roads, irrigation canal, and residential properties. He also became a fervent defender of Jansenism, a formidable heretical Christian sect. Having a rather complex theology with undertones of Christian elitism, Jansenism generally appealed to the more intellectual, but despite both this and vehement opposition from the Jesuits, it became widespread and influential. In fact, the bishops of the neighbouring dioceses of Palmiers, Mirepoix, and Foix all became Jansenists too. But why did Pavillon choose Alet? And where did the money come from?

What is more, Nicolas Pavillon, together with St Vincent de Paul and Jean-Jacques Olier, founder of the Seminary and parish priest of St Sulpice in Paris, became joint head of a secret society, La Compagnie du Saint-Sacrament. Created in 1627, it was also known as La Cabale des Devots. Condemned for its political activities – which reached into the heart of Louis XIII's royal family – the Compagnie appeared to be trying to gain control of all the key positions of State. Operating in the shadows of politics and the Catholic Church, the many names under which it went also included the puzzling Les Enfants de Salomon – that is, The Children of Solomon.

A very clear but extraordinary profile begins to emerge as the facts are put together. The abbey at Alet, after all, was founded by Bera, Count of Razès, descendant of the ancient Merovingian/Visigoth/Jewish family alliances we have traced. Alet now becomes the centre of a secret political society dedicated to the infiltration of the corridors of power. What is more, this is associated with the biblical Solomon, builder of the first Temple of Jerusalem. Through Olier, the secret Compagnie is also connected with the church of St Sulpice – which will also be seen to feature in the tangled web of this saga of hidden treasure.

In the twelfth century, the abbey claimed rights over the 'castrum de Blancafort', the Château of Bernard de Blanchefort, a fief of Rennes-le-Château which came within the diocese of Alet. In 1119, at about the time of the foundation of the Order of the Knights Templar, Pope Calixte II personally intervened and ruled in favour of the abbey. Bernard fought this and, after twelve years of struggle, finally compelled the pope to review his decision. Of Visigothic origin, the ruins of Blanchefort today suggest that this was not so much a château as a fortified watchtower surrounded by Blanchefort lands. But most intriguing is the presence of an ancient goldmine, worked by the Romans, that extends deep into the rocky hillside. Was it Blanchefort tower that was so desirable or the mine underneath which could very possibly have contained part of the ancient Visigoth treasure? The nineteenth-century local historian, Louis Fedié, claimed that the wells at the foot of the walls of Blanchefort, give access to the ancient mine. What is more, locals from the Middle Ages to today have believed that the precious metals extracted from the mine came not from a natural vein of gold but from a deposit of silver and gold secreted there by the Visigoths.

Another local story claims that Blanchefort and Rennes-le-Château are connected by an undergroud passageway or stream. Given the distance involved this would seem unlikely. However, a detailed geophysics map, outlining the geological structure and mineral deposits of the region, does show a fault line in the rock strata that extends west from the village of Granès, passing by the bottom of the west side of the Rennes-le-Château hillside before continuing to the base of Blanchefort, and finally on to the village of Arques. This is only one of a multitude of fault lines; the whole area displays such a profusion of geological activity, caused by the formation of the Pyrenean mountain range, that it would not be surprising to find many extensive subterranean galleries and cave networks. Intense geological activity also created the 1230m high Pech de Bugarach, the most commanding peak in the whole region. Considered by some to be an extinct volcano, hot springs and, more puzzling, a salt-water stream, the Blanque, emanate from it.

Despite a lack of contemporary documents and the inconsistency in spelling at this time, it is generally accepted that the fourth Grand Master of the Knights Templar was a Bernard de Blanquefort. An alternative spelling to Blanchefort, it is most possible that the Blanchefort lands in the Razès were part of the family's greater possessions. The seventeenth-century *L'Histoire Générale de Languedoc*, compiled by the monks at Alet, mentions the Blanquefort family too; of which Arnaud de Blanquefort, a valiant knight, is reported to have supported Raymond of Toulouse. It is also said that Bertrand de Blanchefort had initiated clandestine mining activities, specially importing German miners for the purpose so as to restrict communication with the locals. Indeed, they were explicitly forbidden to do so, thus protecting the secret of the contents of the mine.

Blanchefort is not the only visible connection between the Razès family and the activities of that Order of warrior-monks, known as the Knights Templar. Increasingly, these were coming to play a major political role in western Europe – and the Languedoc in particular. Approximately 6.5km south-east of Rennes-le-Château is a rocky ridge upon which the Visigoths had once constructed fortifications and which, like those at Rennes and Blanchefort, kept guard over this isolated valley and its precious deposits.

Indicated on current maps as the 'Château des Templiers', the ruins visible today are considered to be those of the château of al-Bezun (also Albedun or Albedunum). Its lord, in the early twelfth century, was Bernard Sismund d'al-Bezun. Ancient charters carrying the name show variations of Sismund – Sermon and Simon – but as an acknowledged local historian, J.A. Sipra demonstrates without doubt these are all derived from the Visigothic name Sigismund. Bernard d'al-Bezun was a member of the ancient local Aniort or Oth family (the two names often appear as interchangeable), from whom several of the noble families of the Razès were descended by blood or marriage. He changed his surname to one derived from his place of residence – now called Bézu. He was uncle to two brothers, Bonet and Pierre de Redas who were both Knights Templar, and made substantial gifts to the Templar Order, confirmed in a charter dated 22 February 1151. Donations had been made previously by other local lords, as shown in acts to this effect still kept in the abbey at Alet.

However, Abbé M.R. Mazières, a keen researcher of local history, maintains that the château of Bézu (or Albedun), was not actually under control of the Templar Order, despite the close links between them and the Aniort family. But he believes that a fortress belonging to Pierre d'Aniort was sited a short distance away in the village of Bézu, and that it was the farm of Les Tipliers, further down in the valley, that was the site of a Templar commandery; he observes that Les Tipliers is Catalan for Les Templiers. Whatever the exact location of Templar buildings and the precise nature of its fortifications, there is no doubt that Bézu was an important site to any on the trail of the treasure, and that it played its part in the guardianship of the Razès.

The unique village of Campagne-sur-Aude still displays much evidence of its Templar past. Situated only 5km from Rennes-le-Château on the banks of the River Aude, the village has grown around a circular fort, at the centre of which is a church. Its bygone role, to which its road names attest, has been exhaustively researched by local historian, George Kiess, founder of a well-respected Templar research association.

But who exactly were these medieval Knights? What was

the true nature of their activities? And why did they come to have such a strong connection with this isolated backwater of rural France? Nearly 700 years after the suppression of the original medieval Templars, the appeal of these almost mythical spiritual warriors is still strong. Among a proliferation of chivalric Orders worldwide, the modern Templars are possibly the most numerous – and far exceed the number of original medieval knights. A potent mix of military virtues, such as courage, discipline, fortitude, and strength, together with the spiritual values of self-sacrifice, compassion, charity and chivalry, form a powerful archetype, which may explain something of the Order's appeal; a 'knightly' class of some description has existed in most sophisticated cultures throughout the world. A romantic vision of the Templars appeared even in their own time through the works of writers and poets of the troubador tradition such as Wolfram von Eschenbach, who referred to them as guardians of the Holy Grail. This perception was further enhanced through the works of Sir Thomas Mallory, and later, Sir Walter Scott, as well as by their integration into the higher degrees of Freemasonry in the eighteenth century. But these sources have contributed more to the Templar's legendary aspect than to historical accuracy, and without doubt, there was much more to the Knights Templar than a military force defending Christianity against Islam.

Following the political and spiritual unity that Mohammed brought to the Arab world, the new religion of Islam spread rapidly through the Middle East and North Africa, replacing the powerful Roman and Persian Empires. Palestine, and hence Jerusalem, was under the control of the Moslems by 650, and was to remain so for nearly 450 years. However, Jerusalem still operated as a fairly open city, with Jews, Moslems, and Christians free to follow their religious beliefs.

Interestingly, a large number of Arabs converted to Christianity in the pre-Islamic period; to them Jesus was an Aramaean from the area of Gallilee and so, in the strict definition of the term, not a Jew. Furthermore, many Arabs also converted to Judaism. With the multitude of other cults and sects also established in the Middle East, it is easy to understand how Jerusalem became a spiritual centre for many different faiths.

Of course, for the three major religions of Judaism, Christianity, and Islam, Jerusalem held a special significance, the focal point of which was the great Temple, built over the rocky outcrops of Mount Sion and Mount Moriya, and dominating the centre of the city. For Jews it was the holy site of the prophet Abraham's sacrifice, and later, Solomon's Temple which housed the legendary Ark of the Covenant in its inner sanctum, the Holy of Holies; for Christians it symbolized all this and the passion, death, burial and ascension of Jesus; for the Muslims, the rock of Shetiyah on Mount Moriya was the point where Mohammed had ascended into heaven. In honour of their founder, the Moslems constructed the golden-roofed, eight-sided mosque known as the Dome of the Rock. Yet despite being a magnificent building, the Dome was seen as an affront not only to Jews but to the western Christian community and, compounded by the refusal of the Moslem Seljuks to allow Christian pilgrimages, this provided a powerful motive to launch a series of armed missions.

In 1095, at the Council of Clermont, Pope Urban II appealed for a crusade to liberate the Holy Land from the Moslems. The First Crusade was the most successful, bringing Jerusalem under Christian control. A force of knights and men-at-arms, led by some of Europe's finest nobility – and including Raymond, the powerful Count of Toulouse – entered Jerusalem in July 1099, having fought its way from Constantinople, via Antioch. The leader of this victorious army, Godfroi de Bouillon, Duke of Lorraine, was elected ruler of the conquered lands but did not accept the title, King of Jerusalem; this would fall to his younger brother, Baudouin (or Baldwin) who succeeded him the following year. This was for many highly symbolic since it was claimed that Baudouin and Godfroi were descended from the Counts of Razès, hence from Dagobert II, and thus of the Merovingian/Visigoth/Jewish alliance. As such, they could claim a unique legitimacy to the throne of Jerusalem.

Twenty years later, it appears that three knights, Hugues de Payen, Godefroid de Saint-Omar, and André de Montbard, offered their services to King Baudouin II, to provide security for pilgrims travelling on the roads around the Holy City. Joined shortly after by six more knights, they were offered accommodation in a section of the royal palace on the south side of the Temple site, adjacent to the Al-Aksa mosque. Calling themselves the Poor Knights of Christ, they appeared to do little more than carry out their stated duty of protecting pilgrims. However, some accounts have it that they were busy excavating beneath the Temple mount, in the legendary Stables of Solomon.

Other military-religious Orders were also active in Jerusalem. For instance, the Order of Lazarus cared for lepers; the Order of St John ran hospitals, and are still active today; and within fifty years, the German-orientated Teutonic Knights were established. All the Orders espoused a call to duty as defenders of Christianity, but it is the Knights Templar who have entered the realms of fact and fiction as the archetypical noble warriors. Dressed in full armour with a long white mantle on which was emblazoned a blood-red cross, mounted on armoured war-horses and carrying their black and white chequered battle standard, the Beausant, these Knights must have created an awesome sight to both their allies and adversaries.

However, for the first nine years, this fledgling Order consisted only of the nine knights residing in part of the ancient Temple of Solomon. This is confirmed by the Frankish historian, Guillaume de Tyre, writing in the mid-twelfth century. Yet the king's own historian, Fulk de Chartres, makes no mention of the knights or their mission. Does this strange omission hide a secret agenda? Evidence of digging under the Temple comes from a report by Lt Charles Wilson of the

Royal Engineers, who in the late 1890s led an archaeological expedition to Jerusalem, in the course of which he discovered Templar artefacts at the site of the stables. Additional evidence comes from more recent Israeli investigations: a tunnel extending under the Temple Mount was identified as being of Templar construction. Unfortunately, because this area of Solomon's Temple is under Moslem jurisdiction, further excavation has been denied. It is not known whether the Templars had found something of note – treasure, documents, or other artefacts – but speculation is rife, ranging from the recovery of the Ark of the Covenant to the discovery of lost scrolls of Jesus and the early Christian Church.

The surprising scarcity of information about this early period has understandably contributed to the mystery surrounding the Templar's origins and motives. The only authenticated contemporary reference to the Templars is an account of the visit, in 1121, of Fulk V, Count of Anjou who granted them an annuity of thirty Angevin pounds. In 1125, Hugh, Count of Champagne, the powerful overlord of Hugues de Payen, formally joined the Templars, although he had already been on crusade in 1104. This was some fourteen years before the official founding of the Templars; could Fulk have sent Hugues to Jerusalem with a specific mission? The Count of Champagne, like the Count of Toulouse, was an extremely powerful lord, with more power and influence than the King of France himself. It is possible that Hugues de Payen had been sent to Jerusalem with specific instructions to search for some ancient biblical artefact, perhaps the Ark of the Covenant, or even the body of Jesus himself.

Intriguingly, the Count of Champagne had also provided the land for the foundation of the Cistercian Abbey of Clairvaux. This was established by St Bernard, who was the nephew of André de Montebard, one of the founding Templar Knights. Under Bernard, the Cistercian Order flourished and became a most effective international organization, with wealth to match.

It was also through St Bernard that the nine original knights were to be transformed from a motley crew into what would become, a powerful military-religious order.

Just months after the death of Baudouin II in 1126, Hugues de Payen and André de Montebard returned to Europe on what can best be described as a recruiting campaign. They were remarkably successful in not only attracting new recruits and donations of land, property and other wealth but also, and possibly more significantly, in convincing the Church to endorse their new Order. This took place in 1128 at the Council of Troyes in Champagne, only 13km from the birthplace of Hugues de Payen, under the aegis of the energetic Bernard, Abbot of Clairvaux, who also played a crucial role in drawing up the Order's 'Rule'. In 1147, Pope Eugenius granted the Templars, now called the Military Order of the Knights of the Temple of Solomon, the right to wear the now-familiar red Templar cross on their mantle. From then on the Order went from strength to strength, establishing houses, farms and commanderies throughout Europe. Of these about one-third were in the Languedoc; two of the most influential, Douzens and Mas Dieu, had control over the Corbières, Razés, and Rennes-le-Château – and hence by extension, the hidden treasure.

To augment their military and religious functions, the Templars developed a sophisticated administration comprising a hierarchy of posts with specific duties, both military and domestic, clerks, non-knightly workers and even translators of Arabic. These were found throughout their major centres. And by the beginning of the thirteenth century, the Templars had amassed unparalleled wealth in land, goods and precious coins, not simply through donations and revenues but from deliberate policies of financial dealing and management. This necessitated the careful keeping of records and the development of auditing skills, and with these qualifications, the Templars were soon employed on royal financial commissions and as advisers to monarchs throughout Europe. Taking advantage of these opportunities and refining their competence in financial matters, the Templars achieved a unique role as Europe's bankers.

A number of factors were encouraging the expansion of the economy throughout Europe and the East. The crusades had opened up trade routes and facilitated a massive flow of goods and raw materials from west to east and vice versa, and it was not unusual to find adversaries who nonetheless continued to trade. The steady stream of pilgrims to the Middle East also required goods and services, and in this, shipping played a major part. The Templars maintained their own fleet and became expert in maritime trade; they were sure to establish houses in the key ports of southern Europe. Preeminent as merchants, shippers, and financiers, the Templars have left a lasting legacy.

The medieval world was a dangerous one. Law and order were arbitarily applied and afforded very little protection from outlaws and bandits in open country. It would certainly have been inadvisable for anyone to travel with a quantity of money or precious goods without a small army for protection. This insecurity applied as much to ordinary pilgrims as it did to the nobility. The network of Templar fortified houses quickly undertook the function of what today would be considered a banking system. Depositing their wealth for safekeeping at home, the traveller or pilgrim was given a letter of credit redeemable at other Templar centres, which in effect became the forerunner of the modern cheque. It was only a matter of time before the system gained wider applications, and landowners were able to raise credit from the Templars against the security of their lands. Of course, if the owner was unable to repay the loan this swelled the Templar coffers.

Their function as loan-agents caused some disquiet, but this didn't deter the Templars from offering such a lucrative service. Unlike the Jews, the religious beliefs of Christians and Moslems technically forbade usury – that is the loaning of money for interest. A way around this was to add a fixed commission to the initial loan – essentially interest by another name – so the more religious members of the community still found grounds for condemning this activity. Prominent church leaders vehemently spoke out against money-lending as being as evil as avarice; Christians indulging in this practice were accused of being no better than Jews — a distorted 'righteous' anti-Semitism.

Nevertheless, the Templars remained undeterred and continued to accumulate vast wealth; furthermore it did not deter popes and monarchs from using the Templars as their personal bankers, for collecting taxes and even raising loans. Ultimately, political expediency was to swing things against them, leading to the persecution of the Order. But by then, its activities had already diversified. With the fall of the Holy Land to the Moslems in 1291, the Templars lost their original avowed *raison d'être*; it was time they turned their attention to a very different agenda.

Despite expanding their activities throughout Europe, the Templar's main power base was centred in the Languedoc-Roussillon and Aragon region, more or less the ancient princedom of Septimania. The commandery of Mas Dieu, in the centre of this region, had been founded in 1132, only four years after the Order's official endorsement at the Council of Troyes. But with the original sponsors and initiators of the Order from or connected with Champagne, why would it be the Languedoc that was chosen as its principal focus for activities? Was there something special about this region that made it so particularly attractive?

A group as financially competent, and with direct experience of the ancient Temple of Jerusalem, as the Knights Templar, could hardly have been unaware of the tradition, if not the actual detail, of the presence and value of the Jewish-Visigoth treasure in the Corbières. Throughout the nearly 200 years of their existence they were to maintain total military control over this region, exercising virtual sovereignty over its local nobility. They had received donations of a large number of lands and properties, including mills, vineyards, and farms from its lords. They were even given six châteaux by the Count of Barcelona. By the end of the thirteenth century the Templars of Mas Dieu were at the heart of a grand plan that aimed at nothing less than the creation of a fully independent state.

Though nominally vassals of the king of France, the counties of the Languedoc-Roussillon and Barcelona, being far from Paris (the seat of the king), rarely fulfilled their obligations and gradually turned their allegiance to the much closer kingdom of Aragon. As the power of the Templars became formidable, the Preceptor of Mas Dieu commanded much the same authority as either the king of Aragon or the sovereign Count of Roussillon. From their beginning, the Spanish orientated Templars had developed as an independent power and had always exerted a strong influence over the rest of the Order. An opportunity arose to advance their ambition still further when, through a will made at Barcelona in 1162, Jacques I of Aragon, divided his kingdom. His second son was to become king of Majorca. The new kingdom of Majorca included the Roussillon and its neighbouring regions, in which could be found the great power base of the Templars. They had enjoyed a close and trusted relationship with King Jacques, so following the death of the old king at Valence in 1174, the Templars of Mas Dieu were effectively able to establish a sovereign independent state under the titular head of the king of Majorca. Besides the Balearic Islands, this extended from Montpellier in the north to Barcelona in the south.

Rivalries within kingdoms, and between counts and cities, proved a problem for the Templars. Internal division arose as commanderies allied themselves to their local lord. This division of loyalty, combined with the wealth and power of the Templars at Mas Dieu, was to prove instrumental in their downfall.

Medieval kings of all nations were habitually short of money, both from excesses of expenditure on luxury living and from continually waging war – maintaining an army was very expensive. Philippe le Bel, king of France, was no exception. He tried to enter the Templar Order, doubtless with the longer-term objective of becoming Grand Master and to gain control of their military might and enormous wealth, but was denied. In other attempts to reduce his liabilities, he defaulted on loans made to him by the Lombard merchants, extracting huge taxes from them; he employed similar tactics against the Jews, even expelling them from his kingdom. As minority groups these were fairly simple targets; the Templars would require more devious action.

In 1305, Philippe succeeded in manipulating the election of Bertrand de Goth, Archbishop of Bordeaux, to the papacy. Whether by design or by coincidence, Bertrand, who took the name Pope Clement V, was also the grand-nephew of Bertrand de Blanchefort, the Templar Grand Master, through his mother Ida de Blanchefort. It is unknown how divided his loyalties were when he was called upon by Philippe to support him against the Templars. But he did persuade him to leave the Holy Seat in Rome to take up residency in Avignon; Philippe now had the pope fully under his control. Then, with advice from Nogaret, his able but cunning chief minister, Philippe compiled a damning list of heretical practices with which he accused the Templars.

In medieval Europe, heresy was possibly the most serious of all crimes and justified the use of extreme measures. On Friday 13 October 1307, an arrest warrant, issued by the king of France and implemented through Nogaret, ensured the immediate detention of a large number of 'Templars'. (Very few of these would actually turn out to be Knights.) Pope Clement was dismayed at Philippe's actions; heresy was a religious and not secular crime and there was no real evidence of the Templars' guilt. But politics prevailed and, within a year, Clement acquiesced. The Templar Order was officially condemned, and finally dissolved. Without delay, Philippe entered the Paris Temple expecting to seize the Templar treasure: since the Templars had been his personal banker, he assumed they held the royal treasure along with their own. Yet with disbelief he found no trace of it – and very little in commanderies elsewhere (each commandery had its own safety deposit with some reserves of gold and silver). Of course, his principal objective was not to be found in Paris, but some 1,000km south, in the remote valleys of the Corbières.

The château-fortress of Pierre d'Aniort at Albedun (Bézu), as well as the fortified tower at Blanchefort, had been destroyed in the mid-thirteenth century, so the Templars from Roussillon, under the authority of Mas Dieu, established a new fortified base at Bézu within sight of the château at Rennes. There was already a Templar fort at Campagne-sur-Aude, less than 8km away, which came under the jurisdiction of the mother house at Douzens, as well as a number of hilltop forts commanded by local lords sympathetic to the Templars, which provokes the question as to why a new base was necessary. The prevailing and enduring tradition among the locals was that the Templars had discovered and wanted either to exploit a hidden treasure, or to bury one of their own. Certainly, the Templars were to ensure that neither their own nor any treasure of the Temple of Jerusalem would be found by anybody else, including the new king of France. Furthermore, what better place to hide the enormous Templar treasure away from the clutches of King Philippe than in the heart of the Templars' own intended kingdom?

The researches of Corbu and Captier reveal an even closer link between Rennes-le-Château and the Templars. A charter of the Templars of Douzens shows that a Templar family lived at Rennes even before the establishment of Alberdun (Bézu). Called Pierre de St Jean, lord of Rhedae, he became a Templar in 1147, and progressed to Commander of Douzens and Brucafel. Ultimately, he became Preceptor and Master of Carcassonne and Rhedae, between 1167 and 1169.

Not only were their treasuries bare after the Templars' arrest; their fleet had disappeared along with the majority of Knights. Sure indications that they must have had prior warning of Philippe's intentions. An organization as powerful as the Templars with such an extensive network, would doubtless have had an intelligence wing. It is most improbable that they would not have been aware of the factors leading to their demise, and so were prepared to take the appropriate action when the moment arose. Unlike Douzens, Mas Dieu was of course not within the realm of the king of France. It is thus quite logical that the isolated valleys of the Corbières, already containing the legendary treasure of the Temple of Jerusalem, was thus also to be chosen as the last hiding place of the treasure of the Knights Templar.

4

SPLENDOUR AND TRAGEDY
IN THE LANGUEDOC

The Cathars · The Troubadours and the Holy Grail
The Treasure of Montségur · Counterfeiting

THE MYSTERIOUS, WILD and romantic Languedoc, with its curving golden coastline, vine-laden plains, rugged sparsely covered hills, and secluded valleys, has also been home to riches of a quite different kind than those of ancient treasure. It has often been said that knowledge is power; power invariably leads to wealth. Certainly, wealth explains in part the quite extraordinary advance in culture found here in the Middle Ages. Following the checking of the Islamic invasion of the Iberian peninsula at the Pyrenees by Charles Martel, the Languedoc became an interface between the cultures of the Middle East and the West. In addition, Marseilles, Avignon, Narbonne, and Toulouse had been major ports since ancient times. Traffic generated by the crusades and the resulting trade had enabled the merchants and nobles to amass fortunes to a greater extent than elsewhere in France. Together with the material trade enriching the region, a flow of knowledge and wisdom, originating from the ancient classical worlds of Greece and Rome, was allowed to flourish under the Moslems and thus came to be felt in the Languedoc.

Though the Christian Church, both Roman and Orthodox streams, had itself inherited a wealth of learning from the ancient world, it adopted a policy of strict censorship over what knowledge was fit for public consumption, fearful that such learning could constitute a challenge to its own doctrines. It further discouraged the search for scientific discovery and the development of independent thought, opting instead to 'teach' the people what it thought was necessary for them to know. The consequence was the stifling of progress in many fields, including science, medicine, and philosophy, for centuries. But the human spirit and sense of curiosity cannot be suppressed for long, and there were those who ignored, at their peril, the restrictions in the search for truth.

By contrast, the Arab world voraciously absorbed and developed the wisdom of the ancients. Within 300 years of the death of Mohammed, Islamic culture was far more advanced than that of European Christendom. Of course, the Islamic faith also had its sects and internal rivalries through which dynasties would come and go, exerting varying degrees of power and influence. One of the most successful of these was a sect called the Ismailis who arose through a schism in 765, coming to prominence a century later. With a strong intellectual and emotional appeal, and a respect for tradition, the Ismailis drew support from much of the Islamic world. For the intellectuals they presented a philosophical explanation of the universe, drawing on the sources of ancient and especially neo-Platonic thought. For the spiritual, they brought a warm, personal and comforting faith, with a continuous quest for the truth. Recognized as a branch of Islam today, they continue to flourish under their spiritual leader, the Aga Kahn, who claims to be a direct descendant of the Prophet.

The Ismaili cause was given an enormous boost with the emergence of the great Fatimid dynasty (named after Fatima, the daughter of Mohammed), which adopted their faith. At their peak, in the tenth century, they controlled North Africa, Sicily, the Red Sea coast of Africa, the Yemen and Hijaz in Arabia, as well as the two holy cities of Mecca and Medina. Their main base was at Cairo, Egypt. In Cairo, as in other great cities, they established the world's first universities, pre-dating Europe's own by about 200 years. However, by 1090, the Fatimid dynasty was in decline, unable to withstand the challenge posed from the more aggressive Seljuk and later Zangid Sultanate. Yet, despite political upheavals, the Islamic world continued to allow the free transmission of knowledge.

When the Crusaders of northern Europe, indoctrinated with a false vision of pagan Islamic hordes, arrived in the Holy Land on their mission of liberation, one can only imagine their utter astonishment to find such cultural sophistication. This didn't deter them from pursuing their objective with ruthless determination. But there is abundant evidence that they did show some respect for, and even cooperated with, their pagan adversaries. But some Europeans had already made contact with Islamic culture 300 years earlier, on the doorstep of Europe, when the Umayyad Caliphate had swept throughout the Middle East, North Africa and the Iberian Peninsula. Within fifty years the Umayyads were to be replaced, except in Spain, by the Abbasid dynasty, who were to found the great new city of Baghdad, which would become one of the known world's most eminent centres of learning. The Umayyid prince took the title of Emir and, with his capital at Cordoba, established an independent Emirate. As elsewhere, political upheavals continued to cause disruption, but failed to hold back the flourishing Islamic culture. Irrigation enabled new crops such as cotton, rice, and oranges to be grown, as well as orchards and vineyards to be planted, on previously arid land. Spices, silks, and perfumes, all contributed to a variety and comfort of life unknown to the majority of northern Europeans.

Despite the Umayyid independence, a steady stream of scholars travelled between Baghdad and Cordoba carrying with them scientific knowledge, literary and artistic works and, possibly most important, a sophisticated level of philosophy.

Originally of Phoenician foundation, Cordoba became the capital of Islamic Spain, with a population of over a million, and the centre of learning in Europe boasting a library of more than 400,000 books. Such was the enlightenment of its ruling body that even its Christian adversaries, engaged in a continuous crusade in the north, were treated with tolerance and respect. Cordoba, a city of illumination when Europe was emerging from the Dark Ages, attracted seekers of knowledge in their thousands – Arab, Christian, and Jew alike. Schools of music, astronomy, medicine, alchemy, mathematics, and many other disciplines, flourished.

Among those drawn to this beacon of light was Gerbert d'Aurillac, the future Pope Sylvester II. Some French historians have said that Gerbert, the first French pope, was the most learned man of his time to wear the papal tiara. Born near Aurillac, the capital of the Cantal region north of the Languedoc (a name which, as in villages like Orbeilles, Auroux, Les Aurières, and Auriac, evokes the presence of gold though the element *Or*, which is French for gold and derived from the Latin *Aurum*), Gerbert was the son of a poor manager of an estate belonging to the Abbey of Saint-Géraud. As with many figures of antiquity, his life has been embellished with legend; it is not a simple task to extract the facts from the mythology.

According to French author Pierre Jarnac, Gerbert, as a young man tending to his father's flock one evening, was spotted by some monks from the nearby Abbey of Saint-Géraud, staring up at the sky, counting the stars. The monks stopped to speak to him and were amazed at the apparent wisdom of his replies. With the permission of his parents, they adopted Gerbert. In the abbey he would receive a classical education worthy of his intellectual ability. He thus became a Benedictine monk, and gained a reputation as a scholar. After fifteen years, his 'free spirit' compelled him to extend his search for knowledge. In the words of Voltaire, 'science magnified his soul.'

The story continues that Borel, Count of Barcelona, having returned from a pilgrimage to the tomb of Géraud in Spain, visited the Abbey of Saint-Géraud, where he made contact with Gerbert. Fired up by the enthusiastic report of Borel,

Gerbert left the abbey and travelled to Cordoba to 'learn the curious arts of the Arabs who held the key to great secrets'. It is said that he was later employed by the Emperor Othon II as tutor to his son, the future Othon III, and soon enhanced his reputation as a wise teacher. A fascination with alchemy led him into the world of transmutation, the secret of manufacturing gold from base metal, in which he achieved the status of not only initiate but adept. This inevitably brought him into conflict with the hierarchy of the Roman Catholic Church which had developed a paranoia about scientific knowledge. For its own purposes, the Church maintained a virtual monopoly over education and the dissemination of knowledge throughout Christendom, a position that gave it a power that it was determined to protect.

In the Middle Ages, alchemical and scientific knowledge were viewed with suspicion and in some cases its possessors were considered as the devil's magicians. Possibly realizing where his best future lay, Gerbert managed to reconcile himself with the Church. He decided to return to Rheims, site of the baptism of Clovis, where he offered his services to Hugues Capet, claimant to the throne of France. He contrived not only to replace the Archbishop of Ravenna but in 999 to be elected pope, taking the name Sylvester II. Gerbert's political skills and his awesome intellect kept his critics at bay and ensured his survival.

Thanks to his stay in Spain with the Jewish and Arab scholars, he is credited with introducing (or re-introducing) into the rest of Europe, the use of mercury, mechanical clocks with an escapement, the astrolabe for navigation, and even distilled alcohol. Sylvester also brought back to Christendom the basis of our modern numbering system, including the zero (unknown in Roman numbering), and the concept of decimals. But legend also recounts a more telling incident. It is claimed that Gerbert discovered that the river flowing through Aurillac contained small particles of gold mixed in its sediment. By immersing a piece of sheepskin in the flowing waters he was able, through disturbing the sediment, to trap these small flakes in the fleece. Upon withdrawal from the water, the sheepskin glistened with gold, much to the surprise of his on-lookers. Needless to say this became further ammunition for all those accusing him of diabolical powers and, following his death in 1003, he was branded a heretic and virtually expunged from Vatican history. Such was the power and fear of knowledge.

Gerbert was only one of many who returned to northern Europe, having experienced the learning not only of the Arabs, but of Jewish scholars and even Persian philosophers. There were two well-trodden routes from Spain into France: one was the old Roman road following the coast from Narbonne down past Elne, onto Barcelona and beyond to the south of Spain; the other was the pilgrim route from Le Puy in the Massif Central to the great shrine, allegedly containing the relics of St James, established in the ninth century in north-western Spain, at Santiago de Compostela. Both these routes passed through the Languedoc, and where in the eleventh–thirteenth centuries, during the period of the troubadours, there was an unparalleled blossoming of literature and music at the splendid courts of the region's nobility. Using elaborate and elegant language, the troubadours composed long romantic poems of courtly love and noble quests, recited for the pleasure of the lords of the Languedoc and Provence.

Of these great literary works, *Parsival*, by Wolfram von Eschenbach, is one of the best known. It also introduces the theme of the Holy Grail, one of the most enduring archetypes of Christian mysticism. The exact nature of the Grail is still open to debate: to some it represents the blood of Christ or the chalice of the Last Supper; to others it is the quest for inner purity and the meaning of life. It could also be the secret of eternal life, the philosopher's stone, the Ark of the Covenant, or the treasure of the Temple of Jerusalem. Whatever its nature, the Grail is considered priceless, and may only be approached by those that are pure in heart.

Adopted as a Christian symbol by the Catholic Church, the

Holy Grail of Wolfram's poem is given a different provenance. Despite writing for a Christian audience under the patronage of Herman von Duringen, Count of (modern) Thuringia, Wolfram did not hesitate to explain, within the text, that he had learned the story from Kyot, a Provençal troubadour, who had seen the story of Parsival at Toledo, written in 'heathen' – Arabic. He later states that Kyot had himself learnt the story from Flegetanis, 'a Jewish scholar born of Solomon, who could read the movement of the stars'. In conjunction with the rest of the Parsival story, these details of its origins are intended to show how the Grail concept transcends the divisions in the basic dogmas of Christianity, Islam, and Judaism. Wolfram also asserts his belief in a higher mission of the religious-military orders by referring to the Knights Templar as the 'Guardians of the Grail'. Without doubt, the Templars were guarding something in the heart of the Corbières; could it be that the Holy Grail was actually part of the ancient treasure of the Temple? Or is the treasure the Grail itself?

Also closely connected with the Grail stories was the Cathar heresy which mushroomed throughout the region from the mid-twelfth century. Of uncertain origin, the Cathar teachings have much in common with those of the Bogomils of eastern Europe, based on the dualistic philosophy of the Persian Manichaeans and Zoroastrians. Despite a radically different theology in which they believed that the material world was intrinsically evil, the Cathars lived a life that was patently more Christian than the Catholics. This didn't pass unobserved by Rome. Yet, although espousing an austere and spiritual existence, they were rumoured to have amassed a great treasure, and by some to have been in possession of the Holy Grail itself. Evidence certainly shows that the Cathars enjoyed the protection of local Templars, some of whom had family ties. Also, the great lords of the Languedoc, who even if not of the faith themselves, gave them their full support. This policy was to result in a most bloody and brutal persecution.

In July 1209, an army of nobles, knights, and men swept

down from the north to beseige the town of Béziers, led by Simon de Montfort (grandfather of the famous English knight) and Arnaud-Amaury, the Abbot of Citeaux. Upon entering the town, when asked by a knight how he should recognize a heretic from a Catholic, Amaury is said to have replied, 'Kill them all. God will know his own.' This signalled the start of what was to become known as the Albigensian Crusade – named after the town of Albi, site of a particularly vicious attack.

Some forty years earlier, after Catharism had achieved a firm grip on the region, the local Catholic bishops, alarmed by the conversion of their congregations to this new faith, had alerted Rome; but it was to be many years before action would be taken. The king of France, and many of his most powerful barons, preoccupied in fighting the English who at this time held the western half of France, had little interest in an internal crusade. However, the pope offered an inducement in that all lands taken from the heretics would be forfeit to the aggressor. For over a century, the barons of the north had kept their avaricious eyes on the splendid and wealthy culture of the Languedoc, but powerful local counts, like those of Toulouse, Barcelona, Foix, and Comminges, and their vassals, had been considered unassailable. At first, the Catholic Church sent a mission to the region in an attempt to reconvert the Cathars by preaching. Despite being unsuccessful, no further action was taken until the mysterious murder of the Papal Legate, Pierre de Castelnau. Unjustly blamed on Raymond VI, Count of Toulouse, this murder provided an ideal excuse to launch a crusade.

Although Raymond was the virtual overlord of most of the Languedoc, he avoided direct confrontation with the crusading army by the somewhat cowardly strategy of taking on the crusader's cross himself, leaving his feudal vassals to take the brunt. Of these, the young and courageous Raymond-Roger Trencavel, Viscount of Béziers, Carcassonne, Albi, and Razès, attempted to defend Béziers and Carcassonne, to no avail. The crusaders swept through this peaceful and cultured land, looting, burning, torturing and killing heretics; laying waste the châteaux, forts and homes of the nobility. The ruined castles still precariously perched on rocky hilltops are an enduring testament to this bloody episode. Known popularly as Cathar castles, the origins of these predate the Cathars. In some instances, they even have Visigothic foundations.

It is of particular note that seventeen of these castles form an oval ring enclosing an area of some 600 square kilometres. At the centre of this is the imposing and isolated castle of Auriac. And it is within this oval of stark, silent ruins that the treasures of the Temple of Jerusalem, and possibly that of the Knights Templar, are said to remain.

Nine years after the destruction of Albi, Simon de Montfort was killed outside Toulouse following its liberation by Raymond VI. He was succeeded by his son Amaury who, proving to be less competent, was forced to discontinue the crusade and to return home. A period of diplomatic manoeuverings and an uneasy peace followed, the county of Toulouse was annexed to the crown of France. However, by 1240, the crusaders were back and once again the region was subject to the ravages of fire and sword.

Twenty-five years earlier, a Spanish monk, Dominique Guzman, had founded the Dominican Order of Black Friars. Charged with the mission of rooting out heresy and heretics, Dominique created the institution which would come to be known as the Holy Inquisition. Feared throughout Christendom for its extensive and ruthless use of torture, the Inquisition would become the most powerful weapon of the Roman Catholic Church.

The renewed crusade culminated in 1244 at the mountaintop fortress of Montségur ('Safe Mountain'), the siege of which was both tragic and mysterious, and a lasting symbol of Catharism. Following the sacking of other centres, Raymond de Pereille had allowed his castle at Montségur to become the new centre of the Cathar Church. But within a short time the crusading army arrived at the foot of the mountain. Due to its position on the peak, an assault proved difficult, as did the cutting off of supply routes, which gave rise to ten months of siege. But the defenders finally had to negotiate a surrender with an armistice period of a fortnight. During this armistice, two heretics, Matheus and Peter Bonnet (some accounts claim two more) left the fortress by a secret and perilous route. They took with them the Cathar treasure. Speculation as to the exact nature of this has been rife ever since, but one Inquisition account mentions *pecuniam infinitam*, that is, a large quantity of gold and silver bullion. It is reported that there were at least two successful previous attempts to remove parts of this treasure to a place of safe-keeping. Montségur was not the only castle to be associated with treasure; those of Puylayurens and Queribus had similar reports revealed in the Inquisition records. It is quite possible that it was passed into the hands of the Templars for safe-keeping. But it has not surfaced since in any identifiable form. Shrouded in myth and legend, the accounts that remain of both the material and spiritual treasure of the Cathars were even to prompt secret excavations 700 years later.

Among the crusading knights peopling this story, two in particular are significant. The first of these is the noble Guy de Levis, whose name evokes Merovingian/Visigoth/Jewish connections, echoing that of Dagobert's trusted knight Mérovée Levi. The second is Simon de Montfort's lieutenant, Pierre de Voisin, who was to found a new dynasty that was to dominate the Razès.

The de Voisin family took over the mantle of Lords of Rennes-le-Château from the deposed Trencavels and were responsible for rebuilding the Visigoth château and partially restoring the ruins of Rhedae to their former glory. While no doubt aware of the precious deposits within their domain, it is not known for sure whether they knew the actual details of their locations. Further east, beyond Château Blanchefort, they constructed the *donjon* (keep) of the Château d'Arques. This is of course a name with associations to the Ark of the Covenant.

Could it indeed be the Ark that the Templars had found during their excavations under the temple of Jerusalem? And did they bring it here?

The Château at Arques is only 2km east of the old French zero meridian of longitude, established in 1666 on the command of Louis XIV, ostensibly as a rival to the English Greenwich meridian. It extends down the centre of France, striking at the heart of the Corbières like an arrow. It is almost as if the meridian is a symbolic signpost indicating the significance of the region. Less than 1km from the meridian is the mysterious monument known popularly as 'Poussin's tomb', resembling the tomb featured in *Les Bergers d'Arcadie* by the great French artist Nicolas Poussin. Of obscure origin, its earliest recorded mention being in 1903, this tomb has spawned its own mythology. Painted in about 1640, *Les Bergers d'Arcadie* bears a remarkable resemblance to the tomb and its surrounding landscape – suggesting that the tomb existed at this time. Art historians assert that there is no evidence that Poussin ever visited this area and would therefore have not known about the tomb, even if it had existed. However, there is a strong link between Poussin and Arques which is historically documented.

Most of Poussin's career was spent in Rome; during this time Henrietta-Catherine de Joyeuse and her husband Charles de Lorraine had been forced into exile in Rome by Cardinal Richelieu. From her father, Ange de Joyeuse, Marshal Governor of the Languedoc, Henrietta-Catherine had inherited the titles Duchess of Joyeuse, Countess of Eu, Baroness of Laudun, Roquemaure, Couiza, Esperaza and Arques. The last three of these are very close to Rennes-le-Château and Blanchefort. It could very well have been as a result of a meeting between them, that Poussin was moved to paint this symbolic work. From 1640 to 1642, he had been coerced back to Paris by Cardinal Richelieu for whom he was expected to execute several works. The court of Louis XIII was a hostile environment, but Poussin had the protection of Sublet de Noyes, Royal Treasurer and Secretary of State. His father had been financial adviser to the household of the Cardinal of Joyeuse, uncle of the Baron of Arques, who had been exiled to Rome. Thus, Poussin's connections with the Joyeuse family were very strong; could he have not known of the great secret of the treasure, buried in the heart of their lands?

It is said that after Louis XIV had acquired the painting, which he kept in his private chamber, he sent his chief minister, Colbert, to investigate the region. Evidently aware of its symbolism, Colbert is said to have initiated diggings at Blanchefort, Arques, and other local sites, and to have destroyed the original tomb. Some local historians assert that a tomb at this site was mentioned in an eighteenth-century inventory of the Abbé Delmas.

Poussin's *Les Bergers d'Arcadie* is in fact his second treatment of this theme. An earlier version, entitled *Et in Arcadia Ego,* is one of a pair of paintings now part of the collection of the Duke of Devonshire at Chatsworth House, England. This earlier version includes the river god Alpheus emptying a large pitcher of water, symbolic of the River Pactolus. The companion painting illustrates the legend of King Midas attempting to wash away the curse of his 'golden touch' in the same river, overlooked by Alpheus. Was not Poussin, the great philosopher-painter, not working to preserve a great secret, using his prodigious skill in symbolism and art to leave an encoded message that could only be understood by other initiates?

There is also another tantalizing clue that Poussin was in possession of a momentous secret of inestimable value. In Rome in 1656, he received an unexplained visit from the Abbé Louis Fouquet. The Abbé sent a letter, concerning this meeting, to his brother, Nicolas Fouquet, who was Superintendent of Finances to Louis XIV. The letter, which has survived in the archives of the aristocratic Cossé-Brissac family, contains the following enigmatic passage:

> He and I discussed certain things, which I shall with ease be
> able to explain to you in detail – things which will give you,
> through Monsieur Poussin, advantages which even kings would
> have great pains to draw from him, and which, according to
> him, it is possible that nobody else will ever rediscover in the
> centuries to come. And what is more, these are things so
> difficult to discover that nothing now on this earth can prove
> of better fortune nor be their equal.

The contents of this letter have never been conclusively
explained, but could it not be that Poussin was referring to the
Holy Grail or the treasure from the Temple of Jerusalem?

At this time, Nicolas Fouquet was the wealthiest man in
France, having misappropriated taxes collected on behalf of the
king. Following a visit to Fouquet's magnificent château at
Vaux-le-Vicomte outside Paris, however, Louis carried out an
investigation of his minister's activities and, finding him guilty
of embezzlement, had him imprisoned for the rest of his life.
Fouquet, clearly obsessed with the acquisition of wealth, would
have been particularly intrigued by Poussin's secret.

★ ★ ★

Other more tangible discoveries of gold have of course been
made in the area. The most bizarre must be the story, fully
documented in the French national archives, of the counterfeiting of gold coins at the ruined château of Bézu. Some
twenty-five years after the suppression of the Templars in
1314, and ten years into the reign of King Philip VI of Valois,
the king's treasury ministers became alarmed at the appearance
of counterfeit coins in circulation. Their source was a mystery.
But most surprisingly, these coins contained a higher gold
content than the official currency! Extensive enquiries led them
to the Languedoc and to the ancient château at Bézu. Having
withstood the ravages of the Albigensian Crusade and the
Templar suppression, the fortress at Bézu had never been taken
by force, but by 1340, belonged to Jacques de Voisin, the son
of Pierre de Voisin, Simon de Montfort's second-in-command,

who had earned a reputation in the area as a great and honest knight.

The Senechal of Paris, chief official in the royal household, sent Guillaume de Servin, his second-in-command, to investigate these activities. Arriving unexpectedly, he discovered a cave containing minting equipment and a stock of gold ready to use. Of further astonishment was that the perpetrators were not common villains but members of the local nobility: Guilhem Catalini, son-in-law of Jacques de Voisin and a nephew of the reigning Pope Benedict XII; Brunissande de Gureyo, the wife of Jacques; Pierre de Palajan, Lord of Coustaussa (a village on the hill north of Rennes-le-Château); Agnes Mayssene de Caderone; and Dame Francoise, Lady of Niort.

Surprised in their illegal deed, the counterfeiters seized Guillaume and threw him over the cliff. On noting his disappearance the authorities went to Bézu in force, arrested the nobles and brought them to trial. They were sentenced to imprisonment and the forfeiture of their goods. Meanwhile, Jacques de Voisin, who had masterminded the operation, was away, fighting on behalf of the king, in Flanders. Hearing of the plight of his fellow conspirators, he approached the pope and other noble families of the region for their intervention. Eventually, in 1344, the new pope, Clement VI, obtained a pardon for them from the king of France. The act of remission, in which the participants are mentioned, is held today in the French national archives.

A story almost more extraordinary than fiction, this raises a number of questions pertinent to this unfolding story of the treasure hidden in the Corbières. Where had the counterfeiters' gold come from? Why would they mint coins of a greater gold content than the official currency, unless their own supply of gold was colossal, and in a form not able to be publicly revealed? Evidence perhaps of the Cathar treasure *pecuniam infinitam*? But this operation had also involved practically all of the nobility of the Razès, those who would have been most likely to have inherited or acquired the secrets of the treasure of the Corbières. Family connections aside, to receive a full pardon for such illegal activities was quite exceptional. Perhaps they were able to buy their freedom? All of these questions remain unresolved – but above all, the source of the gold has never been established.

LOST GOLD,
SECRET SEARCHES

Nicolas Flamel · Pope Sylvester II · General Dagobert
Napoleon · The Vatican Library

WHILE THE LORDS of the Razès were busy with their counterfeiting operations, a young man was growing up in Paris
who, despite documentary evidence and an autobiography,
would enter the world of mythology. Nicolas Flamel was born
in 1330 at Pontoise and, evidently well educated, became a
scrivener (book copier), finally acquiring a bookshop. At the
age of thirty, he married a woman called Perrenelle. Being an
educated man he was able to profit intellectually from the
many rare books and manuscripts that passed through the shop,
and he became proficient in painting, poetry, architecture,
mathematics, and astrology.

In his autobiography, *Le Livre des Figures Hiéroglyphiques*,
Flamel describes how he bought, for two florins, a book
written by Abraham the Jew. It carried the most bizarre title:
*The Sacred Book of Abraham the Jew, Prince, Levite, Astrologer and
Philosopher to that Tribe of Jews who by the Wrath of God were
Dispersed amongst the Gauls.* This curious book, which would
become famous in the world of those who studied the cabbala
(Jewish mysticism), alchemy and the western mystery tradition,
consisted of twenty-one leaves of beautifully written Latin text
and cryptic illustrations. Nicolas and Perenelle spent twenty-
one fruitless years attempting to penetrate the secret meaning

of these enigmatic writings; in desperation Flamel went to Spain, at that time the centre of cabbalistic and alchemical wisdom, where at Leon in 1382, he met a Jewish cabbalist who had converted to Catholicism, and who could explain the sacred texts to him. Inspired, Flamel returned to Paris. He and Perenelle set to work in his laboratory on the transmution of metals – for this was the secret encoded in the texts. On the 17th January, a date that will occur frequently in later chapters, he claimed to have produced pure gold and silver from base metal. While one may remain sceptical about the effectiveness of these alchemical operations, it is on public record that he became extremely wealthy. He acquired more than thirty houses, endowed hospitals, churches and charities, and had an arch constructed at Saint-Jacques-la-Boucherie, inscribed with symbolic figures, that commemorated his alchemical success.

This remarkable episode contains a number of elements that resonate in the context of the wider picture revealed so far. It is interesting to note that the information that probably led to Flamel's phenomenal wealth came from a Jewish cabbalistic source; a book which referred to a Jewish strain within the ancient Gauls, and that to access this knowledge Flamel had to go to Spain, the ancient kingdom of the Visigoths. It is possible that in so doing, the most significant thing he stumbled across was not the secret of alchemy, but knowledge that allowed him to recover some of the ancient Jewish-Visigoth treasure buried in the Corbières, close to a main route from France to Spain. Given this possibility, it becomes no surprise to learn that he is to be found included in the history of a secret society, today at the centre of a web surrounding the treasure; and that Flamel and his findings drew the attention of men of the calibre of Isaac Newton, and others, who are also likely to have been implicated in this enduring mystery. And, interestingly, despite entering the realm of mythology and for a document supposedly containing such great secrets, the book of 'Abraham the Jew' can be found in the Arsenal Library, Paris.

Researches of Jean-Pierre Deloux and Jacques Brétigny have revealed that, throughout the centuries, the association of gold with the Corbières is undeniable both in fact and in legend. In 746, the mines at Auriac were exploited jointly by the monks of the Abbey of Saint-Martin-d'Albières and the Lords of Rennes; a hundred years later they were obtained by the Archbishop of Narbonne for his diocese, and then, in 898, these rights were confirmed, but included the renewed rights of the Lords of Rennes. The mine at Blanchefort was also being worked in the Middle Ages, again under the supervision of the Lords of Rennes. But the most surprising fact is that these mines, worked from Roman and possibly Phoenician times, were considered to be exhausted of all viable sources; so what was the true source of gold 'mined' and 'minted' over the centuries?

In the mid-seventeenth century the *Memoires de l'Histoire du Languedoc, Tome 1* by Guillaume de Catel related that German workers were imported to excavate the mines near Rennes-les-Bains. About the same time a story began circulating that concerned a shepherd called Jean (in some versions he is called Ignace Paris). Out looking for a lost lamb, Jean fell into a ditch which revealed an underground chamber in which he discovered a quantity of gold coins. Taking some coins back to his village, he was accused by some of the villagers of stealing, and stoned to death. The local lord remained strangely quiet!

In 1734, Lamdignon de Basville was to write, 'The Romans had mines of gold in these mountains but, as the mines were exhausted, the art of finding them was lost and the treasures are now so hidden that it is impossible to find them.' But an article about Carcassonne that appeared in *Le Dictionnaire Historique de Moreri 1759*, reaffirms the possibility of the continuing existence of the Visigothic treasure, including that of the Jews. Then in 1832, a keen traveller on a visit to Rennes-les-Bains, Labouisse-Rochefort, came across a local tale of the treasure of Blanchefort, valued at 19.5 million gold francs and guarded by the Devil, which he then reported in his book,

Voyage a Rennes-les-Bains. Some years later, an archaeologist from the Aude confirmed local treasure traditions and, in 1876, a very well-respected and knowledgeable local librarian, Justin Firmin from Limoux, later to become Conservator of the local library and Secretary of the Society for Arts and Sciences of Carcassonne, carried out a detailed analysis of the known facts and popular stories concerning the treasure, and reached the same conclusion that it must indeed exist.

Some remarkable discoveries add weight to this. In 1860, a very substantial gold ingot, made of imperfectly melted-down ancient coins and weighing 50kg, was found in a field; another 20kg of gold was discovered on a separate occasion in a wood. Since then there have been various finds of ancient silver and gold coins, and it is alleged that some villagers at Rennes-le-Château, at the turn of the twentieth century, benefitted from gifts of Visigoth jewellery and other precious items, uncovered by their parish priest. Understandably, the recipients of these gifts have been reluctant to discuss them, though the researcher Gérard de Sède does claim that they were shown to him. Finally, in 1928, a small partially melted golden statue was found in the nearby River Blanque.

References to treasure buried in the Corbières can also be found cryptically woven into the stories of at least two prominent French authors, Maurice Leblanc and Jules Verne. In 1905, Maurice Leblanc created the character of the gentleman thief, Arsène Lupin. Leblanc's many stories of his hero's adventures contain a remarkable number of indirect references to the mysteries of Rennes-le-Château, especially that of the treasure. The extensive references demonstrate an in-depth knowledge not only of the region's mainstream history, but of the traditions, symbolism and personalities now seen to be connected with these mysteries. But even more noteworthy, these stories were written fifty years before the more recent interest in the Abbé Saunière, Rennes-le-Château and the ancient treasure. A very comprehensive examination of these connections can be found in Patrick Ferté's *Arsène Lupin – Supérieur Inconnu* (1992).

Jules Verne, a household name thanks to *Around the World in Eighty Days* and *Twenty Thousand Leagues Under the Sea*, would seem to be an unlikely participant in the secret of the treasure. Born in 1828, Verne published *Journey to the Centre of the Earth* at the age of thirty-six, which has become a classic in the science fiction genre. But it is a far less well-known work, *Clovis Dardentor*, that links him to the mysteries of the Corbières. An acknowledged master of puns and anagrams, he appears to have encoded messages within his stories, particularly in *Clovis*.

French researcher and writer Michel Lamy has extensively analysed this and other works in his book *Jules Verne – Initié et Initiateur* (1984). It explores how Verne's membership of secret societies and association with Freemasonry probably introduced him to the mystery of the treasure. The title of *Clovis Dardentor* itself contains a strong clue to the hidden message of the book: 'Clovis' refers to that Merovingian king who unified the Franks and defeated the Visigoths at Vouille, pushing them back to the foothills of the Pyrenees; 'Dardentor' can be separated into *D'ardent*, the title given to the descendants of Clovis once they lost their regal power, and *or*, French for gold. Hence the title is in effect describing, 'the Visigoth gold of Clovis and his deposed descendents' – who are none other than the Counts of Razès, the Lords of Rennes and the other ancient families of the Corbières, guardians of the secret of the treasure!

The thread of the treasure surfaces most often in association with the activities of certain groups, families and individuals. Without doubt the ancient noble families of the region have possessed the secret of the presence of the treasure if not its actual locations. And by looking in more detail at these families and their members, key signposts can be uncovered along the treasure trail.

It is in the late eighteenth century, a decade before the

French Revolution, that a very real and illustrious figure enters the scene, whose exploits are to play a major role in the future course of events. Luc Siméon-Auguste Dagobert, later to become a general in the Republican Army, was descended from a long and distinguished line not least of which were the Merovingian kings Dagobert I and II. Retired architect Roger-René Dagobert, now living in Nantes, has compiled a comprehensive history of his famous family after twenty years of research to reveal a previously unknown chapter in the secret of the Corbières.

On 8 August 1780, Luc-Siméon Auguste Dagobert, Marquis de Fontenille, Captain-Commandant of the Royal Italian contingent at Perpignan, married Mlle Jacquette-Claire Josephe, daughter of Joseph-Gaspard Pailhoux de Cascastel, Lord High Justice and a member of the Sovereign Council of Roussillon. The wedding was witnessed by Jean-Pierre Duhamel, a cousin through whom the couple had met. A man of some importance, Jean-Pierre Francois Duhamel was, at that time, Commissioner of Mines and Forges for King Louis XVI, and correspondent of the Academy of Sciences of Paris.

A year before the marriage, Joseph-Gaspard Pailhoux had formed an association with Duhamel and an entrepreneur, Peltier, to engage in mining activities in the region. In August 1779, they obtained permission from the Monastery of Lagrasse to reopen mines on its land, and to construct a forge and works at the Grau de Padern (the ruins of which are still visible). This permission was later endorsed for a thirty-year period by the king. The original of this Act is held today by Roger-René, in his extensive archives.

As a result of his marriage, Dagobert was given a one-sixth share of the forge to which he was to add Duhamel's share having bought it. The third owner, Peltier, unable to meet other financial commitments, was obliged to sell out to Pailhoux and Duhamel. So when Dagobert finally received the gift of his father-in-law Pailhoux's holdings in 1782, he had complete control of the mines and the forges, in an area that extended from Termes in the north to Tuchan in the south, and Cascastel in the east to Roco-Negrè, near Blanchefort, in the west. Since Dagobert was still an officer in the Army, he had to appoint a manager, for whom he provided a house at Villerouge Termenes, to oversee the mining operations. Yet it is a great surprise therefore that, despite this extensive enterprise, no record exists of any extraction of metal or other minerals!

The lands at Blanchefort, in which were found the ancient mines, belonged to the Marquis de Fleury, Lord of Rennes, who had married Gabrielle, the daughter of Marie de Negrè d'Hautpoul Blanchefort. An engineer called Duboscq attempted to reopen these mines without permission; the Marquis protested, but to no avail, for Duboscq's actions were upheld by the Intendance of the Languedoc. In fact, Duboscq already held several concessions on mines in the region, granted by the king's Commissioner – who was none other than Dagobert's cousin, Jean-Pierre Duhamel. It would therefore appear, that Duboscq was no more than a representative of Dagobert, who in effect had been given licence to exploit all the mines in the Corbières. Perhaps it was more than a coincidence that both Dagobert and Duboscq originated from Normandy.

Coming from such a noble and ancient Merovingian family, Dagobert must have been well aware of the secret of the hoarded Merovingian, Visigothic and Temple of Jerusalem treasure and, though his marriage appears to be a love-match, it does also appear to have been remarkably fortuitous. However, to fully understand Dagobert's crucial part in future events it is necessary to look back a little into his family history.

Following the usurpation of the throne by the Carolingians, the Merovingian descendents of the family of Dagobert II remained in the north of France, except for Sigisbert or Magdala, depending on which tradition one accepts, who had been taken to the Razès. Settling in what would become Normandy, this family of ancient royal blood was eventually integrated by marriage into the local nobility. In the mid-sixteenth century the Dagobert family embraced the new religion offered by Luther and Calvin, becoming Protestants; in the course of the Wars of Religion, their manorial family home near St Lô was burned down and their archives destroyed. However, the male members of the family continued their military tradition, and many achieved notable positions in the Royal Army. They also further consolidated their status by marrying into other noble families. To be accepted into the Royal Guard, it was necessary to establish a genealogy that confirmed noble origins; so it happened that in 1728, Robert Dagobert presented his family history to a commission. Despite the loss of their archives in the fire at St Lô, the commission accepted that the Dagobert family were indeed of noble – and even royal – birth.

In 1685 the enlightened Edict of Nantes, which had granted restricted liberties to the Protestants, was revoked, and the Catholics embarked on a new round of persecution. Looking for support, the Dagoberts enthusiastically embraced the newly emerging groups of so-called Freemasons, which attracted free-thinking philosophers, scientists, atheists, Protestants, Jews, merchants, and bankers who were prepared to adopt the principles of Equality, Liberty, and Fraternity. Later to be assembled under the name Grand Orient, these early lodges were committed to the abolition of the absolute monarchy, the reduction of the power of some aristocrats and release from the stranglehold of the Roman Catholic Church; they were later to be blamed by the monarchists for bringing about the French Revolution. Freemasonry at this time had brought together many of the great names of France who had an interest in intellectual and esoteric pursuits. In 1745 the Lodge of the King's Chamber was constituted, made up mainly of officers of His Majesty's staff and even the King's Chaplain. One army officer, Luc-Siméon Dagobert, and his two brothers, themselves officers too, founded the Lodge of the Three Brothers at the court of Versailles, into which the royal Duc d'Orleans, cousin of Louis XVI, was also initiated. Posted to the Royal Italian garrison at Perpignan, Captain Dagobert was initiated into the Scottish Primitive Rite branch of Masonry by his uncle Hector, Governor of the Fort at Salses, near Narbonne. He also initiated the Vicomte de Chefdebien, who came from an ancient minor aristocratic family, formerly of Brittany, with medieval connections to the Lords of Rennes in the Corbières, but who were now established at Narbonne.

This was a time of phenomenal growth in the numbers of secret societies; some were direct offshoots of parent Freemasonry; some of masonic appearance but actually in opposition to regular Freemasonry; and others avowedly chivalric or of a non-masonic basis. Generally in opposition to mainstream Masonry, the chivalric orders and societies tended to support the monarchy, aristocracy and the traditional symbolism, practices and status, if not always the dogma, of the Catholic Church. It was against this background that, in 1771, the Lodge of the Reunited Friends was founded in Paris and within three years had attracted a membership of noble army officers, rich bourgeois and dignitaries. One such initiate, Savalette de Lange, son of the Treasurer Royal, gave up his job as a parliamentary adviser to devote his time to his Masonic interests. This led to his appointment to Grand Secretary of the Grand Orient in 1777. Before this, however, he had persuaded his mother lodge to approve the constitution of a 'Commission of Grades and Archives', to look into the origins of Masonic rites and rituals under his presidency. This was no more than an excuse to found a new lodge, Régime des Philalethes, with the aim of acquiring as many archives from other lodges as possible in order to discover traces of lost or forgotten ancient secret knowledge! Savalette used any means necessary to accomplish his aim and carefully cultivated good relations with other Masonic and neo-Masonic groups, acquiring documents from those that had gone into dissolution.

It was in 1779 that the very experienced Freemason, the Marquis de Chefdebien, Knight of Malta, Colonel of Foot, was also initiated into the twelfth and highest grade of the

Régime des Philalethes – where he would have had access to their extensive plundered records. A year later, the Marquis, in collaboration with his father, founded a new rite which came to be known in Masonic history as the Loge des Philadelphes de Narbonne. Viewed by outsiders with some scepticism for its curious, apparently occult activities, the Philadelphes was in reality set up, as were the Philalethes, to poach the secrets guarded by other lodges. It was a tactic that was to prove fruitful.

In 1789, the future of France was irreversibly changed with the onset of the French Revolution and its aftermath, the Terror, which ironically in the most bloody way replaced the monarchy and aristocracy with a Republic based on the Masonic principles of Liberty, Equality, and Fraternity. It is still a matter for debate as to how much Masonic involvement lay behind the Revolution; but it is without doubt that the outcome pleased a large number of Masonic brethren, though the means may well have alarmed them. The competing Masonic and Chivalric ideologies became the core of French politics, and the most astute of politicians became increasingly adept at keeping a foot in both camps.

Within the ensuing political turmoil, the opportunity was taken by many to settle old scores and bandy about various accusations with little evidence to support them. The extremists, under Robespierre, carried out an almost indiscriminate and paranoid purge of anyone they thought may be a threat. Even the Grand Master of the Grand Orient was executed along with most of the aristocracy and the Royal Family – including the king's cousin, Philippe d'Orleans. Dagobert, accused of treason by virtue of his noble status and for suspected nostalgic sentiments for the *ancien régime*, was imprisoned. Awaiting the scaffold, it is said he was saved by the intervention of his Republican Masonic brothers, who drew attention to Dagobert's popularity and competence as an army officer.

The kings of France had belonged to the Bourbon dynasty, and their cousins, who occupied the throne of Spain, decided to take advantage of the upheavals in France to launch an offensive. France desperately needed competent military officers and so Dagobert was recalled, promoted to General, and sent to join the Eastern Pyrenean Army under the command of the Marquis de Chefdebien, son of the Vicomte and Grand Master of the Philadelphes. Thus two men, ideologically divided, were brought together in an apparently common cause, the defence of France; Dagobert being a Protestant supporter of the Republic and Chefdebien being a Catholic aristocrat. This singular state of affairs was to present the Marquis de Chefdebien, who had somehow managed to escape the scaffold (probably also through his Masonic connections), with a golden opportunity to further his secret ambitions.

General Dagobert's marriage to Jacquette Pailhoux had resulted in two daughters. This lack of a male heir prompted him to leave his archives, the *Arcanes des mines des Corbières* – containing the great secret of the hidden treasure, in the care of his Masonic brothers of the Grand Orient. In the event of his untimely death – such a threat was ever present during war – they could be put to good use in support of the Masonic ideals.

Welcomed back by his troops in the Roussillon, General Dagobert had some initial success in launching his plan for the invasion of Spain; but on 18 April 1794, he died. Some eight days earlier at Montella, he had been suddenly struck by an inexplicable fever; the effect of food poisoning according to some accounts, but the mysterious circumstances have led others to believe that he was deliberately poisoned. Nobody else became similarly ill at the time, and Dagobert's cook suddenly disappeared some days before the general died.

With their family seat established at Narbonne, less than 40km from Cascastel and Dagobert's mining operations, the

Marquis de Chefdebien would have been well aware of the exploitation of the mines; it is unlikely that he would not also have known of the traditions referring to the buried treasure. The extent and secrecy of the Masonic network enabled him to gain more information about Dagobert's enterprises and eventually to acquire his archives through the Grand Orient – having possibly contrived the removal of their owner. The name of Chefdebien will crop up later in this strange history, again in mysterious circumstances.

Quite coincidentally, the demise of the celebrated General Dagobert (whose tomb at Mont Louis in the eastern Pyrenees near the Spanish border is surmounted by a stone pyramid memorial, a reminder perhaps of his Masonic interests) heralded the rise of another great French officer; a general who would affect the future not only of France but most of Europe, and even further afield. Earning the nickname the 'little corporal', Napoleon Bonaparte conjures up an image of the people's soldier, an officer who rose from the ranks and who never forgot his roots. The reality is quite different.

Napoleon was born at Ajaccio on the island of Corsica in 1769, the fourth son of Carlo Buonoparte, a lawyer, and his wife Letizia Kamolino. His father's family was of ancient Italian nobility from Tuscany who had emigrated to Corsica in the sixteenth century. Though truly Corsican, Napoleon was educated in France from the age of nine and continued his education in three military schools, including the military academy in Paris. He graduated in 1785 and was made a second lieutenant of artillery in the regiment of La Frère, a sort of artillery officer training school, where he continued to expand his own education in military matters. After a chequered military career tinged with political activity, he joined a Jacobin lodge whose goal of a constitutional monarchy he supported. Napoleon was finally promoted to brigadier-general following his succesful recapture of Toulon from the British in December 1793.

Napoleon's military skills were then used to quell monarchist civil unrest. As a result of his success, he was given command of the army of the interior, and henceforth became acutely aware of all political developments in France. Though ostensibly loyal to the Republican Directory, he appears to have had a separate agenda, and also to have received patronage from non-Republican sources. There is no doubt that he was violently opposed to a return of the old monarchy, but he seemed equally unhappy with the system that had replaced it, the five-man executive with absolute power known as the Directory.

Successful campaigns in Europe enhanced his reputation, but his Egyptian campaign, apparently mounted to gain control of the trade route to India, proved to be a disaster. His fleet was destroyed by the British Navy while at anchor in Abu Qir Bay in the Nile delta. Temporarily confined in Egypt, Napoleon proceeded to utilise his innate political flair to introduce Western political organization, administration and technical skills into the country. For over two centuries philosophers and scholars had been fascinated by this ancient and mystical land with its unique hieroglyphs, which they considered to contain lost ancient knowledge. Thus the campaign to Egypt had drawn support from many quarters, including that of some Freemasons. Napoleon was accompanied, and possibly financed, by counter-revolutionary nobility such as the Hautpouls of the Razès and the Chefdebiens – whose lodge, Les Philalethes, was dedicated to the discovery of ancient knowledge.

During his stay in Egypt, Napoleon initiated an extensive survey of ancient sites which became the basis for much later archaeology. The most important find was a stone tablet inscribed with three parallel ancient texts that enabled the Egyptian hieroglyphs to be deciphered. According to the researches of Barbara Watterson, formerly of the Department of Egyptology at Liverpool University, the stone was found near the town of Rosetta by a soldier named Hautpoul – a name inextricably linked with Rennes-le-Château.

It has been suggested, however, that Napoleon had a less benign motivation than the search for knowledge for his Egyptian campaign. An article that appeared in the *Gazette Nationale ou le Moniteur Universel* on 22 May 1799 reported that Bonaparte had issued a proclamation to Jews to join him in the restoration of ancient Jerusalem. From his experiences of the Revolution and the part played by the Jacobin and radical Masonic lodges, which were said to have had Jewish financial associations, Napoleon had doubtless grown wary of such secret networks, and was determined that the new State would not remain vulnerable to further subversion. So, despite later adopting a more tolerant attitude to the Jews, it is possible that initially, Napoleon wanted to establish a Jewish State in or near Egypt to which he could exile all Jews – for their assumed support for Masonic lodges – from France. This was a strategy that may even have been acceptable to some of the more orthodox Jews, who had always dreamed of regaining a homeland.

Indeed, in 1811 James Rothschild, one of the five sons of the Jewish banking giant Meyer Amschel Rothschild, arrived in Paris to help finance the restoration of the Bourbon monarchy; an action that would have alarmed Napoleon. In general, banking and financial institutions find a monarchy more favourable for their business, since republics or state-controlled systems of government tend to put restrictions on private enterprise.

Putting principles and loyalties aside, the Hautpouls and Chefdebiens, with their eyes firmly on the eventual recovery of the Jewish treasure in the Corbières, would also have seen the advantage of removing the Jews, the rightful inheritors of the treasure, from France. One can understand now more easily why they would have wanted to – and it is claimed, did – finance Napoleon's Egyptian campaign.

In November 1799, Napoleon carried out a *coup d'état* with the support of two of the five directors disaffected with the old administration. They set up a consulate which effectively gave

Napoleon political control of France. It became clear he did not believe in the sovereignty of the people, in the popular will, or in parliamentary debate, but instead believed that a firm and enlightened purpose, with the support of the military, could achieve anything.

Despising and fearing the masses, he imposed a military dictatorship on France with a constitution which omitted any guarantees of the rights of man or the principles of liberty, equality, and fraternity. He introduced a reform that was to be known as the Code Napoleon, that is still the basis for French civil law; but he paid most careful attention to his army who were, after all, his instrument of control. And realizing the 'necessary' role of religion for the people, inspired by Voltaire, Napoleon entered into an expedient accord with the Vatican, restoring restricted rights of worship. Though he himself was indifferent to religion he evidently, during his stay in Egypt, intriguingly expressed a desire to become a Muslim. In fact some of his officers did convert to Islam.

In time, and after surviving a British assassination plot, Napoleon came to realize that life consularship was not secure enough endorsement. In May 1804, on the advice of Joseph Fouche, his Chief of Police, he proclaimed France an Empire, and himself its Emperor. Despite his cynicism for religion and his previous loyalty to the Republic, he wanted to be consecrated by the pope himself, so that his coronation would be more impressive than those of the former kings of France who had never received so direct an anointing. In 1653, the tomb of the ancient Merovingian king and father of Clovis, Childeric I, had been discovered and was found to contain arms, treasure, and regalia. Among the riches were 300 miniature gold bees, a symbol sacred to the Merovingians. Napoleon had these same bees specially sewn on to his coronation robe. Equally outrageous to royalists and supporters of the Republic alike, the ceremony took place in Notre Dame cathedral on 2 December 1804, in the presence of Pope Pius VII, who was denied the actual crowning when Napoleon seized the crown and put it on himself. Claiming a legitimacy not only from the 'grace of God', as had the Bourbon kings, but also by the will of the people, he was far more powerful than any monarch before him. His court expenditure was also to exceed that of the extravagant Louis XIV, the 'Sun King'.

Princely titles were restored for members of his family as well as an imperial nobility of hereditary counts, barons, and chevaliers. Always looking to secure and consolidate his position, he surrounded the empire with a ring of vassal states ruled over by his relatives. Additionally, to gain control of the secret world of Masonic lodges who many believed to have been instrumental in the Revolution, Napoleon contrived to place his brothers as successive Grand Masters of the Grand Orient.

Possibly as a result of Napoleon's mistrust of the Masonic and neo-Masonic societies and his desire to re-invent an aristocracy, there emerged a renewed interest in Chivalric Orders. The most discernible example of this was the renaissance of the Knights Templar.

Following the dissolution of the Knights Templar in 1314, little is written about an underground survival of the Order until around 1804. Just five years after the Revolution, two doctors, one named Ledru and the other Bernard Raymond Fabré-Palaprat, claimed to have discovered documents that confirmed the Order's continuation in secret since its dissolution. They alleged that the Order had resurfaced at a convention in 1705, from which they had discovered statutes revealing the election of the Duc d'Orleans as Grand Master. But forced underground yet again due to the upheavals of the Revolution, the Order remained dormant, its archives protected by its regent, the Chevalier Radix de Chevillon. On its alleged rebirth, Fabré-Palaprat became the new Grand Master. Under Napoleon's regime, the renovated Templar Order was permitted to flourish, and succeeded in attracting some of the most prominent public figures who ensured its protection.

On 28 March 1808, Knights, resplendent in full Templar

regalia, assisted at a memorial service at the church of St Paul and St Louis in Paris for Jacques de Molay, the last known Grand Master of the Templars, martyred in 1314. This ostentatious and lavish service, endorsed by the authorities and supposedly by Napoleon himself, was attended by an elderly and respected priest, the Abbé Pierre Romains Clouet, who was described as the 'Primate of the Order'. So the leader of the Republic and a new empire was apparently happy to accept the re-emergence of a military-religious Order that had been the sword-arm of the Catholic Church, and a relic of the medieval age of feudal kings, lords, and barons. Did Napoleon believe that the Order had indeed survived undercover for the previous 500 years, and with it, the great secret of its treasures?

Napoleon's interest in the Merovingians appears to have extended beyond his coronation. According to documents deposited in the Bibliotheque Nationale in Paris, he commissioned a study of Merovingian descent from Dagobert II, who had been assassinated in 679, specifically from his offspring, Sigisbert, who had settled at Rennes-le-Château. And, when dissatisfied with his childless marriage to Josephine, Napoleon repudiated her in order to marry Marie-Louise, daughter of the Austrian emperor Francis I – of Merovingian descent. Yet Napoleon considered himself to be the heir to the empire of Charlemagne, whose dynasty had deposed the Merovingians. Was there an altogether separate explanation for his fascination with the Merovingians?

In 1810, Napoleon ordered the seizing of the Vatican archives and their removal to Paris. About 3000 boxes of material were brought back to the Arsenal Library in Paris where they were examined and catalogued by Charles Nodier and his colleagues. Nodier, born in 1780, achieved quite a reputation in literary circles having written several books, including a multi-volume compendium of sites of antiquarian interest in France. In this he devotes a large section to the normally little-mentioned Merovingian epoch. He also wrote, anonymously, a book entitled *A History of Secret Societies in the Army under Napoleon*, in which he refers to the Philadelphes, which he states to be the 'supreme' secret society, presiding over the others. Whether this is the lodge founded by the Marquis de Chefdebien, or one of the many other Masonic groups, or even a group possibly founded by Nodier himself in 1797, is not made clear. Yet the coincidence is striking. Presumably unknown to Napoleon, he was also steeped in esoteric circles. A friend of Eliphas Levi, the renowned occultist, and mentor of Victor Hugo, Nodier eventually became an esteemed Master Mason; in 1824, he was appointed chief librarian of the Arsenal, which contained the greatest collection of medieval and occult manuscripts in France.

The common thread that appears to run through these centuries of conflict and collusion is the search for information; specifically that from the Merovingian epoch, a period of history which by the time of Napoleon was somewhat forgotten and omitted from standard historical works. The repositories of this knowledge seem to have been the secret archives of the Catholic Church and those of Masonic and other secret societies with connections to either the Merovingians and their descendants, or to the region of the Languedoc. The logical conclusion must be that Napoleon, aware of the existence of the Corbières treasure, was attempting to acquire whatever information he could about it, as had many before him. Yet he was also working to establish a legitimacy of ownership should he manage to recover it.

However, this aspiration was never to be realized. Napoleon's other agenda of maintaining and expanding the empire was finally to bring about his downfall. Following defeat at the Battle of Waterloo, he was forced to abdicate in favour of his son on 22 June 1815.

Following the passing of General Dagobert and the Emperor Napoleon, the quest for the legendary treasure was of course to continue. But it is through the bizarre activities of a simple country priest some seventy years later that this hidden thread physically resurfaces. These suggest that vital documents that could have shed light on the presence of the great treasure had been carefully hidden in a secret crypt, in 1781, some eight years before the French Revolution.

THE CURÉ DE MILLIARDS

Saunière and Rennes-le-Château · Boudet
Bigou and the Hautpoul Secret · Strange Deaths

ON 1 JUNE 1885, the Abbé Bérenger Saunière arrived at his new hilltop parish deep in the Corbières. No longer the royal fortress and vast encampment of the Visigoths, or even, in their turn, the seat of the Counts of Razès, the Hautpouls and the de Voisins, Rennes-le-Château was by then only a small and neglected village of about 300 inhabitants. From the highest point of the village, adjacent to the ancient château of the Hautpouls, Bérenger Saunière could look down on the town of Couiza, with its impressive sixteenth-century château, ancestral home of the Ducs de Joyeuse, which during the Peninsular War with Spain, had been temporarily converted into a hospital for wounded soldiers on the orders of the late General Dagobert.

Overlooking the town, on the hillside north-east of Rennes, are perched the château and houses of Montazels, the village in which Bérenger had been born; the eldest of the seven children of Joseph Saunière, who held the enviable position of managing the estate of the Marquis de Cazemajou, a co-lord of Niort and cousin of the Hautpouls. In his childhood, Bérenger is said to have displayed leadership qualities and led his friends in games, of which the most popular was searching for buried treasure in the surrounding countryside.

Coming from a family of dedicated Catholics and loyal monarchists, it is not surprising that Bérenger and his younger brother, Alfred, decided to enter the priesthood, to the delight of their parents. Entering the Grand Seminary in 1874, Bérenger successfully completed his five years of study and, after his ordination, was appointed Assistant Priest to the prestigious parish of Alet, site of the great ruined abbey, former centre of the heretical Jansenist faith and its great advocate, Bishop Nicolas Pavillon. In 1882 he was sent to the remote village of Clat, which could only be approached by a long winding track from the town of Axat, some 23km south of Couiza and Rennes. Little is known of his three-year ministry in this isolated parish.

In direct contrast, his appointment to Rennes-le-Château has generated a virtual industry of mystery and speculations. But what is really at the heart of the mystery and how can the irregular activities of this simple parish priest be explained?

On arrival in the village, his heart must have sunk at the sight of the delapidated state of the little church dedicated to St Mary Magdalene. With holes in the roof, broken windows and crumbling masonry, the building had actually been con-demned as unworthy of renovation and only suitable for demolition by the architect Guiraud Cals in 1883. But with a youthful confidence and determination, Saunière set about creating a 'house worthy of the Lord'. With only a modest monthly stipend of 75 francs, he was obliged to borrow some money from the Commune for the essential repairs. But within months of taking up his post and commencing the most urgent repairs, he was suspended from his parish duties for making anti-Republican speeches from the pulpit and was obliged to spend nine months teaching at the Seminary in Narbonne.

Upon his return to Rennes he continued with his work even though his financial state resulted in debts with local shopkeepers. However, in 1886 he received a welcome dona-tion of 3000 francs from no less a person than Maria-Thérèse, the Countess of Chambord, widow of Henri, the last Bourbon claimant to the throne of France. At first sight it appears strange to see such munificence on the part of such a distinguished person as the Habsburg Countess Marie-Thérèse towards an unknown, humble priest in a remote backwater, but it soon becomes clear that the same tentacle-like network of connections encountered elsewhere in this story can also be discerned here.

Saunière's connection to the Count of Chambord and the (monarchist) aristocracy began through his father who, working for the Marquis de Cazemajou, was a loyal servant and as an ardent monarchist eagerly awaited the return of Henri, Duke of Bordeaux, Count of Chambord, as the legitimate claimant to the throne. The Cazemajou family had been co-lords of Niort since 1696, with their cousins, the Negrè d'Arbles. The daughter of François de Negrè d'Arbles, Marie, married François d'Hautpoul-Rennes in 1752, thus linking the Cazemajou with the Hautpoul family, Lords of Rennes and Blanchefort – whose château is found adjacent to the church at Rennes-le-Château. Félines d'Hautpoul had been a tutor to the young Count of Chambord and, in 1843, the Marquis Armand d'Hautpoul had accompanied him on journeys to Germany and London where he was warmly received by Queen Victoria. It must also be recalled that the Hautpoul family were descended from the Visigoth king, Atulph, who had arrived in the Languedoc just a couple of years after the sacking of Rome in 410 and the removal of the treasure.

As with all other monarchists, the Count and his wife supported the Catholic Church and the renewed mission of the Sacred Heart; a Catholic institution central to the rejuvination of the Church in France and which was seen as integral to the restoration of the monarchy. In 1870, Rohault de Fleury had initiated a scheme to erect a massive new church, dedicated to the Sacre Coeur (Sacred Heart), in order to focus attention on this growing cult. Building commenced five years later on the hill above Montmartre, in Paris. Some years before his death in 1883, the fervent Count of Chambord donated 500,000 francs to the project, thus becoming its largest single donor. Whether his widow, the Countess Marie-Thérèse, had heard of Saunière's endeavours through the Hautpoul connection or whether he contacted her directly is not known, but either way the donation must have seemed like manna from heaven. Saunière's own devotion to the Sacred Heart and the monarchy is in evidence throughout his former domain. It must also be recalled that Rohault de Fleury was a member of the de Fleury family that held the lands near Rennes-le-Château on which can be found the Blanchefort mines.

With fresh funds, Saunière was to continue with his refurbishment and turned his attention to the ancient altar consisting of a stone slab supported by two carved pillars, probably dating from the ninth century. According to existing receipts, he was given another small donation with which he was able to purchase a new altar; he later placed the original altar slab in a private chapel and put one of the two carved pillars in a small garden in front of the church.

It was during the replacement of the altar that Saunière appears to have made his first important discovery. Actual details are sketchy and various authors give slightly varying accounts, but the consensus is that he uncovered a tomb covered by a sculpted stone, placed face down in the nave in front of the altar. In the tomb he is said to have found some bones, some jewels, and a pot of gold coins which he told the workers present at the time were only worthless medallions.

An actual record of the restoration is not available but a rough chronology of works can be pieced together from surviving receipts. By 1891, which appears to be a critical year in the mystery of Rennes-le-Château, the stained glass windows had been replaced, and the porch, with its ornate carvings and inscriptions, had been added. But it is a number of other factors that have made this year a turning point in the life of the Abbé Saunière, and a key in our quest for the web of gold.

In June that year, he organized a first communion service

at which some men of the village carried a statue of the Virgin
Mary on their shoulders, in procession from the church and
around the village, until they arrived back at the church garden.
There they placed it on top of the ancient pillar. Normally this
would have been an unremarkable event, except that the pillar
had been deliberately placed upside down, (evident from the
carving of a processional cross and an alpha and omega on its
front face). On part of the pillar Saunière had had inscribed,
'Penitence, Penitence', and in another spot, 'Mission 1891'. If
the pillar is turned the right way up, then the date reads 1681
– which is also found inscribed in 'error' on the tombstone of
the last Hautpoul to live in the château. Marie de Negrè
d'Ables d'Hautpoul actually died in 1781, but the inscription
on her headstone reads MDCOLXXXI (1681). Given that this
is factually incorrect (not to mention there being no '0' in the
Roman numbering system), could there be another meaning
in the inscription? Intriguingly, it could be interpreted as,
1–681, that is, January 681, the date on which Dagobert's
surviving heir was believed to be brought to Rennes-le-
Château. The gravestone itself is not in evidence today; it is
said to have been defaced by the Abbé Saunière, who wished
to conceal its hidden message. Fortunately, however, the
original inscription had been copied by a local antiquarian and
was published in the seventeenth edition of the bulletin of the
Société des Études Scientifiques de l'Aude, in 1906. Further, it is
the rescue of the young Sigisbert and his arrival at Rennes-le-
Château that may be the subject of the sculpted stone slab
found upside down by Saunière in the nave.

Later in the year, Saunière wrote in his diary that he had,
'discovered a tomb'; not a particularly unusual event in the
renovation of a church, so one must conclude that this tomb
carried some special significance. Even more enigmatic is
another entry in his diary, 'The year 1891, carries to the
highest the fruit of that which one speaks.' Two events
occurred at this time, one or both of which may help to shed

some light on these entries, their possible significance undoubtably lying at the heart of the Abbé's later activities.

In the course of replacing the pulpit, he seems to have uncovered yet another tomb, evidently of some importance, because he dismissed the workers engaged in the restoration for ten days, during which time he is said to have undertaken secret diggings in the church. Then there is the story related by his old bellringer, Antoine Captier, in which he tells how he discovered a small rolled-up parchment hidden in a glass vial that had been secreted in the top of a wooden post. This post, which originally formed part of the altar rail, had been removed and cast aside during the renovations. As a result, a small fillet of wood had become dislodged, revealing a cavity in the top of the post. In this Captier found the vial. It is said that the parchment contained information as to the access to the crypt, and the nature of its contents. According to some accounts, the entrance to the crypt was under the 'tomb' in the nave under the Knight's stone. The 'tomb' had been deliberately arranged to conceal the entrance to the crypt, presumably for extra security.

These precautions had been taken by the parish priest of Rennes-le-Château, one hundred years before Saunière's arrival. In 1780, when General Dagobert married the noble Jacquette Pailhoux de Cascastel, and his father-in-law had formed the association for the re-opening of the Corbières mines, Marie de Negrè d'Arbles, Dame d'Hautpoul de Blanchefort, feeling that the end of her life was near, had summoned her parish priest, the Abbé Bigou, to her château. Having no male heirs, she had decided to confide the great secret of the treasure, handed down through the centuries, and shared only by a handful of local noble families, to Abbé Bigou. She also entrusted him with the family jewels and documents of considerable importance, requesting that these be passed in turn to someone worthy. A few years after the death of Marie, sensing the impending upheaval and danger of the Revolution, the priest placed these jewels and documents in the church crypt. This already contained the sepulchres of the Lords of Rennes and other notables. He then carefully concealed the access, leaving instructions hidden in the top of an altar-rail post. Entries in the old parish register, now on display in the museum at Rennes, confirm the existence of a 'tombeau des seigneurs' (tomb of the lords) and the approximate location of its entrance. This tomb, in which the Lords of Rennes have apparently been interred, may well be a concealed crypt.

From unpublished original documents, Jean-Pierre Deloux and Jacques Brétigny continue the story of Abbé Bigou and the Hautpoul secret. Fearing for his life due to his monarchist sympathies, in 1792 Abbé Bigou fled to Sabadell in Spain when the Revolution turned bloody, where he was to remain until his death eighteen months later. However, he had already passed on his great secret verbally to Abbé François-Pierre Cauneille, formerly priest of Rennes-les-Bains, who in turn confided it to two others. One of these, the Abbé Jean Vie, was parish priest of Rennes-les-Bains from 1840 to 1870, and the unusual inscription on his tomb in the church cemetery highlights the date 17 January – that recurrent date in the Rennes mystery. The other colleague, Abbé Émile-François Cayron, became the parish priest of St Laurent-de-la-Cabrerisse. According to the obituary column of *La Semaine Religieuse* in 1897, Abbé Cayron had, '. . . almost completely reconstructed his church in beautiful gothic proportions . . . nobody knew from where he drew the funds to finance such great repairs.' Furthermore, he also financed the education of the young Henri Boudet of Axat, who was to succeed Abbé Jean Vie as priest of Rennes-les-Bains in 1872, some thirteen years before Bérenger Saunière arrived at Rennes-le-Château.

Before continuing to investigate the unusual activities of Saunière, it is instructive to look a little more closely at his elder colleague in the neighbouring parish. In 1886, after nine years of research, Abbé Boudet published at his own expense a book entitled *La Vrai Langue Celtique et le Cromlech de Rennes-les-Bains*, copies of which are still available. It sets out to show that the true Celtic language was English, and that the key to the origin of Celtic lies in the pronunciation of words and not their spelling. Boudet was a well-respected local scholar, a member of the local Society for Scientific Study of the Aude, and so it is surprising that his book contains a number of illogicalities and wild speculations, which have led many researchers to believe that this work had a very different purpose. Evidently, he considered his book to be of some importance since he sent a copy to Queen Victoria, who replied with a note of thanks through her representative in France. A copy of the book has also been discovered in the Bodleian Library at Oxford University, accompanied by a handwritten letter from the author. Nevertheless, most researchers consider that the text of the book contains an encoded message, that refers to the great secret of the Hautpouls and the treasure. Indeed, the Abbé Vannier wrote, 'The Abbé Boudet is the keeper of a secret which could be the cause of *major upheavals.*'

After his death, Boudet was buried with his brother in a family tomb at Axat, upon which is a curious headstone in the shape of a closed book bearing the weathered inscription I X I O Σ, that may possibly be the Greek word for fish (used as a symbol by early Christians). If, however, the inscription is turned upside down it becomes 3 0 I X I, which may well refer to pages 301 and 11 of his book; by a strange 'coincidence', in the original edition, page 301 is a map of the valley of Rennes-les-Bains. Signed by his brother Edmond, who is considered to have drawn it, the map contains a number of anomolies, names and features that have either been deliberately removed since, or which were purely imaginary or symbolic in the first place. Meanwhile, on page 11, there is an intriguing passage referring to 'keys' being obtained through linguistic interpretations of French, Irish, and Scottish dialects. Taken in conjunction with the place names on the map, these linguistic keys when correctly applied may reveal hidden meanings.

Disappointed at the reception of his book by his peers, Boudet seems to have thought of another more novel and permanent way to immortalize his secret. To do this he enlisted the help of his younger neighbour at Rennes-le-Château, the Abbé Saunière, who had just embarked, with energy and enthusiasm, on the renovation of his little church.

A very full and documented analysis of the building works can be found in a book by Jacques Rivière entitled *Le Fabuleux Trésor de Rennes-le-Château! – Le Secret de l'Abbé Saunière* (1995). By the dedication service in 1897, attended by his superior, Arsène-Félix Billard, the Bishop of Carcassonne, Saunière had completed the structural renovation of the church and adjoining presbytery; reorganized the cemetery, much to the alarm of his parishioners; laid out a geometrical garden in which was placed the ancient altar pillar surmounted by the statue of the Virgin Mary; and constructed, about 15m from the Virgin's statue, a Calvary cross. Within the church, Saunière appears to have let his imagination run riot with lavish and, in some respects, bizarre decoration. Many types of symbolism can be found; some are purely Catholic, in the St Sulpician style in vogue at the time; others are possibly Masonic, Rose-Croix, or Templar. And within this profusion of decoration, the message of the Abbé Boudet is thought to have been carefully encoded.

As in all Catholic churches, the walls are hung with the fourteen Stations of the Cross, but here they are very detailed, and were ordered specially from Giscard & Son, sculptors and statue manufacturers, in Toulouse. Giscard was a dedicated Freemason, and his house, next door to his workshop at 27 Rue de la Colonne, is covered in masonic symbols clearly visible today. With this in mind, various attempts have been made to decipher the individual Stations with interesting and persuasive results, but as yet no definitive conclusions have been reached (or publicized), except perhaps for Station number one, which seems to strongly indicate the existence of the mine at Blanchefort. Saunière further commissioned from Giscard a large wall fresco, on the theme of the Sermon on the Mount, which occupies the top half of the west wall and appears to contain several further 'clues'. First, the hill is strewn with flowers, a hint that the location is a hill on the land of the de Fleury family; second, on the ground at the foot of the hill, there is a draw-string bag with a hole in it, through which can be seen the glint of gold; furthermore, the cross mounted on the confessional deliberately draws attention to the bag of gold. Finally, in the scenery on the left can be seen a flower commonly known as Solomon's Seal, possibly a reference to the treasure of the Temple of Solomon.

But the most unexpected feature is to be found just inside the entrance door to the church, and supports the holy water stoop: a hideous, horned, grimacing devil, in a half crouch, bearing the heavy shell-like dish. A drawing of an almost identical figure, found in a book from the library of Abbé Saunière, is labelled as being Asmodeus. In Jewish mythology Asmodeus was king of the demons and guardian of Solomon's treasure!

Statues and other decorative features abound throughout the church, but it is St Anthony of Padua, whose help is sought by the faithful to recover lost items, who is given a special plinth of four supporting angels; possibly a gesture of gratitude by Saunière for his important discoveries. Yet another surprise awaits the visitor to his sacristy, where part of the shelf unit on the left side opens, like a door, to reveal a small room. It was said by the villagers that the Abbé Saunière would lock himself into the sacristy after he had returned, bearing a knapsack full of stones, from long walks in the surrounding hills. Why the secrecy? What was the nature of these stones? Why construct a secret room?

The strange entry in Saunière's notebook, concerning the year 1891, is accompanied by an illustration taken from the journal *La Croix*, of a baby being lifted into heaven by three angels. Below this is another illustration showing the adoration of the Three Wise Men with the following comment: '*Melchior; Reçois, O Roi, l'or, symbole de la royauté. Gaspard; Reçois la myrrhe, symbole de la sepulture. Balthasar; Reçois l'encens, o toi qui es Dieu*'. ('Melchior; Receive O King, the Gold, symbol of Royalty. Gaspard; Receive the myrrh, symbol of the burial place. Balthasar; Receive the incense, to you who is God'.)

Saunière's interest in this legend (the names or number of the Wise Men are not actually mentioned in the Gospels) takes on a new significance in light of the fact that three rocky outcrops, dominating the northern entrance to the valley of Rennes-les-Bains, were known in medieval times, as Melchior (Rocco Nègre), Balthasar (Roc Pointu) and Gaspard (Blanchefort); could this be yet another reference to the ancient goldmines of Blanchefort and Rocco Nègre with their secret deposits?

The church of Rennes-le-Château was thus almost certainly the focus and repository of three important secrets. First, the Hautpoul documents, the contents of which appear to reveal some details, though not the actual locations, of the deposits of treasure, as well as genealogies which attest to the survival of the Merovingians through their descendants, the Lords of Rennes. Second, the Hautpoul heirlooms, precious jewels, artefacts and coins, the sale of which enabled Saunière to continue the renovation and decoration of his church, and some of which were given as gifts. Third, the decoration of the church with its hidden references to the locations of the legendary treasure. The keys for deciphering these clues were evidently known and guarded by the Abbé Boudet, but apparently not revealed to Saunière until the later years of Boudet's life, if at all.

Saunière's discovery of ancient parchments in the crypt has given rise to much speculation as to what information they really contain and also over the actions of Saunière following his discoveries. Two of the four parchments, copies of which are revealed for the first time in a book by Gérard de Sède entitled *L'Or de Rennes* (1967), retitled in a later edition *Le Trésor Maudit*, are Latin texts from the New Testament which could well contain coded messages. De Sède says that, being sure of this but unable to decipher them himself, Saunière went to St Sulpice in Paris where experts in such matters could help him. The Seminary of St Sulpice had achieved a reputation as the foremost Catholic centre for occult studies. However, there is no evidence that he did go to Paris and even the provenance of the de Sède copies is in doubt. On this basis, many have dismissed these documents as worthless fabrications. On the other hand, messages can be decoded within the passages which concur with other known evidence.

In particular, the shorter parchment has a direct reference to the thread of the Jerusalem treasure: '*A DAGOBERT II ROI ET A SION EST CE TRESOR ET IL EST LA MORT* ('To Dagobert II, King and to Sion, is this treasure, and he is there dead'). The parchment also contains the words, *Redis bles*, where *Redis* may refer to 'of Rhedae', the ancient name of Rennes-le-Château, and *bles* translates to corn or bread. In French slang this also means, money.

Finally, its last words, *solis sacerdotibus*, can be translated as 'only for the priesthood'; indicating perhaps that the secret should only be passed on through priests, which has certainly been the case since Marie de Nègre d'Hautpoul de Blanchefort confided in the Abbé Bigou.

Bérenger Saunière's brother, Alfred, having become ordained as a Jesuit priest, secured a position as tutor and chaplain to the family of the Marquis de Chefdebien in Narbonne – grandson of the founder of the Masonic lodge, the Philadelphes, who had acquired General Dagobert's archives. According to Bérenger's account book, Alfred had used his aristocratic connections to obtain donations for his brother, and among a number of entries is one for 30,000 francs, collected within the period 1895–1903, attributed to Alfred. There is also an anonymous entry of 20,000 francs in the period 1895–1905, from a mysterious M.de C.; generally thought to refer to the Marquis de Chefdebien. It is not impossible that Saunière was being financed to continue his excavations and researches with the intent of recovering the treasure hidden within his and neighbouring parishes. However, according to the Chefdebien family's recollections, Alfred lost his post with the Marquis after being caught rifling through private family papers – but probably not before passing on his finds to his brother! Thus, through Alfred's covert activities, Bérenger came to know the secrets held in both the Hautpoul and the Dagobert archives.

Meanwhile, having completed his work on the church property, Bérenger Saunière turned his attention to the creation of a private estate adjacent to the church. In two distinct parts, one comprised a villa with ornamental garden, the other a cliff-top terrace, with the appearance and dimensions of a rampart which connected a three-storey mock gothic tower and a glasshouse, all of which enclosed yet another ornamental garden. Both buildings were well appointed with the best furniture and *objets d'art*, and the recollection of villagers was that he lived like a lord, frequently entertaining visitors at the villa, a claim substantiated by large bills for alcohol and other luxuries. His expenditure by this time was astonishing, and it has been estimated that a deficit of expenditure over declared income amounts to at least 250,000 francs. The source of these funds, quite considerable for their time, has been the subject of much debate by researchers. No explanation is more persuasive than the discovery of a hidden cache of money, gold or precious items, given the number of clues that point towards this.

* * *

Despite being subjected to the most intense pressure by his new bishop, Mgr Beauséjour, who replaced the aimiable Mgr Billard in 1902, Saunière refused to divulge the source of his wealth. Disciplinary action was taken against him and at first he was ordered to move to the parish of Coustouge some

40km north-east from Rennes as the crow flies, but he refused to go, having taken on a new lease of the presbytery (which was the property of the commune). He was then suspended from all priestly offices and replaced by the Abbé Marty; but Saunière was so popular with the villagers that they continued to attend private services at his villa, held in the conservatory that he had arranged as a chapel. When a further attempt was made by the Diocesan authorities to confiscate his property, it was revealed that everything was in the name of his house-keeper and confidante, Marie Dénarnaud, and therefore untouchable. Saunière thus managed, at some cost to his health, to withstand the formidable and unrelenting efforts of his bishop to force him to either be moved or stripped of his wealth. Why was it so important for him to remain in Rennes-le-Château?

Throughout his ordeals, Marie Dénarnaud supported Saunière. Sixteen years his junior, she became his most trusted and loyal companion. Originally from the village of Esperaza, she had arrived at Rennes with her family in 1892 and, for reasons not yet explained, the four were given lodgings by Saunière in the presbytery which he had hastened to renovate. After a while, she gave up her job at the hat factory in Esperaza to attend to the priest's domestic needs. There is some evidence that her mother, Alexandrine, was unhappy with this arrangement but seems to have been powerless to stop it. Marie stayed with Saunière until his death and remained in the villa until her own demise in 1953.

As far as the villagers were concerned, they were in no doubt that their priest had stumbled across a small fortune. In fact Madame J. Vidal, a great friend of Marie (who even gave her a room in the villa on her wedding night), reported a conversation with her in which she had said, 'With what the Monsieur le Curé has left, one could feed all of Rennes for a hundred years and there would still be some left.' However, when asked why she was living such an austere life after the death of Saunière if this was so, she replied that she could not touch it. At another time she had said, 'The people who live here are walking on gold without knowing it.'

In 1925 a young female teacher came to take up a post in the village school. The commune was unable to provide suitable accommodation for her, so Marie Dénarnaud agreed to let her lodge at the villa. During her four-year stay, she too became very close to Marie, but found her reluctant to speak about her days with Saunière. However, her pupils were more forthcoming, and told her that their parents firmly believed that he had discovered hidden treasure. Anecdotal though this evidence is, the power of a village grapevine should not be underestimated!

The war of attrition with Bishop Beauséjour finally took its toll on the Abbé Saunière, and he died, aged 65, five days after a sudden heart attack on 17 January 1917. In the five days before his death he was treated and comforted by his close friend and physician from Rennes-les-Bains, Dr Paul Courrent, who stayed at the villa during this time. Dr Courrent, like Saunière's other friend the late Abbé Boudet, was a respected member of the Society for the Scientific Study of the Aude and so it is quite natural that Saunière should have bequeathed to him all the Hautpoul and Dagobert archives that he had discovered or acquired. As is customary in the Catholic Church, he was given the last rites in his final hours, but his old friend the Abbé Rivière, who performed this solemn duty, was said by those present at the time, to be so shocked by Saunière's last confession that from then on he was a changed man.

Secrecy had followed Saunière around like a shadow; many of his actions being clouded in mystery and innuendo with no attempt by him to dispel them. However, he was not alone. Besides the Abbé Boudet, who without doubt was a key figure in his activities, other priests appear to have shared his secrets. There is the Abbé Grassaud to whom he gave a very beautiful chalice. Grassaud was the priest of Amelie-les-Bains at the time but was later appointed priest of St Paul-de-Fenouillet, a village south-west of Rennes, where he also attempted to renovate his church. The intriguing entry in Saunière's diary for 21 September 1891 reveals another possible collaboration. Only eight days after the discovery of an unspecified tomb, Saunière wrote, '*Vu curé de Névian – Chez Gélis – Chez Carrière – Vu Cros et Secret*', references to meetings with certain colleagues, at which they probably discussed his latest discovery. Nearly twenty years later, two surviving letters from these close friends refer to the fact that Saunière had access to specific money, and that nobody had the right to accuse him of any wrongdoing. They also indicate that he had a duty to guard a secret which could not be revealed at that time.

It would also appear that guarding this secret was a dangerous, and in some cases fatal, affair. The aforementioned Abbé Gélis was priest of the village of Coustausa, which nestles on the hillside just to the north of Rennes, dominated by its magnificent ruined château. In 1897, the elderly Abbé Gélis, who lived on his own, was viciously attacked and killed in the kitchen of his presbytery; evidently not for theft, since nearly 800 francs was found undisturbed in drawers. However, there was evidence that his private papers had been searched and perhaps some removed. Even stranger was that the corpse had been laid out straight, with the arms neatly folded across the chest, and a small cigarette paper, upon which was written '*Viva Angelina*', was found next to the body. The priest's nephew was accused but acquitted at his trial. The incident remains unsolved.

Yet another strange death had occurred earlier in 1732, when the Abbé Bernard Monge, priest of Niort-de-Sault (not far from Le Clat, the second posting of Abbé Saunière) was found lying dead by his presbytery garden gate, having received a fatal blow to the head. The murderer was found to be François de Montroux, the appointed guardian of the young Marie de Nègre d'Arbles, who was later to marry François d'Hautpoul, the Lord of Rennes and Blanchefort. Montroux was banished for his crime, but was found to have lent money to François d'Hautpoul in order to purchase the presbytery.

Three generations later, when the author and researcher Gérard de Sède interviewed the erudite local historian and former lawyer Abbé Mazières, he was warned that, 'This Rennes affair is very gripping, but I must warn you it is also dangerous . . .' With this in mind, was the death in 1905 of Bérenger Saunière's younger brother Alfred, aged less than fifty-five, due entirely to natural causes? That Bérenger himself should be struck down on the symbolic 17 January, raises similar doubts.

UNSEEN HANDS
AND OCCULT INFLUENCES

Freemasonry · Martinism · Visions of the Virgin Mary
Synarchy · The Habsburgs

THE SECRECY SURROUNDING Saunière and his activities is symptomatic of his deep involvement in a world not acceptable to the ruling establishment, his wider local community or to his village congregation. Most probably he inherited from the Abbé Boudet the burden of the great secret of the Hautpouls. This was not only the knowledge of the existence of the legendary treasure but also the true fate of the ancient Merovingian dynasty, which had assumed the mantle of a potent archetype of monarchy. Besides this, he evidently shared a vision of France that was in direct opposition to the liberal democratic Republic in which he lived.

This vision was of a society with echoes of feudalism in which a partnership between the Catholic Church, the aristocracy and the monarch would provide a paternalistic government for its people. It looked back to a fusion of the pre-Revolutionary state of the Bourbon monarchs, the Holy Roman Empire of Charlemagne, and even the age of the unification of the early Franks by the Merovingian king, Clovis I.

Living under a Republican administration openly antagonistic to monarchical aspirations, it was inevitable that the existing network of lodges or secret societies would prove irresistable for infiltration by those dedicated to realizing this vision. Even previously non-political but influential networks could be subtly infiltrated at an administrative level and exploited either for their contacts or to provide a cover for another agenda.

The dissent harboured in, and indeed nurtured by, the times in which Saunière lived was one that had brewed for centuries. Following the Reformation in the sixteenth century, the Catholic Church had found itself an adversary in Protestantism. This could not be suppressed by the traditional means it applied to heresy, vigorously wielded by the Inquisition. Even the founding of the austere Society of Jesus by Ignatius Loyola in 1534, commonly known as the Jesuits, dedicated to the defence of Catholicism, could not stem the flow of conversions to Protestantism. Modelled on the old Order of Knights Templar, the Jesuits were the sword arm of the Church, except that skill at arms was replaced by intellectual study and debate. In time they were to become a major influence within the Vatican, involving themselves in diverse strategies for undermining and destroying enemies both within and outside the Church. After a succession of religious wars and persecutions, both Catholics and Protestants remained firmly entrenched in European society and politics. In France the Church of Rome remained in overall control until the Revolution which dispossessed it of its extensive property, and many of its wealthy aristocratic supporters by means of the guillotine during the Terror. Even after Napoleon's accord with the Vatican, the Catholic Church never recovered its former power.

In Great Britain, the religious battle for the monarchy had been won by the Protestant Hanovarians following the final collapse of the Stuart cause. Nominally Catholic and with a history of dynastic marriages (Mary, Queen of Scots, daughter of James V and Mary of Lorraine, had married the Dauphin, afterwards Francis II of France), the Stuarts, with Scottish roots, looked to their French cousins for support. Following the execution of Charles I, his family sought protection in France and were granted a safe haven at the palace of St Germain-en-Laye, outside Paris. It was not long before the royal guests were joined by members of the Scottish nobility and Jacobite supporters who, determined to restore their monarch and power in Britain, organized a network of Masonic lodges through which they could communicate and conspire. Becoming known generally as Scottish Rite Freemasonry, independent lodges proliferated throughout France. By 1730 there were some lodges that had no direct link to the Stuart cause, their members being attracted by the rites, rituals and social benefits. And being mainly Catholic and aristocratic, these lodges attracted the flower of French nobility. It was inevitable that a rival system would be established, and one soon grew, affiliated to the Hanoverian Grand Lodge in London (formed in 1717). This drew its members from Protestants, Jews, minor aristocrats and the bourgeoisie. Soon, this French wing, displaying typical Gallic independence, decided to break with the English administration and formed their own Grand Lodge of France.

The majority of lodges and their members were not in fact politically active; by and large their motives were social, an extension of the gentleman's club. However, part of the attraction was in the sense of mystery, maintained by an element of secrecy and a strict hierarchical structure; the concept of initiations and degrees of office engendered a powerful feeling of exclusivity and elitism. Itself this could be considered harmless, but it was these aspects, coupled with the widespread network of lodges, that made Freemasonry and other similar secret societies so attractive and vulnerable to exploitation by subversive agents. This potential has certainly been exploited over the past 250 years, and it still gives outsiders cause for suspicion and alarm.

In effect, the French Revolution, though essentially atheistic, could be seen as a victory for the Masons of the Grand Lodge of France. These had a closer affinity with the aims of the Revolutionaries than those in the Scottish Rite and the other neo-chivalric Orders. In fact, the convergence of their aims led to accusations that the French Revolution was inspired, if not led, by Masonic politics. There was indeed a network of left-wing 'Jacobin' political clubs, named after the Jacobin convents in which they held their first meetings, who actively campaigned for popular support; their agitation led to the escalation of internal conflict and ultimately, full revolution. But these clubs have never been shown to be Masonic in nature, although it is possible that some of their members were also Masons.

By the time of the Abbé Saunière, French politics were polarized between republican and monarchist camps, each with its own supporting network of Masonic lodges; but despite having temporarily lost power the monarchists were hopeful of an early restoration. An investigation of many prominent supporters of both sides reveals no clear distinction between aristocrats and commoners and their relative affiliations; Napoleon's new aristocracy, created mainly from the military and the bourgeoisie, did not necessarily support a monarchy.

But the choice between a king or a president was not merely a political decision, for the monarch was considered by many Catholics (and of course the Church itself) to rule by divine right. This implied that a monarch could enlist the spiritual help of heaven. To monarchists, theirs was the only possible option if France was to be protected from her enemies. By implication, French politics were once again experiencing the manipulation of the unseen hand of the Church of Rome.

* * *

Evidence has recently come to light through the researches of the French writer André Douzet, that the Abbé Saunière had spent much time in the city of Lyon, known as the occult centre of France. In this context 'occult' refers to an interest in the supernatural, magical and mystical aspects of life; not to be confused with black magic or Satanism, though the boundaries of each sometimes become blurred. Correspondence addressed to Saunière shows that he was in contact with a secret society in Lyon, called the Martinists, and that he often stayed at a house two doors away from that of Joanny Bricaud, a prominent Martinist. As is typical in Lyon, their houses were even connected by an underground passage allowing unseen movement between houses.

Employing a strange blend of esoteric magic, initiatory rites and Catholic symbolism, the Martinists attempted to connnect with the invisible, that is, the spiritual world. Martinism had started in the mid-eighteenth century with Martines de Pasqually, a Portugese Jew whose family had converted to Catholicism, and who claimed to have obtained secret knowledge from an old Dominican family. The Dominicans were responsible for operating the Inquisition, in the course of which they had amassed a huge quantity of so-called heretical documents, from which they were able to build up a corpus of secret and unpublished knowledge. This knowledge could well have included some details of the treasure, from information obtained during the Cathar inquisition. From his interest in mystical Christianity, Pasqually had also developed a cosmogony built around the figure of Christ, but which also introduced elements of esotericism and the Jewish cabdala, resulting in his founding of the neo-Masonic Elus Cohen ('Elected Priest', where Cohen is the Hebrew word meaning priest). It is interesting to note the choice of Jewish symbolism in this otherwise mystical-Christian society, and the elite status of his initiates.

He was succeeded by his former secretary, Louis Claude de Saint-Martin, who had been initiated into the Elus Cohen in 1765. On an outwardly spiritual level, the original Martinism offered a system by which 'man' could reconnect with his divine self, and so attracted those seeking such a spiritual goal. Saint-Martin maintained the focus on Christ but added elements of magic and initiation – which brought Martinism closer to the world of freemasonry. However, despite its avowedly spiritual role, Martinism was soon to play a political role of some importance.

By the time of Saunière's involvement, Martinism had come under the control of Papus, the pseudonym of Dr Gérard Encausse, a healer and occultist who had organized a Martinist lodge system of which the majority of members were priests interested in mystical Catholicism. But, as with many secret societies, break-off groups founded their own sects. Even the Philadelphes, founded by the Marquis de Chefdebien a century earlier, and dedicated to the acquisition of Masonic secrets and archives, are shown to have displayed Martinist influences. Saunière's affiliation can be seen in an illustration, on what is believed to have been his personal bookplate, that depicts the Martinist symbol of two interlocked triangles like a Star of David, but with one white and one black triangle. Within this were his initials, B.S. This symbol of interlocking black and white triangles – inexplicably added to the plain blue shield of the crest of Rennes-le-Château – appeared in an illustration found in the secret dossier of another secret society that surfaced in the mid-twentieth century, as we will discuss later in this chapter.

The interlocking triangles form not only the Jewish symbol of the Star of David, otherwise known as the Seal of Solomon, but also the symbol of hermeticism representing the philosophy of 'as above, so below', meaning that the state of the heavens is reflected on the Earth. This philosophy is considered to have been passed down from ancient civilizations who are thought to have had a greater knowledge of man and his place in the cosmos; and to have had access to sacred techniques such as astrological divination, alchemical transformations and the ability to transcend the physical world. For Christians, this ancient knowledge or 'gnosis' is thought to be contained in the teachings of St John the Divine, especially in his *Revelations*. This is the basis of esoteric Christianity which appealed to the more intellectual, endorsing the belief that the Catholic Church was a repository for such lost knowledge.

It was generally held in the occult world that the Martinists possessed arcane secrets and that they followed a hidden agenda. Despite the profusion of Masonic and secret societies, the Martinists attained a pre-eminent status attracting and influencing some of the greatest names in occult circles as well as a large number of Catholic priests. The involvement of priests was not frowned upon, for Martinism was not a Masonic organization and didn't suffer the same condemnation from the Catholic Church. In fact, in view of its predominant Catholic and monarchist affiliates it may even have been encouraged by the Church. Certainly, after the time of Sauni-ère's involvement, Martinism appeared to be becoming increasingly more political than spiritual, participating in the veiled world of occult politics.

★ ★ ★

Yet another prominent devotee of esoteric Christianity, Jose-phin Péladan, had also been initiated into Martinism. Shortly afterwards, he founded the Order of the Rose Cross and the Temple and the Grail with the support of Papus, head of the Martinists, and an imaginative occult poet, the Marquis Stanis-las de Guita. This was an attempt to revive the ancient Rosicrucian brotherhood of the early seventeenth century; a mysterious and unidentified body that as well as promoting a subversive philosophy had also been credited with the possession of ancient secrets. Rosicrucian symbols are to be found in profusion in the church at Rennes-le-Château; an indication that Saunière – or his mentor – was actively involved with this neo-Rosicrucian revival.

Taking the pseudonym sar Merodack (of Assyrian origin; *sar* meaning king, and Merodack, an Assyrian god), Péladan established the Salons de la Rose-Croix in Paris, in which he mounted exhibitions with the aim of restoring what he considered to be 'Ideal Art' based on traditional and Catholic influences. Very successful for five years, the Salons attracted many accomplished and distinguished exhibitors; it is even reported that Debussy would arrive almost every day to play the piano. The connection with Debussy is significant since he is cited as a Grand Master, like Nicolas Flamel and Charles Nodier before, of the secret society that claims to have acted as guardian of Rennes-le-Château and its great secret.

Péladan himself left a considerable body of literary work dedicated to Catholic occultism, mysticism and magic. In 1889 he had made a visit to Jerusalem and on his return claimed, without any supporting evidence, to have discovered the true site of the Tomb of Jesus; not in the Holy Sepulchre as generally believed but under the Mosque of Omar. That site, one may recall, formed part of the dwelling occupied by the Knights Templar on their arrival in the Holy City. No further explanations were ever given publicly, but despite his devotion to the Catholic faith, he firmly believed in the mortality of Jesus. As well as his Martinist and Rose-Croix affiliations, Péladan had connections with the Order of Knights Templar since he had been invested into the reconstituted Sovereign and Military Order of the Temple of Jerusalem, and according to the Order's history, became Regent for two years (in place of a Grand Master) in 1892.

By the late nineteenth century the French occult world was a close-knit group of often competing lodges, sects and individuals, with alliances being continuously formed and broken. Out of this mêlée of esoteric mysticism, Templarism and Masonry, a new network of secrecy and influence arose that was to become highly significant in later French and European politics. This very same network became inextricably linked with the acquisition and transmission of archives relating to the hidden gold. But another fascinating phenomenon, directly connected with the Catholic Church, also manifested itself and came to play a major role in the politics of the time: that of miraculous apparitions.

The Catholic-backed monarchist cause came to a head in 1876 with the French national pilgrimage to Lourdes by monarchist supporters to crown the Virgin Mary as Queen of Heaven, thereby enlisting her spiritual aid in their cause. Lourdes, located in the foothills of the French western Pyrenees, had been the site in 1858 of the famous visions of a young shepherdess named Bernadette Soubirous. She claimed to have seen the Virgin Mary no less than eighteen times in a grotto above the Gave de Pau river; and miraculously, a spring of fresh water began to flow which has apparently healed the afflictions of the faithful that have visited the site ever since. Whatever the truth behind the events of 1858, Lourdes has become a powerful symbol of the true faith, and one of the leading tourist sites of the world, attracting in excess of four million pilgrims annually (supposedly more than visit Rome or Mecca). Through unashamed commercialism, Lourdes has become a very rich town.

The Catholic monarchist movement had already moved into higher gear, as previously mentioned, through the cult of the Sacred Heart. Resurrected by Rohault de Fleury (whose family were intimately linked with Rennes-le-Château and Blanchefort), the cult of the Sacred Heart drew its original inspiration from the prophetic visions of a nun, Sister Alo-coque, who in 1671 claimed to have seen Jesus with his heart exposed and bleeding. He told her that France would only be protected from her enemies if the nation fully embraced the worship of the Sacred Heart.

In 1873 a former nun, Constance Estelle Faguette, also had a vision of the Virgin Mary. Born in 1843 near Châlons-sur-Marne, at the age of eighteen she became a novitiate with Augustine nuns, but was forced to leave after two years having suffered a knee injury. She obtained a position as a servant in the household of the Countess of Rochefoucauld at the château at Pellevoisin. For ten years she travelled between Paris and Pellevoisin until she became ill with a lung disease. She wrote a letter to the Virgin Mary, which was placed at the foot of her statue, asking for succour. During her illness, the Rochefoucaulds paid for her comfort and, not expecting her to live, they also made burial provisions. But, as though on cue, the first of her fifteen visions of the Virgin Mary occurred, which often showed the Devil being overcome by the Virgin, and the request that she erect a marble tablet at Pellevoisin, if she was cured. In the vision the marble tablet appeared with a golden rose in each corner and, at the centre, a heart with flames emanating from the top. Needless to say, Estelle was healed, continued her working life in the service of the Roche-foucaulds, and lived until the age of eighty-three. She had two further visions in later life, one of which endorsed yet another message, one that had been received in 1846 in a vision at La Salette. Pellevoisin never achieved the status of the other pilgrimage sites and remained a rural backwater; the visions were never adequately investigated, and, indeed, the whole episode is highly suspect. Interestingly, the Count Antoine de la Rochefoucauld was a founder member with Péladan of the Order of the Rose-Croix Catholique, and initially financed the Salons de la Rose-Croix.

Among its profusion of curiosities, the domain of the Abbé Saunière at Rennes-le-Château contains a number of clear indications of his devotion to the monarchy and the Sacred Heart. For example, in a niche high above the door of his villa is a large statue of Jesus revealing the Sacred Heart, while on the two painted glass windows immediately above the door are lurid depictions of the Sacred Heart by itself, surrounded by the crown of thorns; at the apex of the gable ends of the villa, the royalist symbol of the fleur-de-lys can be seen; and engraved around the plinth supporting the Calvary cross are the opening words of the ancient coronation hymn, '*Christus Vincit, Christus Regnat, Christus Imperat*'. Moreover, the deco-ration of his little church is ablaze with Sacred Heart and Rosicrucian symbolism.

But one of the most enigmatic of his religious features is that ensemble of the statue of the crowned Virgin Mary placed on the upside-down ancient pillar, on which he had engraved the words, 'Penitence, Penitence' and 'Mission 1891'. Whereas the crowned Virgin relates to the visions of Lourdes, the 'Penitence, Penitence' exhortation refers more appropriately to the vision witnessed some twelve years before those of Bernadette Soubirous in September 1846 at La Salette, near Grenoble in the French Alps. There, the Blessed Virgin appeared to a poor, innocent, fourteen-year-old shepherdess, Melanie Calvet, and her young companion, Maximin Giraud. The message revealed to these two naïve children, as interpreted by their confessor Jean-Marie Vianney, the Curé d'Ars, was a warning that if the French people did not reform their ways and return to the teachings of the Church then they would be abandoned by Jesus Christ. A final part of the message, known popularly as the Secret of La Salette, is said to have been passed only from pope to pope and never revealed; it is alleged to be a political criticism of the Church and the papacy. As with the vision at Lourdes, the story has a monarchist undertone. One Charles Naundorff protested that he was the natural son, previously assumed dead, of Louis XVI and backed by a sect of Catholic Church reformers, the 'vision' of La Salette appears to have been stage-managed to promote his cause.

The nine-year-old shepherd boy, Maximin, later confessed to Jean-Marie Vianney, the Curé d'Ars, that he did not actually see anything and had to some extent been led along by Melanie. The Curé, upset by this, complained to his superior, Philibert Brouillard, the Bishop of Grenoble, who advised him to return home and say nothing. It later transpired that the 'vision of the beautiful lady' was really Constance de la Merlière, a local eccentric who enjoyed dressing up, and who after the 'apparition', was spotted in several places wearing the same dress as described by Melanie. Accused by two priests of deception, she brought about a defamation case which she subsequently lost despite the efforts of her lawyer.

The case highlights a strange collaboration. Constance de la Merlière was a fanatical monarchist, but her lawyer was Jules

Favre, an ardent republican and member of the Les Coeurs Reunis lodge of the Grand Orient at Toulouse. Reconciling this courtroom collaboration is somewhat of a puzzle, except that the outcome of the trial appeared to discredit both the Church and the restoration movement, to the obvious satisfaction of Jules Favre, who probably suspected this result from the outset. Despite this revelation of trickery, La Salette continues to be a pilgrimage site drawing thousands of pilgrims each year; a practice that has never been discouraged by the Catholic Church.

Still more coincidences arise from the La Salette incident; a rare statue of Jean-Marie Vianney, the Curé d'Ars, can be found in the little church of Bézu, a village near the old Templar commandery only 6.5 km from Rennes-le-Château. Melanie Calvet, the young shepherdess, turned out to have a famous relative, the opera singer Emma Calvé (originally Calvet but changed for professional purposes), who was closely associated with the Paris occult circles with whom the Abbé Saunière is believed to have made contact.

A certain mystery surrounds Emma Calvé. Born in 1858 at Decazeville, she spent much of her adolescence in the mountain village of Bastide-Pradines, which is close to the preserved Templar commanderies of St Eulalie-de-Cernon, La Cavalerie and La Couvertoirade. After her initial success in the opera, she donated money to finance a sanatorium at Cabrières, north of Millau, but by the end of 1893, her diary shows that she was 100,000 francs in debt. However, a year later she had paid this off and had begun the purchase of the delapidated château at Cabrières.

Though at one time the lover of the renowned Paris occultist, Jules Bois, her rapid change in fortune has been attributed to financial help from the Abbé Saunière, with whom she was alleged to have had a close relationship. They are said to have met during his visit to Paris. While researching the history of her ancient home, she also discovered that the old family of Cabrières had possessed a copy of the ancient alchemical and cabalistic work of Abraham the Jew, the text studied by Nicolas Flamel. Confirmation of this can be found in a book, *Trésor des Recherches et Antiquites Gauloises et Françaises* by Pierre Borel, published in Paris, 1655. During a visit to M. de Cabrières' château, Borel claims to have seen the original book used by Flamel.

Towards the end of her life, Calvé experienced further money problems and sold the château to Madame Aubin, a former tutor to the Habsburgs. She died after an illness in 1942, in an apartment in Millau. Although it has not been possible to verify her alleged relationship with Saunière, there is no doubt that they frequented the same occult circles.

Other members of these circles appear to have had a direct influence on Saunière; such as the eccentric Eugene Vintras and his devotee the Abbé Boullan, who had a strange relationship with the nun Adéle Chevalier, a friend of Melanie Calvet whom she had met at La Salette. For their rites and rituals they adopted the symbol of the upside-down cross, which represented not only the martyrdom of St Peter but also the secret inner teachings and traditions of the Catholic Church. This could explain Saunière's action in placing a crowned Virgin Mary over an upside-down cross.

Although the events at Rennes-le-Château took place only a hundred years ago, and some sons and daughters of Saunière's parishioners are still alive, teasing out fact from fiction proved remarkably difficult. One analyses the available evidence together with suggestive but unproven allegations in an attempt to discern the truth, but the secrecy surrounding many of Saunière's activities inevitably compounds the problem. Gérard de Sède in his book, *L'Or de Rennes* (1967), provides an account which helps to provide a credible overall picture.

Having discovered the parchments in the crypt and realizing that they had a potential value, Saunière made accurate copies and attempted to decipher them. After a couple of years of studying them without success, despite the assistance of his colleague Abbé Boudet, he sought the advice of his co-operative bishop at Carcassonne, Mgr Billard. It was Billard who suggested that Saunière take the parchments to the church of St Sulpice in Paris, where he would find experts in ancient and esoteric documents. He gave him a letter of introduction to the Director of the Seminary of St Sulpice, the Abbé Bieil, and advanced him his travelling expenses. (Though proving elusive to confirmation, other researchers claim that his trip to Paris and St Sulpice is recorded by entries in a Mass book.) During his stay in Paris, while the parchments were being studied by specialists, Saunière is believed to have stayed with the nephew of Abbé Bieil, one Monsieur Ane, a creator of religious imagery. It is here that he is said to have met another nephew of the Abbé, the young novice priest, Emile Hoffet, who later became an expert on occult matters and Free-masonry, amassing a prodigious library of esoteric works. As well as encounters with Emma Calvé, Claude Debussey, and others involved in the Parisian occult circle, it is also alleged that he met and maintained regular correspondence with a journalist, Charles Plantard, who had visited the Razès on several occasions and become friendly with the Abbé Boudet. This association will be shown to be crucial in the future unfolding of the Rennes mystery, especially considering the involvement in it of Charles's grandson, Pierre Plantard, some fifty years later.

But just as the accuracy of the story of the trip to Paris is questionable, so the fate of the parchments themselves is mysterious. Those supposedly taken by Saunière to St Sulpice were evidently confided to Émile Hoffet for further study probably after the death of his uncle and remained secreted in Hoffet's library until his death in 1946. The parchments were then acquired – whether bought or stolen is not clear – by a group claiming to be representatives of the London-based League of Antiquarian Booksellers, who applied, and apparently received permission, to export three of the documents to England where they were deposited in a strongbox at Lloyds Bank International. Other accounts add that these three documents were at first inherited by Saunière's niece, Madame

James, who then sold them, not appreciating their value, to the League of Antiquarian Booksellers. Certainly, after the death of the Abbé Hoffet, Marius Fatin, archaeologist and owner of the château at Rennes, received a letter from this enigmatic League stating that his château was a site of great historic importance, having been the home of Sigisbert IV following the murder of his father, King Dagobert II. The letter also refers to the purchase of the parchments from the library of Émile Hoffet by the League, and even their initial discovery by Saunière.

But why would a British antiquarian book society be so interested in parchments relating to a somewhat obscure (especially for the British) Merovingian line? What was their interest in the fate of their descendants and the château at Rennes? Meanwhile, Saunière's own copies, and the documents stolen by his brother from the Marquis de Chefdebien, were confided to his friend and physician, Dr Courrent, just before the priest's death.

The trail of the parchments, the conspiracies to acquire them, and the extraordinary figures behind the League of Antiquarian Booksellers are fascinating in themselves. But this is more than an adventure story: its twists and turns have far-reaching, and increasingly sinister, implications.

The Abbé Saunière's initiation into the Martinist Order brought him into the midst of a shadowy world of secret societies, whose devotees' activities can be detected throughout Europe. At first sight these mystical preoccupations appear no more than harmless and even laudable (or laughable!) attempts to acquire spiritual knowledge and development through secret teachings, rites and rituals. However, a closer look soon reveals that the hard edge of politics is never far away.

In the tangle of nineteenth-century occult societies some individuals stand out from the rest. One of these was Alphonse Louis Constant (later adopting the name Eliphas Levi). Born in Paris in 1810, he entered the higher seminary of St Sulpice at Issy to complete his training for the priesthood. It was here that he found an interest in magic. However, having fallen in love with a young woman he was obliged to resign from the ministry. He then met Flora Tristan, a leading light in working class and feminist movements, through whom he was introduced to the great novelist, Honoré de Balzac, a Catholic occultist much influenced by Martinism. Influenced by these and other philosophies Levi, dedicating himself to a transformation of society and the abolition of social inequality, wrote a number of books which at times brought him into conflict with the Catholic Church. He was much admired for his openness and belief in occult sciences by progressive artists (and later by the Surrealists), who coincidentally also admired the alchemist Nicolas Flamel. Levi firmly believed that through the practice of magical rites he could enlist the help of 'higher powers' to bring about desired personal and social changes and even miracles to rival those of the authorized religion.

One vision of social change was called 'synarchy' or joint sovereignty; a tripartite government comprising three essential functions based on education, justice and economy. Synarchy was the idealistic brainchild of Saint-Yves d'Alveidre, who had married Balzac's second wife, through whom he acquired considerable wealth as well as the title, Marquis d'Alveidre. He also believed in the tradition of Agartha, the existence of an underground city in the centre of Asia, the home to great masters of science and wisdom, from where would come the enlightened King of the World. He wrote a number of books, including *Les Missions des Juifs* (*The Mission of the Jews*), and *La France Vrai* (*The True France*), in which he develops his synarchist ideas. The concept of synarchy would later be adopted into Masonic politics, and when integrated with Martinism produced the esoteric and politically active Ordre de Martiniste-Synarchique.

But of all the extraordinary personalities involved with these esoteric societies, one of the most remarkable and influential was Papus. Born in Spain as Gérard Encausse, but brought up in Paris, he began his career studying medicine but abandoned this to study occultism. He was initiated into Martinism, which he then started to reorganize, setting up a network of lodges, the first of which was in Lyon; and which would have existed at the time of Saunière's participation. He assisted Péladan, the fanatical Catholic monarchist, to found the cabbalistic Rosicrucian order, and became a central figure in the distribution of occult ideas, writing no less than 260 works. Returning ultimately to his medical interests he developed and published a philosophy of anatomy, and in 1897 opened a school of hermetic sciences. Acquiring a reputation for alternative healing and medicine derived from the occult, he was summoned to the court of the Russian Czar Nicholas II where esotericism and spiritualism had become as popular as they had in the salons of other branches of European high society. From the early 1800s, secret societies, including Martinism, had enjoyed changing fortunes at the Russian court and even during most influential periods was mistrusted by those fearful of subversive or revolutionary politics. At a magical seance held by Papus, he supposedly invoked the spirit of the Czar's late father Alexander III, from whom he interpreted advice on how to deal with the growing social unrest in Russia.

But this was not the court's only source of advice and influence: the Czar and Czarina had fallen under the spell of the 'mad monk' Rasputin, following his alleged cure of their son from haemophilia. Many were alarmed at the enchantment of the Russian royal family and court by this dirty, unkempt and apparently amoral sham holy man; some believed that he was the representative of secret Masonic societies plotting to bring about the downfall of the ruling Romanovs. Papus himself warned against the power of Rasputin and the danger of listening to his advice.

It is at this time that the highly anti-Semitic *Protocols of the Elders of Sion* also appeared at the Russian court. This document was purported to be the minutes of a World Jewish Congress that had taken place at Basle, Switzerland, in 1897, at which a plan had been agreed by Jews and Freemasons to achieve financial, and hence political, world domination.

Generally regarded as a fake, the origin of the *Protocols* remains unknown. It is possible that they were composed and published by the Martinists to discredit the growing Jewish and Masonic influences bearing on the court. As in the case of Rasputin, these influences were also considered by the Martinists to be aimed at weakening the power of the Czar and to bringing down the Romanov dynasty. Whatever the reality of their origin, the *Protocols* have been used as justification for continued anti-Semitism by many right-wing nationalist organizations ever since.

Geographically, St Petersburg is a great distance from Rennes-le-Château. But the network of lodges and secret societies brings them much closer together than the map shows. Saunière's Europe at the turn of the twentieth century was one of competing inter-related dynasties; the Habsburgs ruling an Austro-Hungarian Empire, Germany united with Prussia under Bismark, the Romanovs reigning over Russia, Great Britain and her Empire ruled by cousins of the Russian czars and German kaisers, the Bourbon kings still on the throne of Spain, even if displaced from France by the Revolution. However, the sands of time were running out for many of the 'old order'; rumblings of discontent from the people about the way they were ruled, the fragile alliances between these competing dynasties, were to sound the death knell for some, and major upheavals for others. Against this background it is easy to understand why secret societies proliferated and in many instances became drawn into the political arena, taking up positions supporting conflicting factions with separate agendas.

In 1889, yet another curious and unexplained episode enters the mysterious history of Rennes-le-Château. It concerns the visits to Abbé Saunière of an individual who called himself Jean Orth, but who was in reality the Archduke Johan Salvator von Habsburg. A nephew of the Emperor Franz

Top right: The Arch of Titus, showing the treasures of the Temple of Jerusalem being carried off to Rome. The story begins . . . (© Ronald Sheridan/Ancient Art & Architecture Collection)

Right: The medieval abbey of Sion in Switzerland, former seat of the bishops and counts of Sion, and the site of a Merovingian mint.

Below: The walled city of Carcassonne today.

Montségur's hilltop château, site of the Cathar massacre in 1244 and Otto Skorzeny's excavations in 1944.

Rennes-le-Château. The remains of the medieval château, with Visigothic foundations but rebuilt in the thirteenth century. Former home of the Hautpoul family.

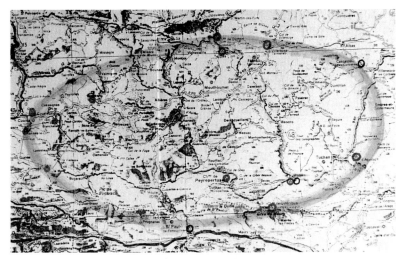

Ancient castles, many with Visigothic foundations, ring the area in which the lost treasure is thought to be located.

The late thirteenth-century *Dalle des Chevaliers*, or Knights' Stone, excavated by Abbé Saunière in his restorations of the church at Rennes-le-Château, 1891. The Templar legacy is rich in the region.

Above: Nicolas Flamel,
1330–1418, alchemist.
(Mary Evans Picture Library)

Right: Portrait of Nicolas
Pavillon, twenty-ninth bishop of
Alet-les-Bains, 1637–77. (Property
of the Mairie, Alet-les-Bains)

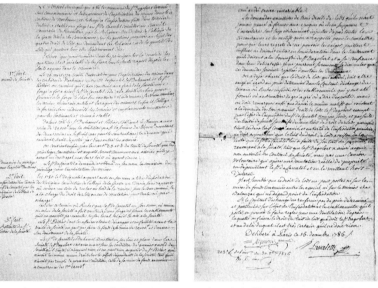

First and last pages of the 1785 Act signed on behalf of the monks of the
Abbey of Lagrasse, granting to General Dagobert and his colleagues permission
to reopen the ancient mines situated on their lands.

Villerouge-Termines: the house built by Dagobert in 1785
for the manager of his mining operations.

Above: The ruins of the forge and mine buildings established by Dagobert at Padern in the Corbières.

Right: Dagobert's memorial at Mont Louis in the Pyrenees.

Left: Roger-René Dagobert, descendant of General Dagobert, photographed in the village of Cascatel, home to the general's wife. He is holding the marriage register that records his ancestors' marriage.

Below left: Marie-Thérèse, widow of Henri, Comte de Chambord and Pretender to the throne of France, who enjoyed the support of Saunière and his family.

Below right: The nineteenth-century opera diva Melanie Calvé, habitué of Parisian occult circles.

Joseph, Johan was also cousin to Crown Prince Rudolph, whose death in 1889 at a hunting lodge at Mayerling was believed to have been a suicide pact with his mistress Mary Vetsera. The suspicious circumstances have prompted several alternatives. Shortly after this tragedy Johan renounced his inheritance and titles, incurring the wrath of his uncle, the emperor, and exiled himself from the Empire. He took the surname Orth from the name of his family château. His arrival in Rennes was recorded by the local police at Couiza, who were informed by Doctor Espezel from the neighbouring village of Esperaza. Concerned by some aspects of Saunière's public life, Doctor Espezel was suspicious of any strangers who visited the priest. It is said that Jean Orth and Saunière opened accounts in the same bank with consecutive account numbers, and that a large sum of money was transferred into Saunière's account. Then in 1890, having acquired a master's certificate in the merchant navy, Johan set sail for South America on the *Saint Margaret*; there is no reliable evidence to indicate that he was ever seen again.

Two further facts, though in themselves obscure, link the mystery of Rennes with the Habsburgs. First, the Count of Chambord (whose widow had donated 3000 francs to Saunière) and the Archduke Johan Salvator were cousins by virtue of sharing their maternal grandfather, Francis I, king of the Two Sicilies. Second, after his unfortunate death, Rudolph had left behind a locked strongbox, said to have contained coded documents and other items of great importance to the Habsburg Empire. This was later passed to Johan, who gave it to his faithful mistress, Milli Stubel, for safe keeping. Mystery still surrounds the fate and contents of the box, though Otto von Habsburg, his oldest surving descendant, claims to possess it. The Habsburgs had already acquired the legendary 'Spear of Destiny', said to have been used by the centurion Longinus to pierce the side of the crucified Jesus (though modern dating techniques disprove this conclusively), so it is quite conceivable that, being aware of the great biblical and symbolic treasure hidden near Rennes-le-Château, Johan, perhaps on behalf of others, wished to support Saunière in his researches.

By way of a footnote, 1975 saw a visit to Rennes-le-Château by Mgr Archduke Rudolphe of Habsburg, the sixth child of the Austro-Hungarian Emperor Charles IV and Empress Zita. According to the authors Gérard de Sède and Jean Robin, and confirmed by the researcher Pierre Jarnac, Rudolphe interviewed well-informed locals concerning the Saunière affair about which he already appeared to have extensive knowledge. He then interviewed two Rennes experts at Carcassonne, Mgr Boyer, the Vicar General, and the Abbé Mazières; Rudolphe paid particular attention to the story of his ancestor's visit to Saunière. Jarnac's researches further reveal that a police file still exists containing some details of a judicial enquiry, following Saunière's death in 1917, into the source of his revenue. Although the nature of the evidence is now unknown, the enquiry did conclude that he had been 'trafficking in gold with Spain'. So did Saunière indeed find some part of the ancient treasure?

SPIRITUAL QUESTS AND
THE LEGACY OF ZION

*Spiritualism · Hieron du Val d'Or · Judaism and Zionism
Order of the New Templars · Nazism*

SO, BY THE dawn of the twentieth century the mountain village of Rennes-le-Château had recovered a little of its past glory. An extract from a report of a visit in 1905 by the Society for Scientific Study of the Aude states: 'Suddenly, we discovered a beautiful crenelated wall, a beautiful villa, a recently constructed tower . . . a beautiful pleasure garden sheltered by a beautiful terrace from which one may enjoy a beautiful panorama; without contradiction, an oasis lost in the middle of a desert . . . *All this is the beautiful domain of the Abbé Saunière.*' Furthermore, the villagers spoke of important strangers to the village who were royally entertained by their priest at his new villa, evidence supported by invoices that reveal the purchase of copious amounts of food, wines, and spirits.

There are also several extant letters from priests thanking Saunière for his excellent and generous hospitality during their stay. But what was it that drew such important people to this backwater parish? How could these modest country priests have accepted such a strange and lavish lifestyle from one of their own? The answer may well lie in Saunière's involvement with Martinism.

A central belief of Martinism is that man can rediscover his spiritual or divine self, the state in which he was before the biblical 'fall'. Very closely related to this is a second belief that, with training and enlightenment, one can contact the 'unknown', that is, the spirit world. Initiates were instructed that these were their goals, and both could be achieved through magic rites and rituals, focused on the figure of Christ. Adherents from the priesthood itself would have considered themselves to be on a spiritual quest for an even higher purpose than that which they provided for their own congregations.

The belief in and objective of contacting one's higher nature is common to many occult organizations and philosophies. Coming from America in the late nineteenth century, spiritualism had quickly taken hold in Europe and soon gained notable adherents, such as the writers Victor Hugo and Sir Arthur Conan Doyle. Even Queen Victoria was said to have received messages from her beloved Prince Albert through the mediumship of John Brown, a worker on her Balmoral estate. There is no doubt that she developed a very close relationship with John Brown, but always remained devoted to her late husband. Papus, that great organizer of Martinist lodges in France, achieved great influence through holding seances and invoking spirits. It is quite conceivable that, having become immersed in Martinist activity at Lyon, Saunière himself had founded what was essentially a lodge at Rennes-le-Château where personal spiritual development and seances could take place. However, being aware of the remarkable history of the region, is it not also possible that Saunière and his compatriots believed that through contacting the spirits of the ancient lords of Rhedae, or perhaps the Knights Templar, they could discover the exact locations of all the legendary treasure?

For Saunière this would not have been for mere personal gain. It would have enabled him and his associates in realizing their passionate objectives: the restoration of both the power of the Catholic Church and their lost monarchy. Ownership of the treasure would have both funded their cause and given it sanction, considering its symbolism. Belief in the ability to contact the 'world of spirit', and the active involvement of Saunière, may well also explain the actions of his confidante, Marie Dénarnaud, after his death. After all, in *L'Héritage de l'Abbé Saunière* (1995), Marcel Captier and Claire Corbu recount that Marie would go to the cemetery and the grave of her priest every night, as if she had a pre-arranged meeting with him. They also note that immediately after the death of Saunière on 22 January 1917, she went around the village, in obvious distress, shouting, '*Mon dieu! Mon dieu! Monsieur le curé est mort . . . Maintenant tout est fini . . .*' ('My god! My god! The curé is dead . . . Now everything is finished . . .'). Had Saunière had psychic abilities? Had he himself acted as a medium for his initiates? According to the accounts of his parishioners, their priest certainly had great charisma – a quality often found in psychics. He was also adamant about remaining at Rennes-le-Château, despite the enormous pressure exerted on him, by his later bishop, Mgr Beauséjour, to account for his wealth and lifestyle. Surely something of great magnitude was keeping him there.

By way of further confirmation that Saunière had created a spiritualist centre at Rennes-le-Château, a close examination of the ground plan of the domain, painstakingly surveyed by Alain Féral, artist, researcher and long-time resident of the village, reveals a remarkable and complex underlying geometry. Buildings and features of the estate have been very deliberately laid out to create regular pentagons in the church garden and the villa garden respectively, and an irregular but cyclic pentagon in the Tour Magdala garden. All three are perfectly integrated with a giant regular pentagon which dominates the complete site – such a rigid geometrical construction cannot possibly have been accidental.

The pentagon is arguably one of the oldest and most universal of symbols. Pentagonal geometry contains the 'golden section', a constant ratio (like that of pi) often found in nature, which was revered by architects and philosophers of the ancient world as a manifestation of the divine. It is also the symbol for man within the universe, as illustrated in the famous drawings of Albrecht Durer and Leonardo da Vinci. But the pentagon, and its derivation the pentagram (a five-pointed star), are most popularly known from their use in magical rites, and are exemplified by the hermetic drawing of Eliphas Levi. This prominent occultist and magician of the mid-nineteenth century, believed that 'the original alliance of Christianity and the science of the Magi are essential'. In other words, the path to spiritual truth is found in a fusion of Christian teachings with knowledge and wisdom from the classical world – a belief parallel to that of the Martinists.

By comparison with another site, this pentagonal geometry takes on a further significance. Paray-le-Monial, a town in the north of the Massif Central and site of the Sacred Heart visions of Sister Alacoque, became a major pilgrimage site from the late seventeenth century, attracting many thousands of the faithful. Sharing the site with the monks and nuns at the eleventh-century basilica was a secretive institution, Hiéron du Val d'Or, which had an ambiguous relationship with its devotion to the Sacred Heart. Esoteric in nature, it laid great emphasis on adopting ancient Celtic sites and the use of sacred geometry; it even occupied a building arranged in the shape of a pentagon. The unusual name of Hiéron du Val d'Or has never been convincingly explained, but it is possible that du Val d'Or ('of the Valley of Gold') referred specifically to an important location. Could it be perhaps, the valley in which a treasure has been hidden?

Among those connected with the Sacred Heart centre was the writer, artist and archaeologist, Louis Charbonneau-Lassay. Attracted by the world of Christian symbolism, heraldic signs and sacred geometry, Charbonneau was particularly interested in the Knights Templar and the possibility that they had discovered some ancient knowledge. Over the years he accumulated a priceless collection of weapons, jewels and coins, from the Gallo-Roman and medieval periods. The exact source of these finds is unknown, but since Saunière and Lassay were both devotees of the cult of the Sacred Heart and probably both members of the Hiéron du Val d'Or, it would not be surprising if he had discovered some in the region of the Corbières.

Jean-Luc Chaumeil claims that one hidden agenda of the Hiéron was the creation of a new Habsburg and Vatican-dominated Holy Roman Empire, very much on the same model of a hierarchical, paternalistic elite favoured by many monarchists and aristocrats at the time, yet in direct opposition to the liberal democracy of the Republic of France, which they identified with evil. From his pulpit in October 1885, during local elections in the Aude, the Abbé Saunière fulminated against the Republic, encouraging his parishioners to vote against it saying, '*Les Republicains, voilà le Diable a vaincre et qui doit plier le genou sous les poids de la Religion et des baptises. Le signe de la croix est victorieux et avec nous . . .*' ('The Republicans, there is the devil to conquer and who must bend under the weight of the Religion and the baptised. The sign of the cross is victorious and with us . . .'). This leaves little doubt of his opinion of the Republic and its non-Catholic supporters.

The superiors of the Sacred Heart cult at Paray-le-Monial produced a magazine called *Regnabit* (He Will Reign), with articles submitted by Charbonneau-Lassay and such famous Christian-esotericists as René Guenon, a great adherent of spiritualism and, initially, Freemasonry. Guenon got to know Papus and other esotericists but also found himself drawn to Hinduism, Sufism, and Islamic esotericism; eventually, after the death of his first wife, he converted to the Sufic branch of Islam. He also considered all branches of esotericism to have the same roots. However, as a traditionalist, he was involved in extreme right-wing activities and wrote: 'History clearly shows that the failure to recognize a hierarchical order (based on the supremacy of the spiritual over the temporal) has the same consequences in all places at all times; social instability; confusion of duties; domination by the lower orders; and intellectual degradation.' Guenon was also a disciple of Saint-

Yves d'Alveidre whose synarchic concept of government was adopted into Masonic politics. Later, synarchy became allied with Martinism, and is now the esoteric agenda of anarchists. Guenon also adopted Saint-Yves' belief in the Central Asian-centred underground kingdom of Agartha, which he believed could be either actual or symbolic. Further, these metaphysical obsessions led him to an association with another strange occult group called the Polaires, whose origins – actual and legendary – are as obscure as its beliefs.

The Polaires and their relationship with other occult societies and individuals are reviewed in detail by Joscleyn Godwin in *Arktos: The Polar Myth* (1993), which reveals some interesting coincidences. The sign of the Polaires is quoted as the sign of two interlaced triangles, the same symbol as that of the Martinists and of course of Judaism. But more significant is that during 1929 and 1930, this group is alleged to have undertaken excavations and research for historical documents in the ancient Cathar region south of Carcassonne around the valleys of the rivers Aude and Arriège.

Also at this time, an awareness of the significance of the Cathars had slowly developed in England, within the esoteric society the White Eagle Lodge. At seances held in the lodge, the spirit of Conan Doyle was believed to have communicated, through the medium Grace Cooke, that he was working on the astral plane with a Rosicrucian initiate supporting the work of the Polaires. Later messages, received in 1937, revealed that something of great importance, but not actually defined, was hidden in the Cathar region, and that members of the Polaires should mount another expedition to the area. There they would make contact with someone called Walter.

This person can be identified as Walter Birks who, having studied history at Oxford University, taught in England and France, until his unexplained decision in 1937 to go to the Pyrenees to recover the lost traces of a 'Brotherhood'. His stay in the Arriège and the people he met are recounted in his book *Treasure of Montségur* (1987), written with the collaboration of R.A. Gilbert, today a high-ranking Freemason and occultist. Much space is devoted to examining the nature of a 'spiritual' treasure, but confirmation is also given of a huge material treasure possessed by the Cathars. Walter Birks, later to be an army major and recipient of an MBE, claimed also to have worked for British Intelligence and it seems hardly credible that such a man should undertake this sort of venture in so remote a region of France without a very substantial reason.

But seven years before the arrival of Walter Birks, another grail devotee had made his mark. Hard on the heels of that first group of Polaires in Cathar country, was a young German named Otto Rahn who in his search for the Holy Grail was to find himself involved in a sinister and ultimately fatal agenda. Evidently blinded by idealism, Rahn initially supported a regime dedicated to German national regeneration. The pursuit of this aim was to dramatically affect world history through the horrors of World War II, but its roots can actually be found in European events some sixty years before.

While young Bérenger Saunière was growing up in the little tranquil village of Montazels, perched on a sunny hillside overlooking the sparkling River Aude, the great dynasties of Europe were already edging towards disaster. France had of course already experienced a bloody revolution, and had substituted an absolute monarchy, for the relatively democratic Republic. However, in most of the rest of Europe, the power still resided in hereditary dynasties. The Romanovs remained in Russia, the Habsburgs in Austria and Hungary, the Ottoman Empire of the Turks persisted and kaisers still ruled Germany. But the Crimean War of the 1850s saw the beginning of the disintegration of these empires, completed after the 1914–18 war. Even so, the effect of Napoleon's conquests, both those successful and those attempted, resulted in a sense of insecurity that stimulated a fierce sense of nationalism which would dictate the foreign policies of most European countries.

Preoccupation with expansion of territory or the protection of existing borders took priority over domestic policy; increasing symptoms of social unrest went unheeded.

This was also a situation easily exploited by the secret societies now gaining political influence. Conventional historians tend to overlook the role of secret societies in these turbulent events, not believing that they have any real effect or significance in politics. On the contrary it can be well argued that the majority of political activity in any era is motivated by hidden agendas conceived in secret.

The other major influence is of course that of religion. For nearly 2000 years Europe has been a virtual battleground of competing sects: Roman Catholicism, Arianism, Protestantism, Calvinism, Jansenism, Islam, and Judaism – to mention just the most prominent. While for centuries the Catholic Church may have dominated, it was also continually under threat. Despite acting as a universal monarchy claiming spiritual authority over the temporal powers, it found itself subjected to restrictions by governments, even in countries where it was the state religion. But this meant that it was forced to resort to clandestine methods and expedient alliances to continue the struggle to reclaim its former power. Nonetheless, the Catholic Church continued to lose ground during the process of national unification taking place throughout Europe.

At the same time, the Jewish communities of Europe were starting to enjoy a temporary lifting of restrictions and greater freedom of movement. In less economically developed countries, particularly in eastern Europe, this emancipation provided an opportunity for the Jews to move into the mainstream of commercial and industrial enterprises, and to be accepted into the professional spheres formerly denied to them. But this very success was to provoke an extreme anti-Semitic reaction. In the commercial and financial sectors, failures and bankruptcies were attributed to parasitic Jews taking advantage of adverse conditions. Policies embracing more tolerant attitudes were soon denounced by the traditional Right; Catholic conservatives even contended that Freemasonry had been invented by the Jews as a cover for their financial and political activities! The assassination of Tsar Alexander II in 1881 was labelled a Jewish plot, and the ensuing pogroms stimulated a mass exodus, to western European cities, of the mainly orthodox and Yiddish-speaking Jews (Yiddish, a language derived from high German dialects with Hebrew and Slavonic additions, had gradually evolved out of a desire to maintain a separate cultural identity). To its shame, the Catholic Church was quick to appreciate the benefits of anti-Semitism and, by also labelling Jews as the killers of Christ, they sought to reunite the masses into the Catholic faith. An event such as the collapse of the Catholic Union Générale Bank in 1882 was a gift to the anti-Semites who could unjustly attribute it to Jewish manipulation of the money market. In short, the Jews were set up as convenient scapegoats by the ruling political, religious, and financial establishments, for all the social, financial, and political ills of the time.

But the arrival of huge numbers of Jewish immigrants, the majority of whom were known as Ashkenazim, into western Europe also created problems for the long-established and integrated Jewish communities. Contrary to popular belief, Jews do not form an homogenous racial or religious group. For centuries, those known as Sephardim had formed communities throughout western Europe where they could trade, usually in the large towns and cities near the Mediterranean. Despite periodic persecutions by the ruling elite, usually to steal their wealth, they worked hard to integrate with their fellow citizens.

It is from the Sephardic community in Marseilles and the towns of the Languedoc that the ancient Jewish princedom of Septimania had been formed. Sometimes restricted to living in ghettos, these Sephardic Jews were, in the main, content to adopt the nationality of their host country; they retained their religious and cultural traditions, but did not seek an individual national identity. By contrast, the Ashkenazic influx brought with them a call for a renewed national identity, and even the demand for a separate independent homeland. This was greeted with alarm by the Sephardic community who, having established a fragile but workable accord with their non-Jewish neighbours, feared a resurgence of anti-Semitism and restrictions on their lives and lifestyles.

Such an understanding of the differences between the Sephardic and Ashkenazic communities is crucial to the appreciation of the tensions between them, to the later emergence of Zionism, and also to the rise of rampant anti-Semitism throughout Europe. Correcting some of the popular misconceptions regarding Jewishness and the origins of many European Jews, also has a direct bearing on deciding the rightful ownership of the lost treasure of the Temple of Jerusalem.

For this understanding, we need to re-examine the biblical account of the formation of the nation of Israel by the patriarch Jacob, and its division into twelve regions each occupied and ruled by one of the families of his twelve sons. Of the twelve tribes, three are of particular relevence. The Levites were not actually granted a region of their own but scattered throughout the other areas; however they later receive some compensation in being the tribe chosen as a hereditary priesthood (Numbers, 3), and as the only ones considered by God worthy to carry the Ark of the Covenant. The tribe of Judah was honoured with the duties of ruler and lawgiver, and it is within their territory that the holy city of Jerusalem is found. Moreover, this was also very close to the border with the land belonging to the tribe of Benjamin.

For several generations the united nation of Israel was ruled by a succession of kings from the House of Judah, of which David and Solomon are the most famous. Following the death of Solomon the monarchy passed to his son Reheboam, who became the new king of Israel. However, his harsh reign was to provoke a rebellion from ten of the tribes, among which were the descendants of the ancient patriarch Joseph, Jacob's son. Only the tribes of Judah and Benjamin supported Reheboam, while the others united under a competent warrior, Jeroboam, who returned from exile in Egypt having previously challenged Solomon unsuccessfully. The account in 1 Kings 12–14, tells of a continous battle between the two, in which Reheboam is specifically named as the king of Judah and Benjamin, whereas Jeroboam is accepted as king of Israel. A clear distinction is thus made between those of Jewish origin, that is from Judah, and the other Israelite tribes.

In the *Jewish Encyclopedia* it is written that, 'Joseph and Judah typify two distinct lines of descent' and adds that Judah was 'in all likelihood a non-Israelitish tribe'. Furthermore, the Chief Rabbi of the British Empire in 1918, the Very Reverend J. H. Hertz, in responding to a query on this point said: 'The people known as Jews are descendants of the tribes of Judah and Benjamin with a certain number of desendants of the tribe of Levi.' This suggests that 'Israel' is quite separate from 'Judaism', and that only those from the tribes of Judah and Benjamin, and some Levites, can be accurately referred to as Jews.

The situation is further confused by the Babylonian captivities and the Diaspora, when Jews and Israelites became scattered. Even back as far as the Exodus from Egypt, it can be seen that the Hebrews, when entering Canaan were moving into a land already populated with a number of other Semitic and Hamitic-speaking peoples, and even Celtic tribes. That inter-marriages took place between these different tribes is illustrated by Solomon himself who, according to 1 Kings 11, had married or had relationships with women, from many different racial tribes. Thus it is highly improbable that any group exists that is exclusively descended from any of the blood-lines of the original twelve tribes.

The separation between Judah, with its capital Jerusalem, and the rest of Israel, was quite marked by the time of Jesus. Divided into three main areas – Judah, Samaria, and Galilee, and a small desert region south of Judah called Idumaea – the whole country, renamed Palestine, was under Roman domination. The Romans had allowed a Jewish aristocracy, which was just as unpopular for their exploitation of its fellow citizens as the king, Herod. Appointed by the Roman Senate, Herod was actually of Idumaean descent. The Judean attitude to its neighbouring groups was also fractuous. Feelings towards the Samaritans are summed up in the parable of the Good Samaritan; the attitude towards the Galilean farmers and fisherman was little better.

A gradual departure of Israelites and Jews from the rigours of Roman oppression turned into a virtual flood following the sacking of Jerusalem by Titus in AD70, and many made their way to the great city of Alexandria on the Nile Delta, or further afield to European cities, where large Sephardic communities flourished. Later, usually as a result of persecution or coercion, large numbers of Sephardic Jews converted to Catholicism, but many of their descendants continued to remember their roots, even after several generations. In Spain, in 1492, it is estimated that about 70,000 Jews were given the stark choice of conversion or expulsion – many left. The legacy of the Visigothic, Merovingian and Jewish relationships can be found in some of the noble families originating in the ancient Jewish princedom of Septimania, now the Languedoc; and it is these few families that are alleged to have held the great secret of the hidden treasure of the Temple of Jerusalem.

It is through 'conversion' that another group, practising a form of Judaism, appeared in central and eastern Europe. The Khazars, of Turkish origin, occupied a large territory in the Volga basin, north of the Black and Caspian seas, from the seventh to the twelfth centuries. In the eighth century, for reasons of expediency, their khan (or ruler) adopted Judaism as the state religion, having considered arguments put forward by a Jew, an Aristotlean philosopher, a Muslim and the Christian St Cyril. This extraordinary event, which has a parallel with Constantine's adoption of Christianity as the state religion of the Roman Empire, is discussed by Judah Halevi, a twelfth-century Jewish philosopher and poet, in his *Book of the Kuzari*.

Gradually, under pressure from the surrounding tribes, the Khazar Khanate diminished. By the thirteenth century it had been absorbed completely by the waves of nomadic tribes from the Steppes, although many Khazars migrated westwards to establish communities in eastern Europe – especially in Russia and Poland. These Khazar communities became known as Ashkenazim. Although practising Judaism, they had no direct genetic or racial links to the biblical occupants of the Holy Land (although 'true' Jews, from the Diaspora or other migrations, may have also settled in these regions). Thus a post-biblical kingdom of Jews certainly existed before the Middle Ages, although only through conversion. However, many Jewish scholars are reluctant to accept that it is this group that comprised the ancestors of the modern Ashkenazim. The matter is still subject to vigorous debate.

Understanding the Khazar heritage, as argued by the late Arthur Koestler, explains how while the Ashkenazic culture developed separately from the Sephardic, the religious observances remained largely the same. Support for Koestler's view has come from the work of the geneticist Professor Steve Jones, in whose book, *In the Blood* (1996), it is apparently definitively proven that the great majority of Ashkenazim, from whom most of the American and European Jews are descended, are not, in contrast to the Sephardim, genetically linked to the ancient tribes of Israel.

But these communities, which during the time of the Abbé Saunière were well established in east European cities, brought more than just their culture into western Europe. They brought an aspiration and a dream. To the dismay of the integrationist Sephardim, they talked of establishing an independent Jewish state, to be founded on the land currently occupied by the Palestinians. The name to be adopted by this political movement was Zionism, after its aim to create a Jewish homeland with its capital as Jerusalem, the 'City of Zion'.

The exact genesis of Zionism is not clear, but the work of colonizing Palestine actually started in 1870 with the formation by Alliance Israelite Universelle, of an agricultural school at Mikveh Israel; and in 1884 the Society of Lovers of Zion was founded to promote resettlement on a greater scale. According to some sources, however, Hibbat Zion was founded by a German-educated Jewish doctor, Leon Pinsker, at his home in 1883, with the support of the Baron Edmond James de Rothschild. An echo perhaps of Napoleon's invitation for Jews to occupy Palestine, even if at that time Edmond's grandfather supported a Bourbon restoration. Other sources claim that the term Zionism was actually coined by Nathan Birnbaum to denote the political efforts he identified at work. However, it was from the work of Theodor Herzel, a book entitled *Jewish State* outlining a scheme for an autonomous Jewish commonwealth under Ottoman suzereignty, that Zionism became publicly acknowledged.

Ironically, Palestine at that time was occupied by the Ottoman Turks; the Zionists themselves were largely from the Ashkenazic community, whose ancestors have been shown to be Khazar Turks. However, Theodor Herzel was duly elected president at the World Jewish Congress held in 1897 at Basle, Switzerland. It was from this Congress that the document called the *Protocols of the Elders of Zion* is said to have originated. Allegedly a record of the discussions and the resulting aims and objectives of world Jewry, the *Protocols* are in essence a plan for world financial and political domination. First published in a book attributed to a Russian, Sergei Nilus, in 1905, the twenty-four Protocols proclaim a strategy for weakening the gentile population, the destruction of gentile traditions, and gaining control of vital organs of power, such as communications and finance. By coincidence or design, some of the sentiments expressed have parallels in the Jewish Talmud (the collection of ancient Rabbinic writings, which constitute the basis of religious authority for traditional Judaism). The Talmud, which stems from the root meaning 'to learn', was written or compiled from AD70 (the sacking of Jerusalem) to the third or fourth centuries, with further additions from as late as the thirteenth century. Though the *Protocols* are almost universally considered a forgery, possibly perpetrated by the Martinists or even dissident members of the Czar's secret police, they were obviously compiled by someone familiar with Jewish teachings. The fact that many of the *Protocol's* stated objectives have since been implemented (even if not necessarily by Jews) has been eagerly but unjustifiably exploited by right-wing anti-Semitic factions.

One of the key objectives of the Zionists may also have been to gain control over the extensive mineral wealth of the Dead Sea. According to an article in the *New York Herald Tribune* of 14 January 1947, the proven estimated value of the Dead Sea mineral deposits was 5 trillion dollars. But even in 1911, a German geologist, Professor Blankenhorn, had reported on behalf of the Zionist organization, that the Dead Sea region contained extremely rich deposits of bromine, phosphates, potash and asphalt.

For 400 years Palestine had been part of the Turkish Ottoman Empire. It was not until 1917 that it was to be 'liberated' by the British during World War I. In 1915, however, Sir Herbert Samuel had already presented a proposal, *The Future of Palestine*, to the British Prime Minister, Herbert Asquith. Within a couple of months a plan for the annexation of Palestine and the creation of a national homeland for Jews had been adopted and supported by David Lloyd George, soon to become Prime Minister, but previously solicitor for the Zionists. In 1922, a temporary mandate from the League of Nations placed Palestine under British administration; though Sir Herbert Samuel, later appointed British High Commissioner, had a demonstrable loyalty to Zionism. The wheels had been set in motion for the process whereby in 1948, only eight hours before the expiry of Britain's mandate in Palestine, the Zionist dream of an independent State of Israel was achieved, despite the large resident Moslem population.

Zionism is seen, however, by even many traditional and Orthodox Jews, as a purely secular and political movement, lacking a truly religious dimension. And this political aspect of cultural Zionism has certainly been a contributory factor in the fabrication of many anti-Jewish conspiracy theories.

Adopted by the Zionist organization in 1897, the six-pointed star formed by two interlaced equilateral triangles had been a symbol of Judaism since the seventeenth century. Known popularly as the 'Magen David', the Star of David, or sometimes the Seal of Solomon, this symbol is also to be found in the region of Rennes-le-Château. For instance, on the bedhead of the deathbed of Marie de Nègre, Dables Dame d'Hautpoul de Blanchefort, in the Hautpoul château, is engraved the Hautpoul coat of arms. It incorporates a six-pointed star. The Martinist symbol, displayed at all lodge meetings, is also composed of black and white interlaced triangles, forming a hexagonal star, and the *Dossiers Secrets*, a collection of documents purporting to reveal the true history of Rennes-le-Château, shows the badge of the village with a Star of David imposed at its centre. At the nearby village of Alet-les-Bains, windows of the fifteenth-century parish church next to the ancient cathedral clearly reveal six-pointed stars; and finally, on an external beam of a sixteenth-century house, also in Alet, are engraved a number of esoteric symbols, among which are five- and six- pointed stars.

The Rue de la Juiverie in Alet-les-Bains is a reminder that the village had an important Jewish community in its illustrious past; a past that included the tenure of Nicolas Pavillon as Bishop of Alet, one of the founders of the mysterious and secret Compagnie du Saint-Sacrement, also known as the Children of Solomon, and its connections with Saint Sulpice in Paris – the seminary to which Saunière was said to have taken his parchments. These links are perhaps further confirmation of a strong association between the Corbières and the legendary treasure of the Temple of Jerusalem.

But if it were to be found, or indeed exist, to whom would this treasure rightfully belong? Considering the symbolic value, possession of these ancient religious artefacts would be enormously significant to the Zionists and the Government of the State of Israel. Perhaps, however, its true inheritors should be those Jews directly descended from those who, in the first century AD, administered the Temple of Jerusalem. On the other hand, could a legitimate claim be made by those families of mixed Jewish/Visigothic/Merovingian descent, who for centuries appear to have been the treasure's guardians?

Yet as we have seen, also enmeshed in this story is the continual presence of secret societies. Operating from the shadows, and sometimes carefully concealed within outwardly harmless esoteric or chivalric organizations, the agenda of these groups has included not just the recovery of ancient treasure in the Corbières but political control within other regions of Europe. Driven by greed, ideology, religious zeal or political ambition, these unseen forces can exert powerful but barely traceable influences. Detection of such forces at work is hardly new. Benjamin Disraeli had an interest in secret societies and the occult, and spoke out about the threat that they posed in Europe. In his novel *Coningsby*, he stated that 'the world is governed by very different personages to what is imagined by those who are not behind the scenes' – a statement that shows either great perception or inside knowledge. One of Disraeli's closest friends was Edward Bulwer-Lytton, 1st Lord Lytton of Knebworth. His interest in the occult stemmed from his days at Cambridge. Despite becoming a very active Member of Parliament he maintained an interest in the theatre, literature, and esoteric pursuits. He enjoyed high status in occult circles and he was visited in 1854 by that famous Paris occultist and magician, Eliphas Levi, who considered Lytton to be one of the principal exponents of occultism in Britain. Unconfirmed family sources claim that Lytton was even a Rosicrucian initiate, and without doubt his esoteric book *Zanoni*, is in large measure a reflection of Rosicrucian philosophy. It further enhanced his reputation in occult circles, and had an impact on the anti-Christian esotericism of Madame Helena Blavatsky, the Russian medium who was to found the Theosophical

Society. Attracting members from other esoteric societies, the Theosophical Society was also to take a more political stance under the later leadership of Annie Besant, who campaigned on a number of social issues, and it became affiliated with the Masonic Grand Orient lodge of France.

Bulwer-Lytton's *The Coming Race* had not only even greater impact on the Theosophists but also influenced the mystical elements of German nationalism. From this arose the Vril Society, a German mystico-political group that adopted the swastika as its emblem. This society, and others, associated the writings of Bulwer-Lytton and the occult philosophies of the Theosophists with a dangerous mix of anti-Semitism, extreme nationalism and a belief in root races or racial supremacy. This was also adopted by extreme right-wing groups, of which a prime example was the Ordo Novi Templi (Order of the New Templars), founded by Lanz von Liebenfels in 1907. This promulgated a right-wing, racist, anti-Semitic agenda, using an erroneous interpretation of the medieval Templars' mission as justification. Through a network of similar groups and by supporting pro-Serbian nationalism, the ONT was even able to play a major part in bringing about the assassination that sparked the tragedy of 1914.

During the 1920s, while the seeds were being sown for Adolf Hitler to take power in Germany, the ONT acted as co-ordinators for right-wing groups in Europe. And, although prohibited in 1941 by the Nazis, who had a paranoid fear of secret societies, the philosophies of the ONT, and the later German Order and Thule Society, were readily adopted by Hitler and his inner cabal, forming the basis for the political creed of the National Socialist Party.

The extreme right-wing politics of the Nazi party were in direct contrast to the Polaires and their quest for the spiritual – and admittedly material – treasure of the Corbières. Yet unwittingly, Otto Rahn, driven by a passionate desire to discover this Holy Grail, was to become fatally entangled with the ruthless politics of the Nazi high command.

OTTO RAHN, THE NAZIS AND THE GRAIL

Otto Rahn · Nazi Occultism · Otto Skorzeny
A New Grail Search

THE ENIGMATIC CHARACTER of Otto Rahn, his own quest for the secret of the Cathars and the nature of the part he may have played in the pre-war activities of the Nazi party, now become central to this story. The scarcity and dubious reliability of biographical sources relating to Rahn, and his eventual membership of the SS, has always made an objective assessment of him difficult. However, one can distill that he was much more in the mould of the medieval questing poet than the soldier; the role of soldier was one reluctantly assumed, and with disastrous consequences.

According to his SS file, he was born on the 18th of February 1904, at Michelstadt, to Karl Rahn and Clara (née Hamburger); Otto was Jewish on his mother's side – a fact that may help to explain the mystery surrounding his later SS career and untimely death. In his second book, *Lucifer's Court* (1935), he recalls that, at an early age, he was introduced to the Grail romances by his mother; but his adult passion for Wagner, who had immortalized the story of *Parsival*, led him to study this epic work of Wolfram von Eschenbach. After an extensive academic education, this fascination led him, in 1931, towards the Pyrenees and the Languedoc, where he embarked on research of the Cathars, Templars, troubadours, and Visigoths.

He sought in particular the secret of the Grail that he thought had been known by the Cathars and Wolfram von Eschenbach. He believed, somewhat idealistically, that the power of the Grail could unify Europe.

Staying at a guest-house in Ussat-les-Bains in the Arriège valley, Rahn's thorough investigation of the ancient Cathar sites, including the ruined fortress of Montségur, soon brought him into contact with Antonin Gadal, the acknowledged local champion of Cathar legends. Delighted to have found a fellow enthusiast, Gadal gave Rahn great support in his researches and later the two were to maintain a long-term correspondence.

Parsival is based on the medieval writings of Wolfram von Eschenbach, who himself claims to have based it on the poetry of a Provençal troubadour, Kyot (or Guyot). The troubadours, who travelled from court to court as entertainers, were the principal purveyors of ideas from place to place; their gentle ways and sense of humour gave them free and unimpaired access and rights of passage. Within the story, there is some artistic disagreement as to the location of the Grail castle (Montsalvat, in *Parsival*). Von Eschenbach and Kyot placed it in Toledo, while Wagner favoured the Pyrenees. Not surprisingly, Rahn followed Wagner's lead, and formed the view that the Grail castle was in fact the isolated château perched on the top of the mountain of Montségur. The identification of Montségur as the Grail castle had first appeared in *Le Secret des Troubadours* by Josephin Péladan, published in 1906; and Otto Rahn would have been familiar with this. It therefore also seemed logical to him that the Cathar treasure and the Holy Grail, whatever they might have been, would have been hidden in the nearby caves at Sabarthez in the Ariège valley, which had long associations with the Cathars.

Furthermore, Rahn considered that the characters appearing in *Parsival* were modelled on the actual medieval personalities who had been prominent in the region. For example, he believed Parsival was le Vicomte de Carcassonne Trencavel;

Repanse de Schoye was Esclamonde de Foix; and the hermit Trevrizent, Parsival's uncle, was the Cathar Bishop Guilhabert de Castres. This coincided with a widespread belief among the Languedocian nobility that they were indeed of Germanic blood, on account of their descent from the Visigoths. As we have seen, among these noble families are those whose ancestors had inherited the secret of the ancient treasure.

Rahn continued to receive much help from Antonin Gadal, known locally as the 'Cathar Pope' (Rahn also referred to him as his Trevrizent, Parsival's uncle), and from whom he got many of his Grail theories. However, Déodat Roché, a noted academic authority on the Cathars, was less impressed by Gadal, and became somewhat suspicious of Rahn's motives. Indeed, one incident is reported to the effect that Rahn was discovered faking Cathar engravings. In any case, Rahn's stay in the region came to an abrupt end in September 1932, as a result of embarrassing financial circumstances following the non-payment of debts, partly arising from a lease that he had taken out on the Hôtel Marroniers. After a brief stay in Paris he was forced to return to Germany, where in 1933, he published *The Crusade Against The Grail*. While not well received as an academic treatise, the book immediately found great favour with the Nazi Party. Himmler is reported to have expressed great enthusiasm for it, and even to have given a specially bound copy of it to Hitler as a birthday present.

Despite their lack of academic merit, Rahn's researches and publications must have created a significant impression. On the 29th of February 1936, an SS Divisional General, Karl Wolff, wrote to the SS recruitment office to convey Himmler's personal wish that Rahn be admitted. Evidently his Jewish parentage had not been discovered and he was formally accepted into the SS on 12 March 1936. In the following May, he joined the personal staff of Reichsfuhrer of the SS, Heinrich Himmler. The depth of Rahn's commitment to the Nazi cause is unknowable, but it is generally accepted that, while he supported its ideology and mythology, he was very much less enthusiastic towards its military aspects and the practical application of Nazi philosophy.

Two years later, in 1938, Walter Birks, who had been drawn to the region the year before by his contact with the White Eagle Lodge, visited the Languedoc and was introduced to a character of very different nature. Calling himself Natt Wolff, he presented himself as an American, though the locals were convinced from his accent that he was German and possibly a spy. It soon became apparent to both Birks and the local residents that Wolff was obsessed with the Cathar treasure. They concluded that his sole motive was to profit financially from the Cathars; either by finding their treasure or by exploiting the mini-tourist industry that had developed in the region. Usually surrounded by 'suspicious-looking German and Spanish refugees', Wolff further upset the locals with his general deportment and behaviour, drinking heavily and womanizing. Given this, one wonders how serious his intent in the region was; he also manifestly lacked any entrepreneurial dedication.

The notion has been floated that Natt Wolff was in reality Karl Wolff (later to become an SS general), and that he was indeed a German spy. His purpose being to further investigate the claims made by Otto Rahn, his unpleasant persona could have been adopted as a deliberate cover to conceal his true identity. Possible confirmation comes from assertions in a book by the grandson of Paul Bernadac who owned the guest-house at Ussat-les-Bains where Rahn stayed in 1932. Being an enthusiastic potholer with an interest in the local history, Paul had accompanied Rahn on several occasions; details of which he had apparently passed on to his grandson, Christian.

In Christian Bernadac's *Le Mystère Otto Rahn – Du Catharisme au Nazisme* (1978), it is reported that during his visit in 1932, Rahn was accompanied by Natt Wolff. Travelling on an American passport, he claimed to be on a US government photographic project. According to police files, Wolff used two passports with different details, giving rise even then to the suspicion that he was a German spy; he was eventually expelled on the orders of the Minister of the Interior.

Walter Birks, however, dismissed the possibility that the presence of Rahn and Wolff could have been in any way connected with Nazi ambitions. His distaste for Wolff might be a clue to this, in that his own sense of cultural refinement and academic taste probably barred the likes of Wolff from being deemed anyone of consequence. As he himself put it: 'The man was a chump who thinks he can get rich quickly, but in fact thinks of nothing but his aperitif and his dogs.'

It is not really surprising that following the publication of his books, Rahn should have been invited to join the SS. His quest for the Grail, his interest in romantic and chivalric heroes, his attraction to Celtic/Nordic philosophies, and his commitment to National Socialism would all have endeared him to the Nazi propaganda machine. But even more, he was thought to have uncovered the legend of the lost treasure of the Cathars.

Membership of the SS would necessarily have exposed Rahn to the harsh realities of the Nazi regime. His own scholarly and ideological interests would soon have been at variance with the more materialistic preoccupations of Nazi officialdom. The four-month tour of duty with the Oberbayern, at a training camp in Dachau where guard duty at the concentration camp was regularly assigned, could well have stretched his Nazi sympathies too far.

In March 1939, Otto Rahn was reported killed in an Alpine skiing accident. However, that is itself shrouded in mystery; not least because no body was ever found. Further, an obituary notice in *Berliner Ausgabe*, announcing that Rahn had died in a snowstorm in March, did not appear until 18 May, and a week later on 25 May another obituary appeared in the SS newspaper *Das Schwarze Korps*. Interestingly, both obituaries were signed by an SS officer named Karl Wolff; and it further appears that Rahn had resigned his commission in a letter to Karl Wolff dated 28 February 1939. The day after, Wolff wrote a letter to the SS office of Racial Questions, informing them that Otto Rahn had been unable to produce the required certificate of racial origin. He was officially dismissed on 17 March 1939. But on 17 July, Rahn's father wrote to a German writers' association, informing them that his son had died in a snowstorm at Ruffheim, on 13 March 1939 – four days before his dismissal.

There was also talk shortly before Rahn's death of an enquiry into the nature and outcome of his unsupervised activities in the Corbières. According to Hans Jurgen-Lange in his book *Otto Rahn – Leben & Werk* (1997), Rahn had been visited at the Hôtel Marroniers by the German singer and actress Marlene Dietrich and her friend Josephine Baker, the black jazz singer; both of whom, disenchanted by the society being cultivated by the Nazi party, spent much time in Paris frequenting the occult circles. These were the very same circles which attracted the romanticists, surrealists, esotericists, and free-thinkers of the time; and those that have formed the backbone for the transmission of occult traditions from the eighteenth century to the present day. These same elite intellectual circles had attracted Debussy and Victor Hugo (both supposedly Grand Masters of the Priory of Sion, the secret society at the heart of *The Holy Blood and the Holy Grail*); and the world in which the Abbé Saunière and the opera singer Emma Calvé had found themselves some fifty years before.

A passionate Francophile, Dietrich was a close friend of the great French artist, poet and film-maker Jean Cocteau, also said to have been a Grand Master of the Priory of Sion. By his early twenties, Cocteau had established himself in bohemian occult circles with occasional forays into spiritualism. His World War II activities are unclear, but he denounced the Vichy government and may have worked secretly with the Resistance. It is also said that Dietrich had been a close friend of André Malraux, yet another high-ranking member of the Priory, a Resistance hero and member of De Gaulle's post-war government. Both Dietrich and Baker received the Légion d'Honneur, Croix de Guerre, and the Resistance Medal in recognition of their ardent anti-Nazi commitment. But what were they doing down in this remote region of France in 1932? Are these associations merely another strange coincidence in this mysterious web centred on the Corbières?

Perhaps inevitably, there have been more recent historians who have ventured that Rahn did not die in 1939. It has even been suggested that Otto Rahn transformed into Rudolf Rahn, the German Ambassador appointed to Italy in 1943; and it was SS General Karl Wolff who agreed the German surrender with the Allies in Italy in 1945. If he was indeed spirited away it does suggest that he was up to something, and it is not unreasonable to accept that Karl Wolff, using the pseudonym Natt, was involved with Rahn, and with others later in 1938, in the search for the Cathar treasure. It is unlikely now that the truth will ever be known for certain, and those still alive in the Corbières, with memories long enough to go back to the 1930s, are understandably vague, beyond the lingering distrust of what they see, and still see, as treasure seekers.

It is similarly unlikely that Walter Birks' dogmatic dismissal of any strange activities should be accepted without question. He had first-hand experience of Wolff, and this may have clouded his judgement, both of the man and his purpose. He may also have had his own agenda. In the bizarre history that has coloured the parallel valleys of the Aude and the Ariège, the only sensible conclusion is not to be surprised by anything.

Before moving onto the war years, it is important to this story to grasp why this region, its promise, and these activities would have had significance to the Nazis. And how that significance evolved during their twelve years ruling Germany. During the early years of Nazi rule, the Party was clearly running on a high. Everything was apparently going as planned: the currency had stabilized, affluence was apparent everywhere, *autobahns* (as part of a work creation scheme) were mushrooming throughout Germany, and there was a sense of purpose and vigour. Morale was at its highest level for a quarter of a century. It can be no surprise that Hitler was held in such high esteem by what seemed like the whole of Germany, and that the Nazi Party in consequence enjoyed almost universal support.

The tone of Hitler's speeches makes it very clear that Nazism sought to justify itself by resorting to the esoteric. The 'divine inspiration' for his philosophy included high-blown notions of reincarnated Teutonic Knights (of which Hitler saw himself as one), present-day realization of Nordic folklore, and the perceived supremacy of the Aryan race. It all struck the right chord with the once proud German nation. Success was once again breeding success, and generating yet further success. The return to invincibility, in the face of the current evidence, was impossible to doubt.

Germany was an exciting place to be in during the mid to late 1930s. The seedier side of it, such as the street thug law enforcers, was ignored by the great majority of the population; dismissed as the Fuhrer's wish, and the cost of doing business. But what business! Even the distaste, which many decent Germans undoubtedly felt for the mounting Jewish persecution in particular, was swamped by relentless propaganda justifying that persecution. In short, the Nazi Party at that time could do no wrong in German eyes, because of the manifest pride and achievements being brought to a nation which had been starved of such benefits for a full generation.

Many scholars acknowledge that Nazism became a substitute religion. Its mass rallies were very carefully organized to provide the participants with a mystical experience, similar to that found by many devotees at a Catholic high mass; a great deal of sophistication went into establishing rites and rituals to complete this psychological manipulation. The Nazi salute, the swastika (ancient symbol of the sun), the red Nazi flag, symbolic of the blood of its early martyrs, and the magnificent uniforms and decorations worn by Nazi officers, are but a few manifestations of this.

In preserving this euphoric momentum, it is easy to comprehend the pride with which Hitler presented to his nation the so-called Spear of Destiny, said to be the spear which pierced Christ's side on the Cross. Hitler had acquired this from the Hofburg Palace in Vienna, when Austria became part of Germany by virtue of the Anschluss agreement in March 1938. It was brought back to Germany and housed in the magnificent German National Museum at Nuremberg that was, and still is, the great centre of Germanism, a centre devoted to a pride in Germany and its characteristic traditions. The Spear of Destiny and the royal emblems of the Holy Roman Emperors had been previously kept at Nuremberg from 1424 to 1796; Nuremberg was chosen to host the greatest of Nazi rallies. That it was selected as the site for the Allies' war crimes trials, cannot have been lost on either the victors or the vanquished. Whether the Spear was authentically that used to pierce Christ's side was irrelevant; the national mood of the time was totally receptive to accepting anything that glorified the Reich and its Fuhrer.

The legends and mysteries surrounding the nature and history of such treasure, but most particularly acquiring further such artefacts, must have been music to the ears of the Nazi leadership. Imagine the tempting possibilities of acquiring the Grail cup, supposed to have caught Christ's blood from the Cross, or even the Ark of the Covenant. The sheer symbolic value of such treasures falling into Nazi hands after 1500 years, would have been incalculable.

It is well documented that both Hitler and Himmler had a profound interest in esoteric issues, and the SS was indeed modelled on those ancient warrior-monks, the Teutonic and Templar Knights. Himmler was contemplating a resurrection of a 'Round Table of Knights' which was to have had its headquarters at the small town of Wewelsburg in Westphalia. Throughout the war he continued the restoration of the ancient castle at the centre of the town. The crypt of the north tower of the castle was to contain the sacred flame, representing the centre of the world of the Third Reich, around which his 'Knights' would meet for highly symbolic rituals. Much to Himmler's chagrin, he had failed to gain personal possession of the Spear of Destiny, which he had hoped to keep at Wewelsburg. However, Hitler did allow him to make a copy, which was displayed in a place of honour in the castle.

Nazi activity continued in the remote region of the Corbières throughout the war, even though far removed from the front lines of conflict. In 1943 a group of German scientists, including geologists, historians and archaeologists, camped out below Montségur, under the protection of the local French Milice. It is said that they carried out excavations throughout the surrounding area; the very area researched by Otto Rahn. At much the same time, eye-witnesses recall a Nazi division of engineers involved in clandestine activities at various locations throughout the Corbières, in the region of Rennes-le-Château. Specifically mentioned by local residents to the avid researcher Roger-René Dagobert, were the areas of Auriac, St Paul de Fenouillet, Embres et Castelmaure, Durban and several others – the exact region surrounded by the ring of ancient Cathar castles that encloses the supposed sites of the Visigothic treasure.

Additionally, local residents recall that the SS regiment Von Salza, was employed in some of these duties. A hero in German medieval history, Hermann von Salza was the first Grand Master of the Teutonic Knights. There is also a small village a few kilometres north of Auriac called Salza, adjacent to which, on the southern side, is a site indicated on official maps as Camp Templie, suggestive of a Knights Templar connection.

By the 1940s, the escalating failure of the economic strategy of Hitler's financial genius, Hjalmar Schacht, and the ensuing inability of the military to enable its implementation, had to be resolved. The necessities of sustaining the war effort in the face of growing Allied success were changing the priorities of the Nazi high command. The symbolic value of what might have been hidden in the Corbières may well have been relegated to a poor second place, in the face of the now pressing financial demands of the war. Gold was, after all, gold.

On the other hand, it is more likely that the continued activity in the Corbières was a last-ditch attempt by a small cabal of Nazi superiors, that included Heinrich Himmler, Alfred Rosenberg and Martin Bormann, to acquire for themselves this fabulous treasure before it was too late. Indeed Bormann entrusted this delicate mission to a man already charged with acquiring wealth for the 'Brotherhood'. Known somewhat affectionately as 'Scar', as a result of a facial injury, Otto Skorzeny was the most gifted commando to appear on the stage of World War II.

Skorzeny was one of the more colourful spirits to rise above the more conventional clones of the SS. A flamboyant officer of great courage, panache and initiative, his individualism made him ideally suited to the role of adventuring troubleshooting go-getter into which Hitler cast him. He is best remembered today as the officer sent by Hitler to rescue Mussolini when the Italians, disillusioned with their dictator after a series of defeats, had ousted him and imprisoned him in a hotel atop the Gran Sasso mountain. Skorzeny was later credited as being the man who set up and ran ODESSA, the world-wide organization that successfully helped former SS officers escape from Europe.

Early in 1940, having been seconded to the 1st SS Division – Heavy Artillery – Skorzeny was sent to France. Following the French Armistice, he was granted leave for a 'short and pleasant' interval in the south of France after which he was sent to Holland. In the December of that year, as an engineer officer, he accompanied the 2nd SS Panzer Division Das Reich to France, which was then to be followed by three months of inactivity. Skorzeny's autobiography, *Skorzeny's Special Mission* (1997), is pointedly vague about the purpose of this assignment. However, at a time when the Eastern Front was opening up with initial excitement and success, Skorzeny's own description of his time in the south-west of France as being a period of rest and inactivity stretches the imagination. Furthermore, by his own account, his visit was followed by several further visits. For a man with such a high-flying career, it is unlikely that there would not be a more major significance behind these visits, attractive and agreeable though that part of France undoubtedly is.

Hitler sent for Skorzeny in June 1941, and he was dispatched to Poland to fight the Russians. The turning point in Nazi fortunes had been reached: after an eight-year period of almost incredible achievement, began a four-year period of Götterdämmerung, which was to destroy Germany, leave it humiliatingly divided, and occupied by foreign powers for the next half-century. However, Skorzeny, a born survivor, was to carve out a place in Nazi military legend for himself.

By 1943, having successfully carried out the rescue of Mussolini, Skorzeny was as close as a major could be to the centre of things. Congratulated by Hitler and Himmler, and awarded the Knights Cross of the Iron Cross, the contacts and connections which he had earned and cultivated made it quite certain that he had a better idea than most of the realities of the then current situation. Interestingly, Skorzeny was even to marry the daughter of Hjalmar Schacht. He had been accepted into the heady world of the Nazi elite.

Himmler sent Skorzeny to the Corbières for the last time in early 1944. Not on behalf of Hitler and the Third Reich no doubt, but as an agent and confidante of Himmler himself and his inner circle. This time there was a touch of desperation about the mission, since the Allies had already invaded Italy, and it was an open secret that an invasion of France was coming. Therefore, to find and recover the Corbières treasure would have been a matter of now or never.

It is not known exactly what Skorzeny may have found. However, the American Colonel Howard Buechner in his book, *Emerald Cup – Ark of Gold* (1991), is quite adamant in his assessment that Skorzeny discovered part of the treasure that had belonged variously to the Visigoths, Templars and Cathars. Removed from the Corbières and transported via Toulouse through France to Germany, at least some of the treasure ended up at the unlikely village of Merkers in Thuringen (about 320 km south-west of Berlin). When Merkers fell to the Allied forces on 4 April 1945, a chance encounter by two American military policemen with some local residents revealed that the nearby Kaiseroda potassium mine had become the repository for the Nazis' undeclared wealth and unrefined booty, the gold pending smelting into Reichsbank ingots. As an officer in the advance party, Buechner was well-placed to know the nature and extent of that booty.

Why should Buechner have known this? As far as is known Buechner never met Skorzeny – and had he done so, it is frankly unlikely that Skorzeny would have volunteered anything useful to someone he would have regarded as his enemy. Furthermore, Walter Birks, in *The Treasure Of Montségur* (1987), points out that the Pog, the mountain on which Montségur had been built, was systematically surveyed and explored by the Société Spéleologique de l'Ariège in 1960. Every cave and opening on the rock was apparently explored and nothing remotely resembling a treasure chamber was discovered. But why then did Skorzeny make several return visits to the region, particularly in 1944 when there was certainly much he could have been doing at a critical time elsewhere? As if to back this up, there is also the arrival in the region in March 1944, of the 2nd SS Panzer Division.

There is no doubt of the staggering size of the booty held in the Merkers mine. While some of it had been stolen from concentration camp inmates – before or after their deaths – this was a small percentage when compared with what else Buechner claims was there. His claims must be taken seriously, because it is on record that, following the capture of the town, the top Allied commanders, generals Patton, Bradley, and Eisenhower, took time out to go and inspect the treasure for themselves. A separate account of this incident can be found in the book *Nazi Gold* (1984) by Ian Sayer and Douglas Botting, in which they confirm, from the recollections of General Patton's ADC, Colonel Charles Codman, the staggering amount of wealth in paper currency, gold and art treasures found in the mine. In fact they report that it required thirty-two ten-ton trucks to transport the haul to the Reischbank building in Frankfurt.

The main point of variance between the two reports, is Buechner's assertion that among the treasure were 'gold coins, some of which dated back to the early days of the Roman Empire' and items 'believed to have come from the Temple of Solomon'; a singular omission from all other accounts if it is true. Though, given the momentous symbolism of such a treasure and the circumstances of its discovery, perhaps it is not so surprising that steps were taken to maintain secrecy and its existence officially denied.

General Patton's own interest in the esoteric is also docu-mented; he wore a pair of pearl-handled handguns and reput-edly saw himself as the reincarnation of ancient heroes such as Julius Caesar and Alexander the Great. He was furious to hear that some of the treasure had been stolen during its transfer from the mines. It is known that he had promised a full enquiry: perhaps he appreciated its deeper significance. A few days later, he was involved in a car crash in circumstances that have never been satisfactorily explained, and died in hospital eleven days later. The mystery surrounding the incident, involving such ingredients as unauthorized vehicles making unauthorized journeys, and the lack of an ensuing official enquiry, do perhaps add weight to the notion that there was something to be covered up about what had been found in the Merkers mine.

Buechner is amazingly candid and informative in his book. He even relates how Skorzeny found the treasure on 15 March 1944, one day before the 700th anniversary of the fall of Montségur and the burning alive of its Cathar defenders in 1244. Buechner's account of these events is exciting, although it does cause the odd raised eyebrow. For example, he claims that following his find Skorzeny sent a one-word message 'Eureka' to Himmler in Berlin. The following day, he claims that at exactly twelve noon, a German aircraft flew over Montségur several times, skywriting a Celtic cross. Considered to be the sacred emblem of the Cathars, Buechner reports that this episode had a profound effect on those watching it, including a group of Cathar pilgrims who had persuaded Skorzeny to allow them to climb Montségur on this significant day. Buechner believed that the aircraft might have contained Reichsministers Himmler and Rosenberg. Even had they comprehended the one-word signal, how could two Reichsministers have left Berlin at such a critical time, and fly all the way to the Pyrenees in time for noon the following day? Again, how would Buechner have known about this?

Three other incidents add further intrigue to the events of 16 March 1944. First, Skorzeny was very friendly with Hitler's right-hand man, Martin Bormann, and was in fact a key member of his 'Brotherhood'. Bormann escaped after the war and was never found; it seems probable that he was one of the early beneficiaries of the ODESSA escape network. However, Bormann's wife did not escape with him, but was subsequently arrested by the Allies. In her possession were 2241 ancient gold coins.

Second, General Lammerding's 2nd SS Panzer Division was unexpectedly withdrawn from the Eastern Front and moved right down to Toulouse, in March 1944, ostensibly for retraining. It is strange that such a prestigious tank Division with its celebrated commander should be removed so far from the anticipated Allied invasion at Pas de Calais on the Channel coast. Toulouse is, however, the nearest major railhead to Montségur.

The third piece of the puzzle is the visit of Heinrich Himmler to the 2nd SS Panzer Division in April 1944, so soon after its arrival. With so many priorities at that time – not least the escalating disasters on the Eastern Front and the threat of an Allied invasion – he appears to have taken time out to visit Lammerding and his Division. Surely they were only involved in regrouping and retraining – coupled merely with routine garrison duty. Of course, what took place at that meeting between Himmler and Lammerding will probably never be known; but this meeting could have led to one of the most tragic incidents in wartime France.

The wanton destruction of the village of Oradour-sur-Glane on the orders of General Lammerding has left a deep scar on the psyche of many French people, especially those who lost family or friends in the massacre. But even more, this personal tragedy has also been revealed to be a blow to the French polity, exposing a web of corruption embraced by even the very highest level of government. The roots of this shameful situation can be traced back to the political upheavals throughout Europe following World War I. But in what way was the corruption manifested, who were those involved and what were the actual circumstances that produced it? And how is it that the mysterious past of Rennes-le-Château is found to be at the very heart of the web?

PART TWO

NATIONAL REGENERATION:
A CONFLICT OF INTERESTS

*Europe 1914–18 · Communism · Rise of Hitler
Action Français · Écoles Nationales
De Gaulle and the Resistance · Masonic Politics*

THE DEATH OF the Abbé Saunière, on 22 January 1917, may have been the end of an era for Rennes-le-Château; the culmination of a string of events for this village that, perhaps more than most, had witnessed some extraordinary happenings throughout its long history. But it far from marks the end of this story of power, greed, and elusive treasure.

An understanding of the powerful forces at work in Europe as this story continues to unfold, and what makes its implications as relevant as ever as we embark upon the twenty-first century, may be instructive. At the time of Saunière's passing, Europe was still immersed in the bloodiest conflict ever seen in the history of humanity; the result of a clash of empires, dynasties, and super-powers in the pursuit of expansionism or survival, in a rapidly changing world of industry, education, and social awareness. In a movement that had started with the French Revolution, elite and autocratic regimes were proving no longer sustainable as citizens desired to take more control over their own lives. The outcome of World War I, and the signing of the Treaty of Versailles in 1919, broke up the German empire and that of the Austro-Hungarian Habsburgs. Yet it failed to bring political stability. Great resentment at losing the war, and demoralization through the sanctions imposed by the victors, opened the door to a powerful German and Italian nationalism that was to result in another great war, twenty years later.

In Russia, the war had brought more problems to a country whose financial and social condition was already in rapid decline. Ruled by the absolute power of the Tsar, with the support of a small number of nobles, army officers and government officials, together with the Christian Russian Orthodox Church, her people were subjected to living under an oppressive feudal system little changed since the Middle Ages. But in March 1917, revolution brought about the end of the Tsar's rule. At first the reformists, who admired the democratic parliamentary systems of Britian, France, and the USA, stepped in with ideas for a gradual modernization of Russia following free elections and the eradication of censorship, but they were soon overthrown by the Bolshevik Revolutionaries who were determined to introduce a completely new system, abolishing Capitalism and dismantling the class system. Following social principles proposed by the nineteenth-century German philosopher Karl Marx, the Bolshevik leader, Vladimir Lenin, became the first ruler of a new Russia – and was the first country to fully embrace Communism. The ramifications of this were dramatically to affect European and world politics for the next eighty years, with an even further-reaching legacy.

The adoption of Communism by such a large and influential country, and its spread to Russia's immediate neighbours, sent alarm bells ringing in the Vatican, the Church fearful of the spread of an ideology in which there was no place for it. Over the next eighty years the Catholic Church would become involved in secret and subversive activities aimed at bringing about the fall of Communism, including strategies that would result in the formation of some rather unholy alliances. These of course were tactics that had been adopted throughout the centuries whenever the Church found itself under threat.

The instability of the inter-war years, 1918 to 1939, was to be felt, to some extent, by almost every country in Europe.

The resulting social and financial upheavals were to prove fertile for exploitation by extremist interest groups. Italy, in turmoil following defeat in the World War I, was the first to fall under the fascist spell. The Italian people had little confidence in their fragmented government; the landowners, industrialists and businessmen were concerned about the Communist rumbles in their industries; and economic crisis created huge unemployment and rampant inflation. Into this arena strode Benito Mussolini, a disaffected Socialist. Preaching a doctrine of firm government opposed to Communists and Liberals, his Fascist Party was supported by middle-class Italians, businessmen, factory and property owners, and army officers. Initial progress was slow, but after resorting to bullying and other violent tactics, Mussolini finally achieved complete control of government and, from 1924, his unelected dictatorship.

The Lateran Treaty of 1929 was a master stroke, ensuring the support of the Catholic Church. It agreed that the pope should have complete control over an independent Vatican state; that Catholicism would be the official state religion and the teaching of religious instruction would be compulsory in all schools. But in return, the Catholic Church agreed to recognize the Italian government of Mussolini.

In the same year, an already insecure Europe shuddered from the economic repercussions of the Wall Street crash. With billions of dollars wiped off the stock values in New York, many investors were financially ruined and the American economy descended into a slump. As a trading partner, Britain found a lack of customers for its products; even the removal of the pound from the Gold Standard (lowering the value of the pound to make exports cheaper) did not stimulate sales. By 1932, nearly 20 per cent of the working population was unemployed; the greatest job losses coming from the heavy industries of steel, ship building, and coal mining. However, various political strategies helped maintain some stability and gradually, though patchily, recovery took place, helping Britain avoid some of the extreme turns seen in other countries.

Britain had of course won the war, and still retained its empire; it lacked that fundamental crisis of confidence in itself that might have called for radical political or social reform.

It was a different story on the mainland of Europe. The German response to the Depression of the 1920s was eventually to follow the Italian model. The government that took over from the displaced kaiser managed to suppress a Communist revolution, yet Communism continued to be a significant force feared by many people, and disaffection with perceived weakness in government was strong. Adolf Hitler, an Austrian born in 1889, moved to Munich and joined the German army in 1914; he was wounded twice and awarded the Iron Cross. His interest in politics took him into the German Workers Party where his talent for public speaking brought him to the fore. Having taken charge, he changed its name to the National Socialist Workers Party, or 'Nazi' for short, and in 1920 launched a new twenty-five point programme which included elements of nationalism, socialism, and racism – especially against the Jews. Gradually its socialist objectives gave way to a stronger nationalism, and the economic crisis generated by the Wall Street crash gave Hitler a great opportunity to promote his grandiose plans for national regeneration, laying the blame for the country's ills at the feet of the Communists and the Jews.

He came a creditable second to Hindenburg in the 1932 presidential elections, which assisted the Nazi party in increasing its support among other right-wing groups, while the Socialists and Communists remained divided. Political manoeuvring secured the Chancellorship for Hitler with the endorsement of the commercial and financial sectors who thought they would fare better under Hitler's political stance than under that of the Communists. Almost immediately, Hitler called for new elections and, using dubious tactics, managed to secure a majority; then by expelling the Communists and joining with the Nationalists, he was able to gain complete political control of Germany. The financial sector continued to give Hitler its support, despite the fact that some bankers and industrialists were Jewish (Ashkenazic), and that they must have been aware of his public anti-Semitism. Money and power, especially in the banking and financial worlds, possibly sometimes outweigh principles.

It was at this time that Otto Rahn published his books on his search for the Holy Grail – the secret treasure of the Cathars. But if there was any other interest in the treasures of the Corbières, it remains unrecorded. Probably due to the economic and political turmoil of the times, potentially interested parties were likely otherwise preoccupied.

Following the death of Hindenburg, Hitler assumed the position of President besides that of Chancellor, and was able to control and manipulate all aspects of German society. Massive re-armament took place; agricultural and industrial production was increased; propaganda against Jews, and any other groups considered to be 'undesirable', was introduced into education. It was also made virtually impossible to criticize by word or deed any aspect of Nazi Party policy without risking one's life or that of one's family. Fearing the worst, many tens of thousands of Jews left Germany, having converted their assets into money, gold or precious jewels, much of which was then deposited in ultra-secure Swiss banks for safe-keeping. For those who did this, and for their descendants, this was to have unexpected and tragic consequences.

Having achieved ultimate power and having collected around him a high command of dedicated and ruthless Nazis, Hitler was able to initiate his avowed foreign policy of uniting all German-speaking peoples. This soon turned into a relentless drive to occupy every country in mainland Europe. Inevitably this was to provoke opposition especially from Britain and France, but since neither country relished the prospect of another war, they employed every tactic to delay making decisions or to appease Hitler at as little cost to themselves as possible. The Munich Agreement between Hitler and the British Prime Minister, Neville Chamberlain, was the prime example. This effectively meant that Britain agreed to turn a blind eye to the German invasion of Czechoslovakia; a pawn worth sacrificing to preserve peace in the British Empire. There were even those in the British Establishment who were somewhat sympathetic to Hitler and admired his efforts at national regeneration after the deprivations of the Treaty of Versailles, and in addition saw the Nazi regime as a solid bulwark against the expansion of Communism. Most of the wealth, land and means of production in Britain at the time resided in the hands of an hereditary aristocracy, or a parallel one of industrial giants, financiers, and bankers, many of whom would have felt empathy with (and even envy of) Germany's economic 'miracle'.

The British Royal Family had close ties with its German aristocratic cousins; and although considered to be a democracy, Britain herself did preside over an empire of countries forced to accept a government and a head of state unelected by them. It has been seriously suggested by some historians that Hitler believed Britain, which he admired for its achievements and considered as a natural ally, would eventually form an alliance with him, and that his contact with the abdicated King Edward VIII, the Duke of Windsor, would bring the rest of the British Establishment on side. Weight to this hypothesis is perhaps given by Hitler's personal reluctance to launch a full-scale invasion of Britain, despite the failure of Dunkirk and his military superiority at the time.

Stalin, having been rejected by Britain and France, formed a non-agression pact with Hitler which contained secret clauses providing for the carving up of Poland between them. Upon the invasion of Poland in 1939, Britain and France, honouring a previous agreement, saw themselves as obliged to enter into war.

The French reaction to the Nazi militarization had been to divert huge amounts of public expenditure to the construction of the Maginot Line, a 320 km line of fortifications along its border with Germany that was considered impregnable. On the day that the newly elected British Prime Minister, Winston Churchill, told the House of Commons that he was fully prepared to wage war by land, sea, and air, the Germans launched a *blitzkrieg* attack on Holland, Belgium, and France. Panzer tank divisions rolled straight over Holland and Belgium meeting limited resistance; while other divisions skirted the Maginot Line by advancing through the Ardennes rendering the French defences ineffective. The German occupation of France was to expose fundamental divisions in French society that had their roots back in the Revolution but that had been re-asserted in the early 1920s.

Since the Revolution, French politics had been inclined to the Left, espousing democratic Socialist principles much to the continuing dismay of those who favoured the *ancien régime* – that is, those who still identified with an aristocracy, property owners, the Catholic Church and the many who felt let down by the Republic. Among factory workers, a trade union movement in the form of Syndicalism evolved which rejected the normal parliamentary process for resolving disputes and instead advocated direct action of the labour-force. Furthermore, they sought worker control and ownership of industry; it was inevitable that, after 1918, Syndicalism should become absorbed by its younger and more virile cousin, Communism.

As in the other major European countries the Wall Street crash was to bring about a financial crisis and a loss of confidence in the government; a situation that provided a golden opportunity for disaffected groups to bid for power. When the Conservative prime minister, Reynaud, proposed devaluation of the franc to alleviate the economic depression, he was swiftly and viciously denounced as a traitor by the extreme right-wing Catholic traditionalist-monarchist newspaper and movement, *Action Française*. Political instability followed; liberal democratic government was perceived to have failed. Just as in Italy and Germany, this opened the door to the possibility of a strong authoritarian government. Prior to the German invasion of France, the political scene had become polarized, with public and secret organizations at both ends of the spectrum. These were epitomized by the Front Populaire of the Left, initially uniting the Socialists and Communists, and *Action Française* on the Right, trading in a paranoid fear of Communism. In fact the Front Populaire was denounced by the Conservatives as being a Jewish-Bolshevik plot – that familiar battle cry of the right wing.

The occupation of France finally provided the Right with the opportunity it had been waiting for, and so brought about the formation of the wartime Vichy government. In the first five weeks the Germans took nearly 2 million prisoners, and 6 to 7 million refugees fled to the south. Since the industrial base of France, which Hitler needed to exploit in order to support his war effort, was in the northern half of the country, an agreement was reached by which the southern half could remain under the control of a French government if it were authorized by the Germans. Reynaud resigned and his deputy, a hero of World War I, Marshal Pétain, succeeded him. A virtually unknown protégé of the Reynaud administration, the junior defence minister General de Gaulle departed for England to set up a French National Committee to 'act as the provisional guardian of the national patrimony'. While later highly significant, this went almost unnoticed in France at the time.

The new French government, set up under Pétain in the spa town of Vichy in central France, imitated many of the policies of the Third Reich, including its virulent attitude to the Jews. At the beginning of the war it is estimated that there were about 330,000 Jews in France, some of whose families had been resident for centuries; within two years nearly 76,000 Jews, predominantly those who had fled from the Nazis to France, had been forcibly deported or repatriated to Germany. Despite this, Marshal Pétain, who was himself at the heart of anti-Jewish legislation, received support from the Catholic Church through its representative the Archbishop of Paris, Cardinal Emmanuel Suchard, for his 'National Revolution'. It must also be recalled that the Catholic Church never excommunicated Hitler (who was a Catholic), in spite of his massive abuse of civil rights; according to the Church, he had never broken any Canon Law!

The division of loyalty between the collaborative Vichy government and the exiled resistance organization de Gaulle set up was to divide the French nation so deeply that, even over fifty years later, the wounds are not fully healed. It also provided an unexpected opportunity for those with no loyalty, except to themselves, to achieve the necessary power or influence to pursue their own agendas. This will be seen to include an attempt to gain possession of the documents concerning the secret of Rennes-le-Château, and ultimately, the treasure itself.

Stemming initially from a historical reaction to Jewish usury and envy of the successful commercial enterprises of some Jews, anti-Semitism had become endemic in French right-wing politics. Despite many attempts by the Liberal Democrats, Socialists and Republicans, to integrate them more into public life, the Jewish community was the first to be blamed for any of the country's problems. This attitude was never condemned by the Catholic Church, and was clearly illustrated by the shameful affair of the treatment of Alfred Dreyfus.

A Jewish French army officer employed in the War Ministry in 1894, Alfred Dreyfus was accused of spying and betraying military secrets to Germany. He was court-martialled and sent to the austere penal colony on Devil's Island in French Guiana. Two years later his innocence was discovered but the military contrived to conceal it, even resorting to forged documents in order to strengthen their case. Ardent campaigners, including the future prime minister, Georges Clemenceau, and the novelist Émile Zola, secured a retrial, at which it was found that the real criminal was a Major Ésterhazy, and Dreyfus received a pardon. Finally in 1906, fully exonerated, he was reinstated in his military rank. If Dreyfus had not been Jewish it is most unlikely that this miscarriage of justice would have occurred. This scandal had a profound effect on French society, and re-opened deep divisions.

One of those affected was Theodor Herzel, the founder of a movement called 'Zionism', who maintained that the Dreyfus affair motivated him to write a book that proposed the establishment of a Jewish homeland in Palestine as the only solution to Jewish harassment. Also deeply affected was Léon Blum, a French politician who converted to Socialism in 1899 as a result of this affair, and who in 1936 became the first Jewish and Socialist prime minister of France.

The election of a Jew, let alone a Socialist, to the post of prime minister, was like a red rag to a bull for the right-wing traditionalists, of which the main standard bearer was the staunch Catholic writer, Charles Maurras. He was founder of the newspaper and movement, *Action Française*. Maurras' main enemies were Freemasons, Protestants and Jews; but he also clearly hated all foreigners, the Revolution and the Republic, parliamentary democracy, the proletariat, free education and social justice, and wished to return to the social structure of the eighteenth century. He maintained an ambiguous relationship with the Church, and despite describing the Gospels as having been written by 'four shabby Jews', and Christianity as 'the religion of the rabble', it continued to support him until the Vatican, in 1926, placed his newspaper on the index of forbidden works. This was however rescinded by Pope Pius XII in 1939.

It was the extremism of Charles Maurras that was to become the blueprint for Vichy policies. Founded in 1908, *Action Française* expounded the tenet that the Catholic Church and the monarchy were essential to French civilization, exactly the sentiment so dear to the Abbé Saunière and his colleagues. It is tempting to speculate that Saunière may have been well aware of Maurras' organization, and could have played some part in it.

Charles Maurras was by no means alone in publishing anti-

Semitic material. Many endeavoured to forment hostility towards the Jews, claiming that this was the natural attitude of patriotic Frenchmen. One late nineteenth-century protagonist in this was the Catholic novelist Maurice Barrès who, according to the authors of *The Holy Blood and the Holy Grail* (1982), was another who may have been party to the Saunière secret. A friend of Claude Debussy and Victor Hugo, the young Barrès had been involved in the Rose-Croix circle founded by Péladan. In 1912 he published a novel, *La Colline Inspirée* (*The Inspired Hill*), which despite containing striking parallels to events at Rennes-le-Château, in fact refers to the hill of Sion-Vaudemont, the ancient pilgrimage site in Lorraine. Yet again the hand of coincidence appears to bring Bérenger Saunière and his little village into contact with the worlds of the occult and European politics, and to connect them with those who saw significance in Zion.

It is often thought that because of its collaboration, the Vichy government was entirely pro-Nazi; but Vichy supporters actually considered themselves true patriots, who sought a renewal in independent Gallic pride, and accepted collaboration as a necessary step towards eventual liberation. The French right wing only mirrored German fascism in some areas. However, in policies such as anti-Semitism, some Vichy ministers were to prove themselves to be even more efficient than their Nazi counterparts and apparently required no external motivation. René Bousquet, having been appointed national Chief of Police, demonstrated his ruthless administrative ability by organizing the rounding up and deportation of 76,000 Jews to Germany, for which he won great praise from the Nazis, and came to the attention of SS chief Heinrich Himmler. The two men were to meet in Paris in 1943, after which Himmler stated that Bousquet was a precious collaborator, and would possibly play a leading role in French politics. Fiercely anti-Communist, Bousquet had possibly exercised his power against the Jews more as an example to others than as a callous anti-Semite. Interestingly, however, Bousquet managed to escape the punishments normally received by collaborators after the war, and was to remain a close friend, until his death, of the later president of France, François Mitterrand – who was himself a one-time member of Vichy.

One of the collaborationist government's most fascinating and revealing activities was to take shape some 200 km south-east of Vichy, near the city of Grenoble. Situated in the dramatic and mountainous Rhone-Alpes region, Grenoble is a bustling industrial alpine city; 50 km to its north is the ancient monastery of La Grande Chartreuse, famous for its liqueur. But it was at the impressive Château Bayard, with its twelfth-century foundations, situated east of Grenoble on the high plateau shared by the village of Uriage-les-Bains, that a most ambitious and controversial enterprise unfolded.

Long before the war, the importance of youth education and training had been widely appreciated; even the 'Catholic' scout movement had been manipulated to be militantly patri-otic, authoritarian, opposed to materialism and to liberal and democratic values. Though avowedly non-political, this scout movement was decidedly anti-Republican. At the Château Bayard these sentiments were to form the basis of a curriculum aimed at a 'National Revolution', to be led by an intellectual elite of youths who would replace the old administration and, in the process, purge Jews and Freemasons from positions of influence.

Under the direction of Pierre Dunoyer de Segonzac, a dashing young cavalry officer from staunch Catholic aristocratic roots, this ideological school, called the École Nationale des Cadres d'Uriage, was the flagship of a network designed to prepare a new elite for the control of France following the Liberation. Just like the Catholic scouts, the students were required 'to exercise a heroic effort for the renewal of France, the reconstruction stone by stone of a Christendom of Europe', in the words of Father Marcel-Denys Forestier, founder of the Rover scouts – a group within the larger Catholic scout movement.

John Hellman, professor of history at McGill University, has carried out an extremely detailed analysis of the history of this elite school and the counterparts it spawned, published in his book *The Knight-Monks of Vichy France, Uriage 1940–1945* (1997). The second edition contains an appendix in which can be found important new material concerning former president François Mitterrand's little-known connections with the Uriage group, and how knowledge of these schools has been largely removed from French public consciousness.

The Uriage enterprise spread to other provincial centres, but by the end of 1942, the schools, despite their initial success, came under attack from youth groups and others, possibly out of jealousy, but also concerned at their growing influence and lack of accountability. The aims of the Uriage school had shifted to even greater horizons, beyond Vichy and France, to that of a European New Order. However, the war starting to turn against the Germans, the Vichy regime came under closer supervision and began to lose even more of its fragile independence. The administration of Dunoyer de Segonzac was removed from the school at Uriage and replaced by a far more sinister organization, the Milice.

Selected from an organization founded on the direct orders of Hitler, who wanted an auxiliary police force to maintain internal order, the Milice instructors were mystical fascists committed to a curious, Catholic-Nazi vision of National Revolution. Added to the curriculum were studies of Communist methods, military training focused on guerilla and street combat, and an exhaustive study of the fighting that preceded the advent of National Socialism in Germany. It is very obvious that this military tuition was aimed not at defeating the Germans but at combatting subversives – that is, those who would challenge the system of authority, whether French or German. By 1944, the Milice, according to American intelligence, had become the most formidable pro-fascist political organization in Vichy France, and had continued to maintain the strong religious tone of Catholic monarchists. Retaining

Catholic ritual and tradition, the Milice endorsed national and racial purity; the priority of labour over money; and condemned Gaullism, Communism, Freemasonry, and Judaism, outright.

This frightening and disquieting institution was remarkably successful in its recruitment and it is estimated that during the occupation some 200,000 French citizens actively identified their own interests, and that of France, with Hitler's New Order. It was never systematically purged following the war. One has to ask what influence the former pupils of the Milice may have had on the French post-war politics and even the vision of a united Europe? Its influence appears to have extended as far as the presidency of France. The vision of the New Order is also the same as that adopted by the secret societies found at the heart of the intrigue surrounding the secret treasure of the Corbières. It is too coincidental to find that the same people involved with the core of Vichy policy, especially the youth movements, also seem to surface as those pursuing most ardently the quest for the hidden treasure.

Among the network of provincial schools was a foundation in the Languedoc-Roussillon region. Having been ousted from his position at Uriage, Dunoyer de Segonzac and his colleagues unobtrusively regrouped at the Château de Montmaur, near Gap, to concentrate more on their spiritual values, in a tightly disciplined and hierarchical community. Developing in time into a more formal Order of Knighthood, with accompanying rites and rituals, the 'Knight-Monks of the Uriage' then moved into the Château de Murinais, above the Isère valley in the French Alps, to accommodate Segonzac's new community in relative security. However, divisions between the Order's so-called elite, and those members of the 'Resistance' dedicated to fighting the German occupiers, were soon clearly revealed. Members of the Resistance who came into contact with Segonzac were alarmed at his presumption to provide unelected leadership over the French; on the other hand, members of the Order were advised to deal carefully with the Resistance groups, avoiding their possible Masonic and foreign influences. But the Order's existence was proof that any attempt to return, after the anticipated 'Liberation', to a pre-war form of republic would be fiercely opposed. The Order's attitude to Jews was resolute, unambigously expressed in one Uriage document: 'Israelites were not to be admitted to the Order . . . we ought not to underestimate the danger of a Jewish revenge (organization) nor ignore the existence of a Jewish international (Zionism) whose interests are opposed to those of France.' However, in some contradiction to this the same document continues: 'Our present attitude remains in the framework of an aid to oppressed Israelites.' By the explicit choice of terminology, it would appear perhaps that a distinction was being drawn between the newly arrived immigrant Jews, and those of the old resident communities.

The Order, just as the Milice had at Château Bayard, studied rival groups competing for power in a 'liberated' France. These included Freemasons, the Synarchist movement and the Communist party. In this shadow battle for prospective power, most were to resort to subversive activities, some of which will be seen to continue to the present day. A paranoia even later developed in which more effort was expended hunting down Communists than Germans! Those loyal to Pétain and Vichy were suspicious of the Resistance movement, both for fear of upsetting the status quo but also because they believed it to have been infiltrated by Communists. Perhaps this was indeed so; Henri Frenay, head of the Resistance movement Combat, told Segonzac at the beginning of 1944 that although the Communists were courageous 'Resistance' fighters, they seemed to him, more and more, 'to be preparing to take power'.

By the end of summer 1943 the war had swung dramatically in favour of the Allies. A French army had become united under General Giraud, while in the political arena General de Gaulle was becoming more prominent. The changing fortunes of war and the increased demands of the German occupiers appeared also to bring about a change of attitude and loyalty in Segonzac towards Vichy. He admitted misgivings about the Pétainist vision, even expressing veiled doubts about Pétain's character. In a complete about-face, Segonzac even arranged a meeting with de Gaulle, and offered his service to the Free French forces. At the Château de Murinais a subtle transformation was also taking place. While retaining the lofty elements of Knighthood, the agenda was moving closer to a military and political stance more attuned to the changing situation of the war. Still inspired by the sense of belonging to an elite and the spirit of French regeneration, the Uriage pupils now looked to the Resistance to fulfill their destinies and reached out to establish contact with the local Maquis (Resistance activists). It is not surprising that these overtures were met with a great deal of suspicion; and it was only after the Germans attacked and closed down the school at the Château Murinais, that the former Uriage members became more acceptable to the Resistants. In time, with careful rewriting of its recent history, the agendas of the Uriage school and its provincial satellites were sanitized of their extreme pro-fascist leanings, to become more moderate, with a politically transcendental viewpoint.

This new agenda came to terms with the growing power of Charles de Gaulle and his Free French, now the predominant symbol of liberation and renewal. Segonzac travelled to Algeria, where the exiled provisional French government had established itself in June 1943, in order to meet de Gaulle. Despite a frosty and mistrustful reception, Segonzac came back with a positive and glowing impression, reporting that: 'General de Gaulle has a very strong personality . . . extraordinary . . . its sense of grandeur, spirit of independence carried to the extreme, intelligence, energy, taste for command and nobility of style are its principal characteristics.' Evidently seduced by de Gaulle's personality, he concluded that: 'We of the Order and of the Movement ought to support him; he is our best chance.' He further observed that: 'The Americans constitute a genuine danger for France. It is a very different danger from that which Germany represents and from what the Russians might eventually pose for us. It is in the economic and moral sphere.'

Yet while Segonzac and his Uriage Order switched their allegiance to de Gaulle, they continued to prepare to fill the political void created by the departure of the occupying forces with an ambitious plan to provide *cadres* (educated elite) for a 'Revolution of the twentieth century'; they would continue to oppose the Communists, modern American culture, old-style Republicans, and any others who might stand in the way of the regeneration of France by their select elite.

As D-Day approached, Segonzac firmly established himself within the Resistance and gained command of more than 200 men of the Maquis; old habits die hard, however, and he subjected the group to Catholic and Uriage teachings – much to its amazement, since many were either Protestant or Jewish. However the Uriage group were extremely bright and throwing off their Pétainist image, established themselves at the very heart of the Resistance, without compromising their former principles integral to their vision of a new France. Of all those able to make this astonishing transformation from Vichyite to Resistance supporter, the most important and influential was François Mitterrand, later president of France. His position occupies a critical place in this tangled web.

In parallel to the diverse aspirations of the Vichy government, the Uriage Order, the Communists, the Resistance and the Gaullists, were the aims of a neo-Masonic brotherhood, the Ordre Martiniste-Synarchique (OMS). Prominent in the 1930s such Synarchist groups had demonstrated active involvement in Masonic politics. The OMS adopted as aims (besides the Fraternity, Liberty and Equality, sentiments common to all Masonic groups) finance through capitalism, the use of traditional symbols of the past, influence through covert means, a drive for a united Europe and a worldwide association of countries. This was diametrically opposed to the Vichy/Uriage philosophy, and the OMS became the subject of persecution.

The Nazis, even if they had used secret society methods to gain power themselves, banned such organizations once in power, and the Vichy government was not slow to follow.

An extreme right-wing journalist and anti-Semitic colaborator, Henri Coston, became head of Vichy's Centre d'Action Maçonique and authorized the looting and seizure of Masonic archives. In the course of this he came across the Synarchist programme, which outlined a plan to exploit the turmoil in French politics of 1942 to infiltrate the Vichy administration. The Synarchists, in sympathy with the Resistance, had also established close contact with British Intelligence; the British made use of their secret lodge network for intelligence gathering. Faced with the threat of suppression, the HQ of the Ordre Martiniste-Synarchique was transferred to Switzerland, but its Grand Master, Martin Chevillion, was caught and executed by Klaus Barbie, the 'butcher of Lyon'.

It also appears possible that, from the acquisition of Martinist documents, certain members of the Vichy government as well as some rogue elements in British Intelligence were able to gain knowledge of those ancient parchments which had belonged to General Dagobert, and those found by the Abbé Saunière, which related to the great secret of Rennes-le-Château and the caches of hidden treasure. Certainly, individuals from the Vichy government, Martinists-Synarchists, British Intelligence and SOE operatives, were all to become involved, often in opposition to each other, in covert activity concerning the aptly named mystery of Rennes-le-Château.

CALLED TO ACCOUNT:
COLLABORATION OR RESISTANCE?

Vichy · Mitterrand · Resistance or Collaboration?
Pierre Plantard · Alpha Galates · The Secret of Rennes-le-Château

FOLLOWING THE LIBERATION of Paris, the Allied forces
paraded down the Champs-Elysées on 26 August 1944, led, on
foot, by a jubilant General de Gaulle. This was both emotional
and symbolic: de Gaulle and his provisional government in
exile had triumphed over the collaborative government of
Marshal Pétain. Formerly condemned to death as a traitor by
the Vichy government *in absentia*, de Gaulle was now warmly
received by former collaborators – who by now appeared as
confirmed Resistants. Yet great tensions still existed between
the two camps, even if to the outside world their differences
were hardly apparent now that the war was over. The future
president François Mitterrand, who wrote: 'Seen from the
camps, Pétain and de Gaulle appeared the same. They were
both representatives of official France engaged in battle ...
Seen from Germany, Pétain and de Gaulle did not represent
contradictory policies.' In fact, there are suggestions that both
Pétain and de Gaulle were playing in the same murky waters
in their quests for a rejuvenated France.

Ironically, de Gaulle had actually studied under the World
War I hero and famed military strategist Pétain, at the military
school of Saint-Cyr, and, what's more, was known to have had
some admiration for the old soldier, which was reciprocated.

De Gaulle even ghost-wrote books on military strategy for Pétain. Following the fall of France and the traumatic shock of becoming an occupied country, it had also taken some time for organized resistance to develop. One of the first visible signs, in late 1940, was the clandestine publication of a magazine entitled *Combat* by Henri Frenay, and *Liberation* by Robert Lacoste and Christian Pineau, both of which attempted to create a unity among the potential Resistants. But a closer look at Frenay and *Combat* illustrates unexpected associations.

Henri Frenay had also been a student at Saint-Cyr military school and was both a classmate and close friend of Pierre Dunoyer de Segonzac, the head of the Écoles Nationales d'Uriage set up by the Vichy government. Frenay strongly criticized Pierre Laval and the Vichy government for deporting young French workers to Germany, among other policies, but he stopped short of criticizing the Marshal himself. He maintained regular contact and friendship with Segonzac, for whom in 1943 he acted as an intermediary with de Gaulle; and it was Frenay who told Segonzac in 1944, that although they were courageous fighters, the Communists seemed motivated more by the possibility of taking power after the war.

Combat attempted to recruit new Resistants from among prominent Catholic Pétainists, but it also attracted contributions from some influential right-wing writers such as Thierry Maulnier, who expressed views remarkably similar to those of the Écoles Nationales d'Uriage. Other notable contributors were Drieu la Rochelle, Robert Brasillach, an intellectual fascist, and François Mitterrand, who admitted to reading the works of fascist writers long after the war. He also contributed to the review *France, Revue d'État Nouveau*, founded by Gabriel Jeantet, a former president of the students of Action Française, the extreme right-wing group of Charles Maurras. Jeantet's politics were clearly pro-Pétain and he was virulently anti-Communist, anti-Capitalist, anti-democratic, anti-Nazi and anti-Gaullist. He even claimed that he was an intermediary between Pétain and the circle of German officers plotting against Hitler, and that he later worked as a mediator between de Gaulle and Pétain for a reconciliation after the war. Jacques Laurent, a pro-Vichy novelist, affirmed that Mitterrand and Jeantet were very close, though he further added that Jeantet was a great Resistant; this illustrates how confusing the wartime picture has become. Mitterrand, of course, has gone down in history as a Socialist.

Without doubt, the Pétainist Vichy regime received more support than is publicly acknowledged today. This is partly explained by its stand against Communism, considered worse than rule by Nazi fascists to many sections of society; Nazism also offered a chance for regenerated national pride so damaged in the previous century. It must also have appeared to be the best option in view of the continuing Nazi threat to extend its occupation in France, and the wasteland that fighting Germany in 1914–18 had produced in northern France. Once the war swung in favour of the Allies, and Vichy began to be discredited, many former supporters either claimed to have been secretly active in the Resistance movement or simply denied former affiliation. Inevitably and understandably, a certain mythology has also grown up around the Resistance, encouraged by de Gaulle and his administration. The Resistance episode has thus become sacred, a story both simplified and embellished, from which a new national identity has been built after the traumatic and turbulent experience of the German occupation.

This is certainly not to deny the actions of true courage performed by many French and other Allied Resistants, and their enormous contribution to the ending of the war. And whatever justification is given for the French collaboration, it is mostly seen as responsible for national and individual shame – hence the sympathetic rewriting of wartime history. However, the confusion this has generated, has been exploited by those with subversive or self-serving agendas, and has acted as a convenient smokescreen both for those in prominent positions and those who prefer to remain in the shadows: some of these play key roles in this remarkable story.

The turmoil of wartime provided opportunities for unsavoury pursuits including involvement in the black-market (illegal trading in rationed goods), the settling of old scores, downright criminal activity, and the pursuit of political power. After the war, many of these activities were publicly exposed, especially those of collaboration and profiteering, creating great difficulty to the cause of French unity. A prime example was the allegation by Henri Frenay that one of General de Gaulle's leading supporters, Jean Moulin, had been secretly working for the Communists. In response, Moulin's former secretary, Daniel Cordier, attributed a manifesto to Frenay that showed him to have been a Pétainist, anti-Semitic, a collaborator and supporter of Vichy's National Revolution.

It is certainly sometimes legitimate to hide one's true colours – think of the act of resistance itself. But it also creates grey areas; it becomes difficult to pinpoint the true political stance and beliefs of even the most prominent of politicians; and facilitates the concealing of tracks and recreation of their past. When the politician is also involved in the world of secret or occult societies the situation becomes even more complex. And mirroring the patterns of history, certain major players of the war and post-war years begin to slip surreptitiously between the political, intelligence and occult worlds in order to further their ambitions, usually a combination of power and wealth.

A key figure in the post-war episode of this saga is no less a person than François Mitterrand, President of France from 1981. Born into a rural Catholic bourgeoise family from Jarnac, a village on the River Charente, Mitterrand showed a youthful fascination with politics, and attended rallies and meetings of all shades of the political spectrum. From 1934 he studied at the prestigious Sciences-Po, France's leading school for the political elite. As a product of Jesuit education, it was quite natural that he would eventually drift more towards the Right, and despite his later denials, there is abundant evidence that he supported Action Française. It is also said that he attended meetings of La Cagoule, an even more extremist, active, and secretive organization that endorsed violent means to confront its perceived enemies. In fact it was a prominent member of this group, Raphael Alibert, who obtained for Mitterrand a position in the Vichy government. Without doubt, prior to the outbreak of war, Mitterrand had also established friendships, some of which were to last throughout his career, that were firmly on the right wing of French politics – and even at the extreme end. It is generally accepted that he was a man of many sides, an intelligent but complex personality who liked to keep his entourage guessing. As a natural leader, Mitterrand also adopted the style of an aristocrat, which caused people to regard him later as more of a monarch than a president – an impression he actively encouraged.

In June 1940, he was captured by the German army and brought to the prison camp Stalag IX, near Kassel, in central Germany. According to his memoirs he escaped three times, each attempt more extraordinary than the last, and he claimed to have joined the Resistance on his return to France. Yet some incontravertible facts cast doubt on the accuracy of Mitterrand's memoirs. His period of imprisonment was significant in several ways. First, as he himself recalls, it enabled him to discover that he had a great capacity for survival. Second, it appears that the experience of prison culture, the comradeship, sharing and mutual support, made a strong impression on his political philosophy, which was to influence his later career as a Socialist. However, in spite of this apparent enlightenment, Mitterrand's instincts for survival and political manoeuvering dictated that he would continue in the Pétainist camp for the time being.

It was during this time as a POW that he made contacts that would dramatically affect his future. He met the brilliant young French composer and musician, Olivier Messiaen, whose career was to enthrall the artistic world and transform the concept of organ music, with rythmically complex works, heavily influenced by religious mysticism. Having a penchant for the esoteric himself, Mitterrand must have been fascinated by the thinking of the young composer. Mitterrand's attraction to the esoteric and the world of occult symbolism is investigated in *Mitterrand – Le Grand Initié* (1996), by Nicolas Bonnal. A life-long friendship also developed from his meeting with Roger-Patrice Pelat, who will be shown later to have had a huge influence on his political career; truly a man from the 'shadows', Pelat was later to become involved in suspicious business activities. To some extent he became an embarrassment to Mitterrand. Yet against all advice, he remained loyal to his old friend.

But perhaps for the purposes of this tale, his meeting with Antoine Gayraud and Antoine Courrière was to prove most significant. Both of them had been prominent local Socialist politicians in the Department of the Aude; adjacent to that of Montségur. Through them he probably first learnt of the story of the Abbé Saunière, the treasure of Rennes-le-Château, and the activities of the German SS officer, Otto Rahn, who had apparently died only the year before. This information was clearly valuable; Gayraud and Courrière enjoyed successful political careers under the Mitterrand administration. These and the other friendships that he developed throughout his career increasingly involved Mitterrand in the mysterious web that extends from the little village in the Corbières.

In contrast to the rather heroic and romantic accounts of his escapes from the prison camp, Mitterrand was probably released by the Germans under the terms of the Franco-German armistice, in which French POWs were repatriated. And rather than joining the Resistance, he clearly became an active member of the Vichy government from May 1942 until late 1943, as an official in the Commissariat General for Prisoners of War. During this period he was to add yet more friends to his inner circle who would prove to be instrumental not only in his political career, but in the even shadowier occult world that he chose to frequent. His services to Vichy were obviously of some note, as he was decorated with the Françisque Gallique, a medal awarded by Pétain as a mark of personal favour for contributions to him and to his country. To avoid embarrassment, Mitterrand was later deliberately vague about this award.

Another myth is his alleged welcome into the Resistance and immediate acceptance by de Gaulle. Like Segonzac, Mitterrand was greeted with suspicion and, as de Gaulle confided to the author of his biography (one of his former ministers) Alain Peyrefitte, when he met Mitterrand in Algeria in the winter of 1943, he regarded him as a defector from the Vichy regime, and a likely double agent. His intense dislike for Mitterrand was never to die and, even in 1965 de Gaulle was to refer to him as 'a thug', 'an impostor' and 'the prince of political schemers'. Mitterrand himself always maintained that he was really a Resistance infiltrator and not a true member of the Vichy government, but evidence to the contrary is over-whelming and his denial has never been convincing. However, he did likely eventually work for the Resistance, and Martin Gilbert claims in *The Day the War Ended* (1995) that Mitterrand flew to England in 1943 from a landing strip near Angers and returned two months later by motor gunboat to begin active Resistance contact with French deportees and POWs.

Some of his former Vichy compatriots also managed for a time to achieve high political posts despite their dubious past, but most, like Maurice Papon, a minister under Giscard d'Estaing, were eventually brought to justice. But Mitterrand had staying power. He was a man well able to perform complex mental gymnastics in recreating a past, and in display-ing separate public and private faces, and furthermore very adept at operating in the 'looking glass' world of secret societies and their hidden agendas.

During the period that François Mitterrand was working for the Vichy administration, a newspaper entitled *Vaincre*

('Conquer'), with the subtitle *Pour une Jeune Chevalerie*, edited in Paris, commenced circulation. In issue No. 1, published on 21 September 1942, its founder is introduced, with a head and shoulders photograph, as Pierre de France. A young man of twenty-two years old, his full name is Pierre Plantard; he has at times also added the rather grandiose 'de Saint-Clair'.

An accurate biography of Pierre Plantard has been difficult to assemble as the various available sources are both meagre and at times contradictory; what follows is a synthesis of the most reliable. According to Michel Vallet, who writes under the name of Pierre Jarnac, Plantard was born on 18 March 1920 in Paris, to Pierre, a wine merchant, and his wife Raulo, who died two and a half years later. In 1939 he entered university where he excelled in Greco-Roman archaeology. It was here that he met and developed a friendship with the Marquis Philippe de Cherisey, the son of a minor aristocratic family from the Ardennes. The journalist Jean-Luc Chaumeil reveals that Plantard's full name was Pierre Athenasius Marie Plantard, and that he claimed to be a journalist; available evidence only confirms his work for several years as a verger at the church of St Louis d'Antin, in Paris. He had also tried to establish an anti-Semitic and anti-Masonic organization, presumably without success as no accounts remain of it, but he did lead a group in the Catholic youth movement. This has been dismissed as insignificant by some researchers, but youth groups were considered to be of great importance to the French National Revival; in this capacity, Plantard may well have already achieved some distinction. In 1940, he is also said to have approached Marshal Pétain and started working for the Vichy government. Little is known of this early period because, as in the case of Mitterrand and many others, association with the Vichy government tended to be forgotten after the war. However, his appearance in *Vaincre* illuminates some remarkable details about the strange world of chivalric and secret societies, and their links to Rennes-le-Château and the Abbé Saunière, given his other activities.

Plantard always claimed that he worked undercover for the Resistance, and that *Vaincre* was in fact a Resistance journal in which the articles carried hidden meanings. A close look at the six issues still obtainable shows this claim to be very difficult to substantiate. Many of the articles are openly supportive of Marshal Pétain and Vichy policies. But there are also indeed some strange anomalies. The company that printed *Vaincre* is indicated as being that of Poirier Murat, described as a former officer in the French Resistance, holder of the Medaille Militaire, and Chevalier of the Légion d'Honneur. And surprisingly, the newspaper is of particularly good production quality, especially when one considers that it was produced under the difficult circumstances of the German occupation with its degree of rationing. Its founder and editor, Pierre Plantard, must have had quite some influence, even at the young age of twenty-two.

Each edition of *Vaincre* features a crest, next to the title, which clearly belongs to an organization called *Alpha Galates*; its statutes are printed in full on page four of the first issue. The aim of the *Order of Alpha Galates*, as confirmed in many of the other articles, can be summed up as a French National Renewal. The methods outlined in the statutes are remarkably similar to those promoted by the Écoles Nationales d'Uriage. Thus one cannot escape the conclusion that Plantard and his supporters were actively engaged in this movement for a French spiritual and cultural regeneration. The statutes, declared to the Prefecture of Police as required by law, are dated 1937, and show that Pierre de France is the 'Gouverneur Général', at the tender age of eighteen! One of the most prestigious contributors to *Vaincre*, Professor Louis Le Fur, a right-wing thinker and writer who occupied a central educational post in the Vichy administration, gives Plantard a ringing endorsement as the new head of Alpha Galates. Professor Le Fur also mentions the retirement from the leadership of Alpha Galates, on 21 September 1942, of his old friend, Le Comte Maurice Moncharville, who is described as Professeur de Droit a la Faculté de Strasbourg. Furthermore, Le Fur claims to have been in the Order of Alpha Galates since 1934, and mentions yet another friend, Georges Monti, as a man of great competence.

It was actually Georges Monti who had founded Alpha Galates in 1934. Monti, who assumed the prename 'Israel' (and also adopted the name Marcus Vella for his occult activities), was born at Toulouse in 1880. Abandoned by his parents, he was brought up by the Jesuits. But despite a rigid Catholic education, he developed an interest in the occult and was initiated into the Rose-Croix Catholique by its founder Josephin Péladan, and then into Martinism by Papus – at the very time that the Abbé Saunière had become initiated. It is therefore certain that Georges 'Israel' Monti would have known and associated with Saunière. He would also have been aware of the secret of Rennes-le-Château.

Monti then became initiated into the Ordo Templi Orientis by Aleister Crowley, who later worked for British Intelligence, and who was alleged to have been central to the plan to bring the Nazi, Rudolph Hess, to England in 1941. This allegation is given weight by the fact that Monti and Crowley had established contact with the superiors of several German lodges which had been involved with bringing the Nazi party to power. Not wishing to leave any stone unturned, Monti also joined the B'nai B'rith, a Jewish Masonic organization, in which he used the alias of Comte Israel Monti. He appeared to delight in danger, working as a spy for the Germans in World War I, then for the Nazis, British Intelligence and even for the Second Bureau of the French Intelligence Service. It is not known for sure whether he was a double agent, and with whom his true loyalties lay. It is perhaps not surprising to learn that he was eventually assassinated, dying in a flat in Paris in 1936 from poisoning. Before this he had made the acquaintance of the young Pierre Plantard, however, who, according to an article by Plantard's first wife Anne Lea Hisler, 'was a friend of characters as diverse as: Le Comte Israel Monti, one of the brothers of the Holy Wehme . . .' The Holy Wehme is said to have been an assassination squad. It is thus possible that Monti passed on knowledge of the secret of Rennes-le-Château and the deposits of hidden treasure, to Plantard, who was to become the head of Monti's Order, Alpha Galates. This would help to explain the comment made by Professor Le Fur that he had always hoped to penetrate the 'secrets' of the Order; it also explains how Plantard was to become so involved with the area of Rennes-le-Château some years later. But there is yet another connection between Pierre Plantard and the Abbé Saunière. It is claimed that Pierre's grandfather, Charles Plantard, a journalist by profession and a contemporary of Saunière, spent much time at Rennes-les-Bains where he became a close friend of the Abbé Boudet. In a preface to the 1978 reprint of Boudet's *La Vrai Langue Celtique*, Pierre Plantard recalls that his grandfather recorded a description and impression of Saunière and Boudet that he had gained during a visit to Rennes-le-Château, on 6 June 1892. An original copy of the book, allegedly given to Charles Plantard by Boudet, contains a dedication to him, accompanied by Boudet's signature, which has since been verified by the discovery, in the mid-1990s, of a signed letter from Boudet that accompanied a copy of his book sent to the Bodleian Library in Oxford. The evidence presented so far suggests that Pierre Plantard had been aware of, and perhaps actively involved in, the mystery of Rennes-le-Château from an early age and was considered by his elders to have been a quite remarkable character. Indeed, he appears to have been one in which they could place their trust in the troubled times of the Occupation.

An article in issue No. 5 of *Vaincre* entitled 'Un Homme Nouveau' ('A New Man') by Professor Le Fur, reveals something of perhaps even greater consequence. In commenting on the succession of Plantard as head of Alpha Galates following the death of the Comte Moncharville, Professor Le Fur refers to a meeting with Hans Adolphe von Moltke, who had been appointed German ambassador to Spain, at which he recalled that this '. . . grand homme allemand, maitre dans notre Ordre' ('great German man, master in our Order') was very happy that they had found such a worthy young man as Pierre de France to lead the Order. This is all the more significant given that Hans Adolphe von Moltke was a cousin of Helmut James Count von Moltke, who with his great friend Peter Count Yorck von Wartenburg, founded the Kreisau Circle, named after the Moltke estate, which dedicated itself to planning a reorganization of Germany following the expected fall of Hitler. This effectively places Plantard not just at the heart of a French National Renewal, but in association with German resistance to Hitler and his Nazi party – and, as will be seen, in the formation of a new Christian-based spiritual and moral order for Europe.

The Kreisau Circle was largely formed from members of old Prussian aristocratic families, many of whom had had distinguished military or political careers. Helmut von Moltke, while studying Law at the Inner Temple in London, had established contact with important members of the British Establishment; even before the outbreak of war, he had expected support for opposition to Hitler. In June 1942, he wrote to an English friend indicating his utter despair for Germany under Nazi domination and the bloodshed to come.

Though the long-term aim of the Kreisau Circle was the rebuilding of a European community of nations – almost a blueprint for today's European Union – its most urgent task was the removal of Hitler. On the 20 July 1944 at 12.45pm, a bomb exploded at one of Hitler's briefing sessions with his high command at Rastenburg, 560 km north-east of Berlin. The bomb had been planted by Klaus Schenk Graf von Stauffenberg, a cousin of the von Moltke family and member of the Kreisau Circle. Despite the deafening explosion in the confined space of the briefing room, Hitler, though badly wounded, survived. The plotters were hunted down and within a short time more than 200 Germans were executed, including 21 generals, 33 senior officers, 2 ambassadors, and 7 ministers. Yet this tragic event demonstrates the extent of the secret German opposition to this ruthless regime and the desperate hope for a new Europe. However, even though by this time the Allied Forces had secured a firm foothold in northern France, it would be a further ten months before Europe was completely freed from the oppression of the Nazi regime.

The parallels between the political objectives of the Kreisau Circle and those expressed in *Vaincre*, and the individual aspirations outlined in the statutes of Alpha Galates, cannot be dismissed as they form the basis of a European-wide vision shared by many diverse groups that were, and still are, active. What is more, those committed to recovering the lost treasure hidden in the Corbières have also deliberately entangled themselves within this movement for the spiritual and moral regeneration of Europe, especially in the guise of chivalric Orders. They serve as an effective cover for their own clandestine activities.

A further review of the extant issues of *Vaincre* reveals the use of some extraordinary, but significant, symbolism. On page three of issue No. 1 is an illustration that depicts a knight on horseback riding along a road towards the setting or rising sun. On the road is printed *États Unis d'Occident* ('United States of the West'); within the 'E' is inscribed 1937; while the areas on either side of the road are labelled Bretagne (Brittany) and Bavière (Bavaria). The 'sun' carries the date 1946 with the astrological sign for Aquarius at its centre, possibly representing the 'new age' aspiration of the New Order and its anticipated fulfilment. The mounted knight carries a large standard, with, at its centre, a device called the Cross of the South which is surrounded by seven stars (reminiscent of the original European Union flag).

The Cross of the South, which also appears in other issues, is made up of several parts, among which is the symbol for Aquarius at the centre of the cross and on the arms of the cross, the French monarchist symbol, the fleur-de-lys. The cross stands upon a heart, at the centre of which is the Eastern symbol that represents harmony, the yin and yang. This can also be found carved on the exterior beam of the house in Alet-les-Bains mentioned earlier, which also carries the carving of the Star of David. Significantly, both these symbols can be found on the dungeon walls of the castles at Chinon and Coudray, etched by the Knights Templar during their captivity. It should be recalled that it was these symbols that were of particular interest to Charbonneau-Lassay, the archaeologist involved with the Hieron du Val d'Or at Paray-le-Monial. The use of these details in the symbolism of Alpha Galates and *Vaincre* were presumably carefully chosen to represent the philosophy, beliefs or aspirations of the Order, which could be readily understood by those of like mind.

The Cross of the South would thus appear to represent an ideology which was neither Vichy nor Resistance, but was instead Catholic monarchist, with mystical esoteric elements. The cross standing on a heart is yet another symbol closely associated with the mysterious society, the Hieron du Val d'Or, based at Paray-le-Monial, that had promoted the cult of the Sacred Heart and the restoration of a Catholic empire or kingdom.

Designating the cross to be 'of the South' may refer not just to the southern half of France that had initially remained free from German occupation, but more specifically to the Languedoc-Roussillon region, the ancient Septimania; the exact area in which the Knights Templar had tried to establish an independent state. This, of course, is the region in which is said to be deposited the fabulous treasure of the Visigoths.

By contrast, de Gaulle and his Free French forces adopted the ancient Cross of Lorraine. This symbol was based on an actual relic, housed and protected by the sisters of the Heart of Marie in their chapel at Bauge. Said to be constructed from a fragment of the 'True Cross', this 27cm high double-armed cross was brought from Crete to Anjou in 1244, by a knight named Jean d'Alluye, Lord of Château-Lavallière, who was very possibly a Templar. He donated the cross to the Cistercian Abbey of La Boissière for safekeeping, where it remained until the outbreak of the Hundred Years War, when it was taken to the château at Angers for protection by the Dukes of Anjou. It remained an object of veneration and was adopted into their coat of arms. Following his successful and memorable battle of Nancy in Lorraine, René II, Duke of Anjou, renamed it the 'Cross of Lorraine' in recognition of its power in helping to defeat his enemies. From then on, the Cross of Lorraine became a potent Catholic symbol for the protection of France.

This symbol evidently exercised its magic once again in August 1944, when France was liberated. In November of the following year, General de Gaulle was elected President, and the task of rebuilding and regeneration began. But though the war with Germany was over, new dangers threatened the stability of France and Europe. The Communist Soviet Union, dividing Germany and Berlin and dedicated to expansion, embarked on the Cold War with the democratic West. Meanwhile, France found itself at war with its Indo-Chinese empire and struggled with its troublesome colonies, Algeria and Tunisia.

Once again, circumstances favoured opportunists. Two characters who shared similar wartime experiences in Vichy France, and who were both aware of the secret embodied in the village of Rennes-le-Château, were to reach the lofty positions of power and influence in this sort of climate. François Mitterrand was to become President of France, and Pierre Plantard was to become the Grand Master of a secret society whose tentacles extend throughout the world of occult politics.

The Myth and Reality
of the Priory of Sion

The Priory of Sion · The Value of Archives
The Merovingian Legacy

A STRONG SENSE OF Gallic independence, national identity
and even destiny have long influenced French politics. But the
Republic's public political arena has also been powerfully
influenced by an almost invisible one, the world of the secret
and occult. Under their cloak of secrecy, and as they have
throughout history, various groups have sought, or created,
opportunities to pursue their own agendas, often in league
with prominent politicians and public figures. The agendas
pursued are not necessarily in the public interest.

The liberation of France and the collapse of the Vichy
government left a political vacuum. The new provisional
government, the French Committee of National Liberation,
based in Algeria, had yet to establish control in metropolitan
France, so the door was momentarily wide open for a Communist bid for power. Local Liberation Committees (CDLs)
had been set up in towns and villages; of these, Communists
formed almost a third of the membership, the remainder
Socialists, Christian Democrats, or Gaullists. In early September
1944, six representatives of departmental CDLs met at the
château of Vizille, near Grenoble – where the French Revolution is said to have started – and within a couple of kilometres
of Uriage and the Château Bayard, home to the Order of

Knight-Monks of the Uriage. At this meeting, the six groups formed an association with sufficient potential power to be able to dictate terms to the provisional government. History, as so often in this tale of treasure and conspiracies, seems again to have been repeating itself.

Post-war French politics were in almost permanent turmoil, with twenty-four different governments of the Fourth Republic holding office between 1944 and 1957. A number of conditions conspired against a Communist seizure of power, however – not least the American determination to prevent the spread of Communism in Europe. Thus, de Gaulle managed to retain his status of saviour, and his position as the man best able to bring about the renewal of France. De Gaulle's idea of a national renewal was of a state with a centralized bureaucracy and a strong presidential regime. He had support within his inner circle; in fact, Michel Debré, working in his private office, argued in a pseudonymous pamphlet that, 'the only chance for French democracy is, if the term may be used, a republican monarch'. De Gaulle's desire for a more authoritarian regime would not have received popular support, had it been publicly known, especially from those in the Resistance. Having fought against their German occupiers, they looked forward eagerly to participating in a French National Regeneration, but not necessarily on those terms. But de Gaulle was only following an ancient Gallic tradition which believes that France holds a unique position in Europe, a sort of 'chosen land', that needs to be governed, or ruled, by a divinely inspired leader.

It is against this background that one must judge the curious writings of a certain R.P. Martin; one of his articles, heralding the appearance of a book, was indeed entitled 'The General de Gaulle awaits the return of the Great Monarch'. One could ask though, whether it would have been more accurate to state that de Gaulle considered himself to be this Great Monarch. In another work *The Book of Secret Companions; the Secret Teaching of General de Gaulle*, Martin (who turns out to be a Father Martin Couderc de Hauteclaire) claims that after the war de Gaulle had formed a group of forty-five companions. They were dedicated to the promotion of Gaullism, and were obliged to remain anonymous for ten years after his death. It is possible that the choice of the number forty-five was purely symbolic and represented the formation of the group in 19 '45'. But of particular relevance is the implication that there were links between this group of companions and a secret society in which Jean Cocteau, André Malraux, Marshal Juin, and Pierre Plantard were prominent members.

This secret society, that calls itself Le Prieuré de Sion (the Priory of Sion), is one active at the heart of the Rennes-le-Château intrigue and the search for its ancient treasure.

Martin's article which was published in the magazine *Nostra* (18 October 1982) is actually signed by the unexplained 'Bayard', which could be a coded reference to Château Bayard, the centre of the École Nationale d'Uriage and its Knight-Monks. This is confirmed by the assertion that the initial CDL group was joined by members of the École Nationale which had been founded by Captain (later to become General) Pierre Dunoyer de Segonzac.The group had adopted the apt motto 'More is in us', which highlights their goal of striving for excellence. The purpose of the École Nationale was revealed as the ideological education of the elite youth of France for future posts in an authoritarian and paternalistic government – very similar to de Gaulle's covert intentions for his post-war government. While there is no evidence that the Priory of Sion is the same as, or linked to, the group of the forty-five companions, the article was clearly intended to draw attention to a political philosophy common to de Gaulle, the École Nationale, and the Priory of Sion.

In the article, Bayard states plainly that de Gaulle was not actually a member of the Priory of Sion but was privy to their internal affairs and enjoyed a significant influence. Certainly, Pierre Plantard, Governor General of Alpha Galates, was to become a key member of the Priory, and instrumental in the politics that returned de Gaulle to power in 1958.

* * *

After the death of her priest and life-long companion in 1917, Marie Dénarnaud, then aged forty-nine, continued to live alone in the presbytery which had been leased by Saunière. As was traditional in rural France, she dressed in somewhat sombre clothes but remained smart and alert and, despite living as a virtual recluse, still received the respect of the other villagers. Within a short time, Marie was assailed by various people claiming to be friends of the late priest, but who were likely unknowns hoping to discover the source of his wealth. No doubt taking advantage of Marie's vulnerability, these uninvited guests seem to have been responsible for the disappearance of most of Saunière's books, papers, curios, and ornaments. However, much of his extensive library (the beautifully made bookshelves can still be seen lining the walls of the first-floor room in the Tour Magdala) was bought by a dealer in books, called Derain, from Lyon. This would seem to reinforce Saunière's other connections with Lyon; only through some previous personal contact could the dealer have been likely to know of his valuable book collection.

Antoine Captier recalls that his father, the son of Saunière's bellringer, remembered seeing Marie burning sheafs of papers in the garden in front of the Tour Magdala. Were vital clues to the Saunière mystery accidently or deliberately destroyed? Antoine further confirms that among the surviving papers are letters that suggest he had deposited certain sums of money in various French and foreign banks. From magazines that he had received, it appears that he had also speculated in stocks and shares. It is possible that Marie, being of little education, did not appreciate the value of share certificates and destroyed them along with other papers. This would explain why, although being the sole inheritor of all Saunière's wealth, Marie was to find herself in financial difficulties.

She appears to have managed only with financial assistance from local priests, who had been close colleagues of her former companion, and was frequently encouraged to sell the domain for a more permanent solution. Resolutely refusing this option – perhaps out of respect for Saunière – Marie continued to live a simple life for nearly thirty years, while the domain fell gradually into neglect.

In July 1946, Noel Corbu and his family arrived at Rennes-le-Château to take up residence in the Abbé Saunière's domain. As with many other aspects of Rennes, Noel Corbu and his acquisition of the domain have become clouded in mystery. Noel's daughter Claire, married to Antoine Captier and still connected to the village, has revealed some details in their book *L' Héritage de l'Abbé Saunière* (1995); but possibly because of her young age in 1946, she may not have been fully aware of all the facts. A full and intriguing account is presented in a book by Jean Markale, a professor of philosophy and a specialist in Celtic history. Unfortunately, he doesn't reveal his sources (common in many French books on the subject), but as a man of academic integrity, his account has to be given due consideration.

Noel Corbu, living at that time in Perpignan, was an entrepreneur with an interest in several small businesses, and had even published a detective novel. However, for some reason to do with his attitude to the Occupation – possibly through black-market activity – he found himself in some trouble. Leaving Perpignan in 1944, Noel, his wife and two children, went to live in the village of Bugurach, only 10 km south-east of Rennes-le-Château, at the foot of the mountain. Noel quickly befriended the local villagers, and it was probably from the primary school teacher that he learned of the story of Saunière and the treasure. On a family outing in 1945 they established contact with the elderly Marie Dénarnaud, who showed them souvenirs from her life with the priest. Determined to acquire the property, Noel made several visits to the village and developed a friendship with Marie, eventually making her an offer to buy the domain. In return he agreed that she could remain in her home where his family would look after her. So, on 22 July 1946, an agreement was drawn up whereby Noel Corbu became the legal inheritor of the estate in the event of Marie's death.

Shortly after leaving Marie at Rennes-le-Château, Noel Corbu took a group of young villagers to Morocco, where he had an interest in a sugar factory. Problems with this venture meant only short trips back to France, but his daughter recalls that during one of these trips Marie told him: 'Don't be so worried, my good Noel, . . . one day I will tell you a great secret that will make you a rich man . . . very rich.'

However, a very different version is recounted in *Rennes-le-Château: Capitale Secrète et l'Histoire de France* (1982), by Jean-Pierre Deloux and Jacques Brétigny. According to this account, the Catholic Church engineered the charge of simony (the selling of Masses) against Saunière, as an explanation for his wealth, in order to draw attention away from the reality of a hidden treasure. They state that: after his death they continued to keep an eye on the domain, occupied by Marie Dénarnaud who had legally inherited all Saunière's assets; they had attempted to purchase the estate to no avail, until in 1946 the Church, according to a report from Jania MacGillivray, a journalist who lived in Paris, dreamed up a scheme.

As was believed by the Abbé Mazières, the Church had conceived an elaborate plan to acquire the domain. A certain Abbé Gau, hero of the Resistance, was charged to contact Noel Corbu to ask him to return to Rennes-le-Château and to convince Marie to sell her domain to the Church. Corbu accepted and, duping the bishop, persuaded Marie to sell the domain to him. On 26 July 1946, she made him the sole beneficiary. The Church did not lose interest in Rennes-le-Château to the point that, when Corbu asked for a grant for the education of his children, the apostolic representative, Mgr

Roncalli, later to become Pope John XXIII, returned to the bishop to enquire. A little later the Vatican agreed a grant to Noel Corbu.

This astonishing assertion has proved impossible to confirm, but in much of this story, the facts are often stranger than fiction. Clouds of suspicion have certainly hovered over the activities of Noel Corbu, including charges of collaboration. C.M. Scargill, a genealogical and historical researcher, further alleges that Marie Dénarnaud was a relative of the Corbu family and, despite the lack of any supporting evidence, that Noel was a founder member of the Priory of Sion. If true, this adds yet more fuel to feed the flames of the mystery.

In January 1953, Marie died, aged 85, without having revealed any secrets she may have shared with the Abbé Saunière. Old age and a minor stroke had by then prevented her from passing on any knowledge, had she been inclined to do so. Convinced that a treasure did exist within the confines of the domain, Noel obtained permission from the local authorities to undertake formal excavations on his property (which was necessary because of a blanket ban on unauthorized excavations in the region). To provide income, he turned the villa into a small hotel and restaurant, hoping to attract visitors by promoting the enchanting story of the Abbé Saunière.

Among the steady trickle of visitors to the twin villages of Rennes-les-Bains and Rennes-le-Château was a man, claiming to be an archaeologist, who seemed to be remarkably interested in certain features. According to Professor Markale, the man was none other than Pierre Plantard, the leading light in the Order of Alpha Galates. One of the local features in which he was most interested was the tombstone, or rather the two tombstones, of Paul-Urban, Count of Fleury, owner of the Blanchefort lands in the late eighteenth and early nineteenth centuries. Both are dedicated to de Fleury, but carry conflicting inscriptions; one stating that he was born on the 3 May 1776, and that he died on the 7 August 1836, and the other, that he died on 7 August 1856, aged 60. Even more curiously, he was actually born in 1778; both inscriptions are therefore inaccurate. The later of the two tombs carries two more inscriptions: IL EST PASSE EN FAISANT LE BIEN (HE SPENT HIS LIFE DOING GOOD) and RESTES TRANSFERES (REMAINS TRANSFERRED). The first of these is a typical dedication to a Chevalier of the Rose-Croix, an adept of a neo-chivalric Order; while the second rather more obviously states that his remains have been transferred from elsewhere. The apparent anomaly of the dates has been explained by interpreting them as a deliberate code, referring in some way perhaps to a new location of a deposit. This interpretation may be supported by the reference to the 'transfer of remains'. Plantard is also said to have been very interested in two thermal sources known as the Madeleine and the Bains de la Reine, and to have spent time investigating the cliffs which border the valley of Rennes-les-Bains. This is the very area surveyed in the map by Edmond Boudet that appears as page 301 of Henri Boudet's book *La Vrai Langue Celtique* (1886). These visits, and the locals' impressions of Plantard, are confirmed by the objective researches of René Descadeillas, former director of the municipal library at Carcassonne.

That Plantard should have visited the area is not surprising, since he alleges that his journalist grandfather Charles, had come here often – perhaps in pursuit of a story – and was well acquainted with Boudet and Saunière. There is no evidence that Pierre Plantard ever met Noel Corbu, but it is more than likely that, during at least one of his visits to Rennes-le-Château, Plantard would have called in at the domain, if not the restaurant, that now belonged to the Corbu family. Plantard's researches were evidently fruitful; he was later to buy a large amount of land around the area of Blanchefort and Rocco Nègre, the site of the goldmine where some of the treasure was said to have been deposited.

Except for some odd glimpses, other details of Plantard's activities for the decade following the end of the war are at best sketchy, with only some references from his first wife Ann

Lea Hisler, who died in 1970, and from some of his colleagues. Though independent corroboration of most of the claims – of which some are astonishing – has not been possible, Plantard himself, in subsequent interviews or letters, confirms, or at least fails to deny, the bulk of them.

A key date in this affair is 1956. It was a politically difficult year for Britain and France, as Anglo-French forces, following Israel's initiative, came into conflict with Egypt over the Suez Canal. Rumblings of discontent in Algeria were growing ever louder, while the French were still smarting over the Indo-Chinese debacle, not to mention the failure of successive governments to gain the confidence of the electorate. At the same time, final preparations were being made for the signing of the Treaty of Rome, which would bring about the European Economic Community.

It is against the background of this European and national news that, on 12, 13 and 14 January 1956, a series of three articles appeared in the prestigious newspaper *La Dépêche du Midi*. Compiled by a journalist Albert Salamon, and entitled 'La Fabuleuse Découverte du Curé aux Milliards de Rennes-le-Château' ('The Fabulous Discovery of the Millionaire Priest of Rennes-le-Château') the articles featured interviews with Noel Corbu and the revelation of the life led by the Abbé Saunière and his alleged discovery of a great treasure. In comparison with the millions of words written on these subjects since, these articles are remarkably simple. They focus only on the unexplained expenditure of the priest and his building programme; the discovery of parchments written in Latin, found in an ancient altar pillar, that referred to a treasure deposited by the medieval Blanche of Castile; and the pressure put on Saunière, by his bishop, to reveal the source of his wealth. No other conclusions were expressed in the articles, except that the writer claimed that a contemporary of Saunière, from Carcassonne, had said that he had actually seen some gold coins that the priest had found. Noel Corbu had to admit, however, that though his excavations had revealed some inter-

Above: Symbols carved into the exterior beam of a medieval house in Alet-les-Bains, said to have belonged to the family of Nostradamus.

Above right: Device printed on paper found among Abbé Saunière's papers, thought to have been used as his personal bookplate, and taken from the frontispiece of *The Golden Age Revised* by Madathanus, 1677.

Right: The six-pointed star featured on the rose windows of the church adjacent to the abbey at Alet-les-Bains.

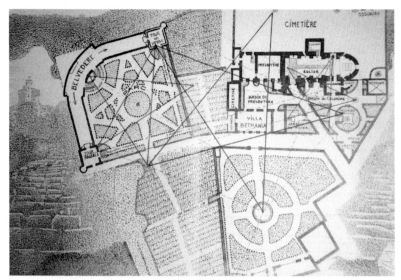

Plan of Abbé Saunière's church and domain at Rennes-le-Château, showing its pentagonal layout. (Original map surveyed and drawn by Alain Feral)

Aerial view of the village of Rennes-le-Château. The domain of the Abbé Saunière is to the left of the photo.

Above: Interior of the Saunière museum, situated under the curving terrace of the Belvedere.

Right: Map featuring the valley of Rennes-les-Bains from Abbé Boudet's *La Vraie Langue Celtique.*

Above left: Bérenger Saunière, curé of Rennes-le-Château 1885–1917.

Above right: Marie Dénarnaud, Saunière's housekeeper and confidante.

Left: The house to which Dr Paul Courrent retired. Saunière's physician, he was entrusted with his papers after his death. These were stolen after Courrent's death in 1952.

Far left: Page from the World War II-era magazine *Vaincre*, edited by Pierre Plantard. It features the Cross of the South.

Left: Another page from *Vaincre*, illustrating the motif of 'The United States of Europe'.

German-born recipient of France's *Légion d'Honneur* Marlene Dietrich, photographed in front of the Arc de Triomphe, 1958. What prompted her visits, and those of fellow ex-patriot heroine Josephine Baker, to the Corbières? (Associated Press)

François Mitterrand, during his presidential campaign, on a visit to Saunière's domain at Rennes-le-Château. (Andre Galaup, Midi Libre, Paris)

Right: Barn at Chaillac, near St Junien. Local *résistants* met here – and could well have planned the raid on the *Das Reich* gold convoy, seen to have such disastrous consequences.

Left and below: The total devastation of Oradour four days after the Allied invasion of Normandy in 1944, preserved as a memorial to this day. Was gold at the root of this attack?
(Robin Mackness)

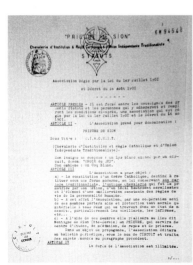

Top left: The Statutes of the Priory of Sion, publicly declared in 1956.

Top right: Pierre Plantard, Grand Master of the Priory of Sion (17 January 1981– 10 July 1984). *(© Michael Baigent)*

Right: Grace Kelly leaves the cathedral in Monte Carlo as Princess Grace, consort to Prince Ranier III of the Gimaldi family, 1956. How aware was she of the activities of the Order of the Solar Temple, with which she became involved? *(Associated Press)*

Left: The BMW which Robin Mackness was driving when pursued by the *douaniers*, riddled with bullet holes. Two years in a French jail followed the arrest.
(Robin Mackness)

Below: The epicentre of this history: the Dome of the Rock in Jerusalem.
(Israel Office of Tourism)

esting artefacts and skeletal remains, no treasure had so far been located.

Five months after these articles appeared, the existence of the Priory of Sion was made public for the first time. In accordance with a law of 1901, that requires all associations to register a copy of their constitutions with the local police authorities, the Priory of Sion lodged a copy of their statutes with the sub-prefecture of police at Saint-Julien-en-Genevois. Confirmation of this is found in the 20 July 1956 issue of the official journal in which such registrations are published. It has been remarked by certain researchers that the public exposure of a supposedly secret society is somewhat strange, but to have operated outside the 1901 law (enacted as a result of suspicion of secret societies due to their supposed participation in the French Revolution and later machinations) could have brought unnecessary difficulties for the Priory. The statutes reveal little about the organization, other than its administration. However, several details are worthy of note.

The sign of the Priory is stated as being the Cross of the South, and its emblem a white cock, both of which are identical to those found in *Vaincre*, the publication of the Order of Alpha Galates, in which Plantard had played such a prominent role. The Priory declares itself a Catholic Order of Chivalry in the 'ancient tradition', dedicated to a moral and spiritual regeneration; without doubt, there are echoes here of the elite Écoles Nationales of the Vichy government. Paragraph (c) of article III of the statutes calls on the members to assist in the founding of a priory as a place for study, meditation, peaceful rest and prayer on the aptly named Montagne de Sion in the Haute-Savoie. But most intriguing is that the Priory's headquarters is stated as being at Sous-Cassan, evidently near Annemasse, on the outskirts of Geneva and the Swiss border. This address has proved impossible to trace, suggesting a front or a pseudonym. Was this a secret location, intended as a contact point for those trafficking goods or money from France to Switzerland?

This is the explanation that becomes probable in the light of an assertion, confirmed by Plantard, that in 1952 he participated in the transfer of gold ingots worth more than 100 million francs from France to the Union des Banques Suisse, Switzerland. Such a transaction was not illegal at the time, but later changes in the law would have necessitated the establishment of a border contact point if other similar transactions were required to take place. Plantard's explanation was that the gold had been transferred on the orders of General de Gaulle as part of a special fund for the use of the Committees of Public safety, of which Plantard was secretary-general. Could this explain why Robin Mackness, one of the authors of this book, encountered such intense interest during his arrest and interrogation in December 1982, when he told French customs officials that he was carrying gold to Annemasse?

The connection with Switzerland reappears in a pamphlet by Plantard's wife Ann Lea Hisler, who states that he had been invited in 1947 by the Swiss Federal Government, to stay for several years in Switzerland near Lake Leman, where a number of other foreign delegates could be found. She doesn't, however, reveal the purpose of her husband's stay, or the nature of the other delegates. She further states that her husband, known under the pseudonym of 'Way', was a director, with Andre Malraux and Michel Debré (under the authority of Marshal Juin), of the Secretariat of the Committees of Public Safety in metropolitan France. These remarkable but uncorroborated statements are given some measure of support by a series of articles that appeared in the newspaper *Le Monde*, in June and July 1958. These articles, in referring to the role of the Committees for Public Safety, affirm the authority of General de Gaulle and the prime objective of 'national rehabilitation'; Plantard, under his pseudonym 'Captain Way', is their signatory. Another article published on 29 July 1958, and reported in *The Messianic Legacy* (1986) by Baigent, Leigh and Lincoln, confirms the connection:

'Captain Way', signatory of this communique, has already published, during the month of May, several appeals and declarations in the name of the 'Central Committee of Public Safety for the Paris Region'. As we have already indicated, he is M. Pierre Plantard . . . who, together with certain friends, took the initiative of establishing this committee.

The 'Movement' which will comprise the successor to the Committee is directed by M. Bonerie-Clarus, a journalist; its treasurer is M. Robin; M. Pierre Plantard is secretary and in charge of propaganda . . .

The Committees of Public Safety were set up to provide support and stability for de Gaulle during the potentially explosive Algerian problem; like those established during the Revolution, they had the potential for great political power. That Pierre Plantard had been appointed to such a prominent position further emphasizes his ability, first seen in *Vaincre*, to become involved at the heart of French politics. Plantard is certainly not a man to be ignored.

The subtitle of the Priory of Sion is 'Chevalerie d'Institution et Règle Catholique et d'Union Indépendante Traditioniste', known in short as CIRCUIT, which became the title of their newsletter. The statutes – signed by P. Plantard in his capacity as Secretary-General – and the contents of CIRCUIT, are little less than a manifesto for Catholic traditionalism in the Vichy mode of Charles Maurras and his Action Française, inheritors of the Sacred Heart cult of the Hieron du Val d'Or with which Saunière was so closely associated.

The considerable volume of works on Saunière and the Rennes-le-Château mysteries that has appeared since 1956, offers an abundance of opinion and information, some factual and some fantastic. But there is no doubt that many of the 'revelations' originate from a common source, and appear to be part of a co-ordinated process of information or more probably, disinformation. The actual facts seem to hide within a profusion of other truths, half truths and fabrications that have successfully masked the reality behind the mystery.

Possibly an objective reality can be deduced; certainly all
genuine new findings seem to fit like pieces of a giant jigsaw
into the known larger picture. The true agenda of the Priory
of Sion, within this overall picture, has been carefully concealed. But patient research has succeeded in lifting the veil a
little. One glimpse is offered in a work by Deloux and
Brétigny, *Rennes-le-Château: Capitale Secrète et L'Histoire de
France* (1982), who report that:

> On the first of June 1967, some months before the publication
> of the work by Gérard de Sède, who relaunched the affair of
> Rennes, Mgr. Boyer, vicar general, published, in 'La Semaine
> Religieuse de Carcassonne', an article entitled 'Mise au point
> et mise en garde'. In this he states: 'One can confirm without
> hesitation that a treasure is hidden in an ancient necropolis, and
> that the bishop of Carcassonne knows the existence of this
> necropolis but refuses to reveal its secret.' Nobody, either from
> within or outside of the Church, has come forward to deny
> this assertion. Is the Catholic Church therefore more involved
> in this strange affair than it would care to acknowledge?

Much of the published material about the Priory has been
based on a series of publications known collectively as the
Dossiers Secrets, which have appeared periodically in a variety
of printed forms since 1956. These documents have been given
considerable status by the authors of the *Holy Blood and the
Holy Grail*. Indeed, they underpin the main thrust of their
thesis. Though a great deal of the contents of the *Dossiers
Secrets* are highly speculative, often dubious and even fabricated, there are certainly some aspects that deserve closer
attention. The central allegation in the *Dossiers* is that the
Priory, founded in the Middle Ages after the Christian liberation of Jerusalem, was formed as a secret chivalric Order, with
authority over the Knights Templar, dedicated to protecting
the bloodline of the Merovingian kings, and to their eventual
restoration to the throne of France. Despite the dissolution of
the Templars, the Priory of Sion is said to have continued to

operate throughout the centuries, adopting various pseudo-nyms and strategies to attain political influence and control. Apparently one of the more effective guises assumed by the Priory was the Compagnie du Saint-Sacrement, also known as the Children of Solomon.

This ties in with another Priory assertion that the descend-ants of the Merovingian King Dagobert II were descended from Benjamin, an ancient tribe of Israel, exiled from the Holy Land. In the light of the analysis of Judaism presented in Chapter 9, it can be seen that the descendants of Benjamin, as those of their neighbouring tribe, Judah, are the true inheritors of the biblical nation of Jews; a fact that is significant when considering legitimacy for possession of the lost treasure of Jerusalem. Much space in the *Dossiers Secrets* is also devoted to revealing genealogies confirming the survival of the Merovin-gian dynasty through the descendants of a few aristocratic families, notably the Lords of Rennes. In addition, there is a genealogy compiled in 1939, by the Abbé Pierre Plantard, Vicar of the Basilica Saint Clotilde in Paris (a relative of Pierre), in which the Plantard family itself is shown to be of Merovin-gian descent. Of very dubious authenticity, this would appear to be no more than a naive, or devious, attempt to establish a claim to a share in the legendary treasure of the Corbières – that symbolic treasure the present Priory of Sion, as self-appointed hereditary guardians, are pledged to locate and protect.

According to the *Dossiers Secrets*, the Priory has been guided by a succession of Grand Masters, referred to as 'Nautonniers' (Helmsmen) in their statutes. A varied collection of twenty-six eminent historical characters, these include René d'Anjou, Leonardo da Vinci, Nicolas Flamel, and Isaac Newton. The antiquity of the Priory and the authenticity of this list of its alleged Grand Masters may be dubious, but the last four on this list, who are said to have presided over the Priory since the French Revolution, share a most interesting and illuminat-ing connection. It suggests that they were chosen, neither at random, nor even to endorse the Merovingian claim, but rather as a symbol of a social and political ideology. Charles Nodier, Victor Hugo, Claude Debussy, and Jean Cocteau, said to have been Grand Masters from 1804 to 1963, can be shown to have had a profound influence on the literary, artistic, philosophical and occult circles in Paris during the nineteenth and early twentieth centuries. These were the very same circles, in the late nineteenth century, with which the Abbé Saunière had become associated.

But the next step through the maze of the *Dossiers Secrets* is to pick up the trail of the archives and documents that were acquired by Saunière and his contemporaries. In view of the unique nature of the archives, documents and parchments, the trail has had to be pieced together from a number of sources, some able to be confirmed, and some more reliable than others. The account rendered here is a 'most probable' scenario which fits the known facts, and offers a measure of explanation for the subsequent activities of those involved with the Rennes affair.

As we have seen, the archives themselves have originated from more than one source. There are the documents of General Dagobert, collected during his tenure as proprietor of goldmines in the eastern Corbières, that relate to the mines and their legendary deposits of treasure. These documents were given to his Masonic brothers of the Grand Orient prior to his departure for military service in the Army of the Eastern Pyrenees. After his mysterious and untimely death in 1794, the archives were acquired by the Marquis de Chefdebien, founder of the Masonic lodge, the Philadelthes, and kept in his family archives.

As we know a century later, Alfred Saunière, a Jesuit priest, was employed as a tutor and chaplain to the family of the Marquis de Chefdebien at their home in Narbonne. He was caught rifling through their family papers, and dismissed. Alfred's action was not as surprising as it may seem since it was considered a mission by some Jesuit priests to infiltrate aristocratic and influential families to 'keep an eye on them'. Documents, stolen by Alfred, were then passed on to his brother, Bérenger, parish priest at Rennes-le-Château, who, like his brother, was dedicated to the restoration of the monarchy.

Of course, other parchments are said to have been discovered by Bérenger Saunière during the initial restoration of his ancient church and the replacement of its ninth-century altar. They were rolled up in wooden tubes secreted in the hollow altar support pillar, having been hidden there by the Abbé Bigou before 1789. The find, apparently witnessed by Elie Bot, Saunière's clerk of works, and two of his workers, is said to have comprised ancient genealogies of the families who had become guardians of the Merovingian bloodline and the fabulous treasure. More recent researches have, however, cast considerable doubt on this account. But on a later occasion Saunière did make a discovery of documents. Due to his sharp-eyed bellringer, M. Captier, who had found the little glass vial containing a small parchment, Saunière gained access to the crypt, in which had been deposited the Hautpoul archives and heirlooms.

In spite of his training in classical languages, Saunière was unable to make sense of two of the parchments. Apparently familiar texts from the New Testament written in Latin, they were composed in such a way as to imply a concealed message. As has been discussed, it appears that he obtained permission to go to the church and seminary of St Sulpice in Paris, where some priests had gained a reputation for an expertise in deciphering ancient and esoteric documents. Evidence of this trip has not of course been confirmed and certain researchers do not accept that it ever took place; though Claire Corbu, the daughter of Noel, is firmly convinced of its authenticity. There is also the unconfirmed claim that Saunière's signature appears in one of the mass books of St Sulpice. Before going to Paris, it would seem Saunière took the precaution of making accurate copies of his curious finds.

According to the writers and researchers Deloux and

Brétigny, Saunière stayed in Paris for five days, staying at the home of a M. Ane, nephew of the Abbé Bieil, director of St Sulpice. M. Ane owned a factory that manufactured religious art and statuary, from which Saunière purchased a set of 'Stations of the Cross' for his church. It was through Ane that Saunière was introduced to Émile Hoffet, the trainee priest who had already acquired a reputation for knowledge of Masonic and esoteric subjects. Hoffet had begun his training at the juniorate of Sion (Meurthe-et-Moselle) before being ordained in 1897, and went on to have a not undistinguished career during which he wrote articles on pontifical theology for a journal that openly supported a restoration of the monarchy in favour of the Count of Chambord. He was also closely involved with the centre for the devotion of the Sacred Heart at Paray-le-Monial, where he would have undoubtably made contact with the archaeologist and historian, Louis Charbonneau-Lassay. Certainly, Émile Hoffet was a member of the Parisian occult circles that had become so fashionable at this time, and so it is quite reasonable to believe the claim that, through him, Saunière was introduced to Claude Debussy and Emma Calvé. Though Saunière's involvement with Martinism and its prime movers, Papus and Péladan, both members of the Paris occult circles, could equally have brought him into contact with Debussy, himself a great supporter of Péladan, and Emma Calvé.

One can only guess what role the parchments and archives played in the last twenty years of the Abbé Saunière's life. The ostentatious lifestyle and his obstinate refusal, not only to reveal the source of his wealth but also to accept a posting away from Rennes-le-Château, still remain at the heart of this enigma. Subjected to the full wrath and sanctions of his bishop, Saunière resorted to all possible tactics to hold his ground. Unquestionably, he had an extremely strong reason to maintain his silence and to remain in his little village.

According to the exhaustive researches of Roger-René Dagobert, the surviving descendant of the family of General

Dagobert, Saunière confided the precious parchments and archives in January 1917 to his old friend Dr Paul Courrent, who stayed with him during the last days of his life. Twelve years later, Dr Courrent retired to a large house at Embres-le-Castelmaure, a little village very close to Cascastel, the home of the Pailhoux family of General Dagobert's wife. The archives were then carefully concealed in the doctor's extensive library.

In 1939, the elderly Marquis de Chefdebien, descendant of the founder of the Philadelphes, deposited his remaining archives, including some of the documents of General Dagobert, with the Archaeological and Historical Society of Narbonne for further study. These were then passed on to their most eminent member Dr Courrent, who now had possession of all the documents found by Saunière and those collected by General Dagobert. Evidence for this deposit of documents can be found in a report of the Commission Archeologique de Narbonne, tome XVI, 1943, which states:

> At a meeting on Monday 16/12/1940, the Secretary read a note relating to the archives of Chefdebien, given to the Commission by the heirs of Marie-Louise de Chefdebien, who died in Narbonne in 1939. Our eminent correspondent has been able to examine a part of these noble archives (including those of Pailhoux and Dagobert). The extreme value draws attention to the importance of confiding them to a specialist archivist for study and the complete classification of this collection which contains particularly rare and precious manuscripts.

It was in the following year that the Germans occupied France, and along with many others, that François Mitterrand was sent to Germany as a POW. During this spell of imprisonment, Mitterrand was to meet Antoine Gayraud and Antoine Courrière, both prominent local politicians from the Aude, from whom he was to learn the fascinating history of Rennes-le-Château and the activities of Otto Rahn. He was also to meet a person, later alleged to be a Grand Master of the Priory of

Sion, Roger-Patrice Pelat, who would continue after the war to play a key role in Mitterrand's political career.

Dr Courrent died in 1952 and his papers disappeared. Once again evidence of this can be found within the archives of the Commission Archeologique de Narbonne:

> At a meeting of 3/02/1954, the Secretary indicated that the Chefdebien family had sought to reclaim the family archives bequeathed by Marie-Louise, who died at Narbonne in May 1939. The Commission was embarrassed since the precious archives had disappeared shortly after the death of Dr Courrent to whom they had been confided.

Furthermore, in the course of his researches, Roger-René Dagobert has learned from the great-nephews of Dr Courrent that the archives had been stolen by some people 'who were aware that these documents could fetch a great deal of money'.

The following year saw the death of Marie Dénarnaud, and it is three years later, in 1956, that the *Dépêche du Midi* articles and *Le Livre des Constitutions* appeared, concerning the history and aims of the Priory of Sion; that year they also registered their statutes with the authorities. *Le Livre des Constitutions*, the first book to mention the Priory, was also published in Geneva by Editions des Commanderies de Genève. Despite efforts by researchers, the existence of this publisher has never been traced, further adding to the mystery that surrounds the Priory. This association with Switzerland is repeated in certain parts of the *Dossiers Secrets*, purported to originate from the Grande Loge Alpina (Swiss equivalent of the United Grand Lodge of British Freemasonry). Another more tangible link with Grande Loge Alpina comes in the person of a fervent esotericist, Robert Amadou. A Martinist and an official in the Grande Loge Alpina, Amadou admits meeting Pierre Plantard while being initiated into Alpha Galates in 1942. In fact he contributed an article entitled 'Situation de la Chevalerie', published in the second edition of

Plantard's newspaper *Vaincre*. In a private letter from Philippe de Chérisey to Pierre Plantard in 1985, there is a reference to the wartime period when Plantard met, among others, Robert Amadou (a former schoolfriend of de Chérisey), Louis Le Fur, and Adolphe von Moltke.

Secrecy and anonymity, long a tradition in Swiss banking and business culture, will be seen to have played a major part in the financial, political and even criminal activities of other groups, at times, involved with those of the Priory.

In 1966, Gérard de Sède managed to acquire part of the archives of Émile Hoffet, who was known to have amassed an extensive and impressive library of books and documents, including many on occult and secret societies. Among these was a dossier that the cleric had compiled on the enigmatic Georges 'Israel' Monti, with whom he had been personally acquainted. Within a year, de Sède published *Le Trésor Maudit de Rennes-le-Château*, in which he revealed the extraordinary history of the village and that two encoded parchments refer to the Merovingian king, Dagobert II, and to the legendary treasure of Sion. This book has been the foundation for many of the subsequent books on Rennes-le-Château; it is almost certainly the result of access to the missing archives. It was also in 1966 that M. Marius Fatin, owner of the château at Rennes, and himself an archaeologist and ardent Freemason, received a letter from the so-called International League of Antiquarian Booksellers in London informing him of the antiquity of his château and its illustrious past.

More light is thrown on the fate of some of the parchments in a document given to the authors of the *Messianic Legacy* by Pierre Plantard, at a meeting in May 1983. The document, officially notarized, contained a request to the French Consulate in London by Viscount Leathers, Major Hugh Murchison Clowes, and Captain Ronald Stansmore Nutting for permission to export three parchments from France. The text states: 'Three parchments whose value cannot be calculated, confided to us, for purposes of historical research, by Madame

James, resident in France at Montazels (Aude). She came into legal possession of these items by virtue of a legacy from her uncle, the Abbé Saunière, curé of Rennes-le-Château (Aude).'

This is not the only written reference to the parchments. In his *L'Énigme de Rennes* (1978), the Marquis Philippe de Chérisey makes an even more detailed revelation:

> . . . Saunière found it – and never parted with it. His niece, Madame James of Montazels, inherited it in February, 1917. In 1965, she sold it to the International League of Antiquarian Booksellers. She was not to know that one of the two respectable lawyers was Captain Ronald Stansmore of the British Intelligence Service and the other was Sir Thomas Frazer, the 'éminence grise' of Buckingham. The parchments of Blanche of Castille are presently in a strongbox of Lloyds Bank Europe Limited. Since the article in the *Daily Express*, a paper with a circulation of 3,000,000, nobody in Britain is unaware of the demand for the recognition of Merovingian rights made in 1955 and 1956 by Sir Alexander Aikman, Sir John Montague Brocklebank, Major Hugh Murchison Clowes and nineteen other men in the office of P.F.J. Freeman, Notary by Royal Appointment.

Finally, a press release on 22 January 1981 concerning the Priory of Sion and announcing Plantard's election to Grand Master, contains the following reference:

> . . . *les parchemins de la Reine Blanche de Castille decouverts par le Curé Saunière dans son eglise de Rennes-le-Château (Aude) en 1891.*
>
> *Ces documents vendus par la niece de ce prêtre en 1955 au Captain Ronald Stansmore et a Sir Thomas Frazer furent deposés dans un coffre de la Lloyds Bank Europe Limited de Londres.*
>
> . . . the parchments of the queen Blanche of Castille discovered by the priest Saunière in his church at Rennes-le-Château (Aude) in 1891.
>
> These documents sold by the niece of this priest in 1955 to Captain Ronald Stansmore and to Sir Thomas Frazer were deposited in a strongbox of Lloyds Bank Europe Limited in London.

These three sources, while concurring with the basic details of the sale of the parchments, do reveal some inconsistencies. First, there is the difference in the date given for the sale of the parchments, that can possibly be put down to a genuine misprint – 1965 for 1955. Second, though one of the versions states that the parchments were only loaned for the purpose of research, the others report their actual sale. Attempts to trace the alleged niece of Saunière, Madame James (actually Jammes) have revealed that she was indeed the daughter of Saunière's younger sister Bathilde (or Mathilde), who married a Jean Oscar Pages; Bertha Pages married Louis Jammes thus becoming Madame Bertha Jammes. But Madame Jammes would have been only nineteen years old in 1917; would her uncle have bequeathed her such a legacy? She was reportedly upset with her inheritance, unable to appreciate its value. If all these accounts were fabricated at the same source – as is claimed by the sceptics – one would not expect to see the differences. It is actually more likely that these are genuine reports with accidental errors. However, from the British names quoted here (all genuine characters who were involved with wartime Intelligence activities), and from other documents concerning the export of the parchments, these reports certainly draw attention to a connection with British Intelligence, which along with the Special Operations Executive (SOE), was very active in France during the war and for some time afterwards.

By some coincidence, an apparently different Madame James appears in an another context elsewhere in this story. In the book *Opération Orth* (1989) by Jean Robin, Madame James is mentioned as someone associated with the literary contributions of Abbé Hoffet, René Guenon and Charbonneau-Lassay to the magazine *Regnabit*, circulated in the 1920s, and its successor, *Le Rayonnement Intellectual*, which published a curious mix of ultra-traditional Catholic views with those of esoteric-occultists. In fact, Madame James wrote that certain circles desired to: '*de ramener l'ordre dans le chaos, en oeuvrant pour un nouveau règne affirme du spirituel sur le temporel ou, plus*

schematiquement, de l'esprit sur la matiere' ('. . . to reduce the
order into chaos, in working for a new kingdom affirming the
spiritual over the temporal or, more graphically, of spirit over
matter'). Here we have confirmation of the thread that runs
alongside that of the parchments, and that of the secret of the
Visigothic-Merovingian treasure: one of occult politics – subversive activity engaged in by the Priory of Sion, tacitly
encouraged by the traditionalist wing of the Catholic Church,
and inherent in French public life over several centuries.

As we shall see, this continues into the present era through
the presidency of François Mitterrand, who even portrayed
himself as a man of mystery. *The Death of Politics* (1994) by
John Laughland is a remarkable and revealing analysis not only
of his political career, but also of the unseen influences of his
close circle of old friends. Always something of an anomaly as
a Socialist, he was considered by many of his contemporaries
as a monarch rather than a president. This chapter has preoccupied itself more with the politics of secret societies and the
ownership of documents than the location and control of
the treasure we have been tracing; however, it is within the
activities of the secretive hierarchy of French government that
the trail of the gold will again reappear.

MITTERRAND'S INNER CIRCLE
AND THE GOLD OF ORADOUR

Mitterrand's Friends · Nazi Funding · Jewish Deposits
General Lammerding and Das Reich · A Gold Hijack
Massacre at Oradour

In 1881, John Emirate Acton, 1st Baron Acton, coined the adage that 'power corrupts and absolute power corrupts absolutely'. In the context of this story, it would be more applicable to say that treasure, wealth, and hard currency are the most corrupting influences. Sadly for the French people, this adage can be accurately applied to at least one former president of the Republic and his circle of close friends.

Elected in 1981, François Mitterrand became the first Socialist president of France. In pursuing what was in effect a continuation of the cause of a French national renewal, Mitterrand appeared to avoid any specific ideology and pursued whatever policies would maintain him and his regime in power. The new French administration acted in striking contrast to its neighbour across the Channel. The British Conservative government of the time showed little interest in conserving Britain's European-based heritage, preferring instead to look to America as a model. Mitterrand, on the other hand, was attracted to a model of French culture that had more in common with pre-Revolutionary tradition than a modern liberal-democratic Republic, and, like most other French politicians, viewed with alarm the encroachment of American capitalistic culture. This substantial difference in attitude and loyalties has contributed to a general political mistrust, by the French and other members of the European Union, that Britain is little more than an agent for the United States.

Initially promising a radical change of life for French citizens, Mitterrand's presidency also talked of the power of a 'tranquil force' which came to mean little more than stagnation for most areas of French life, but also attracted the accusation of creating a climate in which opportunism, corruption and favouritism could flourish. Certainly, Mitterrand assumed a persona that was far less of a dynamic, modernizing and determined politician, but more of a calculating, conservative and complacent monarch. Initially attracted by extreme right-wing doctrines, exemplified by those of Marshal Pétain and the Vichy government, he gradually appeared to move towards the Socialist left. But despite his Socialist stance and public condemnation of unfettered capitalism, his close friends and colleagues, all remnants from his past, prospered under his administration – some are even alleged to have been involved in the most blatant financial scandals. Taking little account of the political embarrassment of maintaining some of these old friendships, Mitterrand not only remained loyal, but used various strategies within his power to protect them from disgrace or even prosecution. The French public had long accepted that corruption was rife among their politicians, but the activities of some within the Mitterrand regime exceeded even this pessimistic view of their leaders. What motivated such loyalty by the President to these shadowy friends?

René Bousquet, a member of the Pétainist Vichy government, appeared to be a most curious choice of friend for a man claiming a Resistance past and affirming Socialist values. Born in south-west France, at Montauban, where his father was a barrister, he then went on to study law in Paris, before making his mark in the Vichy administration. Resolutely anti-Semitic and anti-Marxist, his enthusiastic support for Pétain gained him the Légion d'Honneur at the age of twenty-one and later, during the Battle of France, the Croix de Guerre. Appointed Chief of Police, Bousquet excelled himself in rounding up and deporting 76,000 immigrant Jews to Germany, earning the praise of the Nazi high command in the process. On 22 July 1942, he went to meet General Oberg and other SS officers and concluded an agreement to allow the Vichy government to continue to take responsibility for law and order in France in exchange for the continued harassment and deportation of foreign Jews. Considered a cultured and brilliant professional, the resolute nationalist Bousquet faced up to the Germans; even Himmler, after a five-hour meeting in August 1943, recognized that Bousquet was a 'precious collaborator' and 'would play a leading role in French policy'. Accused of war crimes, he was brought to trial in June 1949, but Mitterrand, who was then Minister for Information, proposed an amnesty for all collaborators just two days into Bousquet's trial. According to Paul Webster in his book *Pétain's Crime* (1990), the British were said to have intervened in the lifting of the nominal sentence of 'five years' national disgrace' given to Bousquet because of his alleged work for the British Intelligence service.

Bousquet supported Mitterrand's electoral campaign against Charles de Gaulle in 1965. At that time, Bousquet controlled the influential newspaper *La Dépêche du Midi*, which had been the first to reveal the strange story of the Abbé Saunière. Once again accused of war crimes, this time by the Nazi-hunter Serge Klarsfeld, Bousquet was due to attend a trial in June 1993; two days before, however, he was assassinated. This gave rise to much speculation. It was said to be almost impossible to 'shoot' him with a camera, let alone gain access to his apartment and shoot him in cold blood. Klarsfeld later remarked that he believed Mitterrand had ensured Bousquet never came to trial; yet once Bousquet was dead, Klarsfeld dropped all investigations. What was it that Bousquet held over Mitterrand that had bought his protection? Was it Mitterrand's ambiguous wartime career, or was it some other deeper secret that they shared?

In 1992, Mitterrand reluctantly appointed Pierre Bérégovoy, one of his Socialist ministers, as Prime Minister in order to quell the growing public storm over corruption within governmental circles. Bérégovoy, one of the only politicians to have retained an untainted public image, announced that after probing investigation he would reveal the names of the guilty politicians. Never having been admitted to the inner circle, Bérégovoy had already tasted the ruthlessness of Mitterrand when, in 1981, the president removed him from a prestigious 'grace and favour' apartment which had been his right as Secretary-General of the Elysée Palace. The apartment was then granted to François Durand de Grossouvre, a close friend and advisor. Bérégovoy innocently accepted a loan of 1 million francs, in 1986, from Roger-Patrice Pelat, one of Mitterrand's closest friends, to purchase a new apartment. This decision would come back to haunt him; it is most likely that the loan was deliberately set up as a a means of future embarrassment. It was obvious that Bérégovoy's appointment as Prime Minister was only a public relations exercise; he was never going to be allowed to penetrate the secrets held by Mitterrand's inner circle. On 1 May 1993 Pierre Bérégovoy apparently committed suicide. He was found on the bank of a rural canal, shot in the head and barely alive. In spite of adverse weather conditions, a decision was taken to transport him by helicopter, not to the local hospital nearby, but to the Val-de-Grace in Paris. Initial reports were that he had died outright; the later official version claimed that he passed away in the helicopter.

Almost a year later, on 7 April 1994, François Durand de Grossouvre, an *éminence grise* during Mitterrand's presidency, was found dead with a gun in his hand, shot in the head at his office in the Elysée Palace. A former Vichy collaborator before entering the Resistance in 1943, Grossouvre had been closely involved in the financing of Mitterrand's election campaigns. However, his later verbal attacks against others of Mitterrand's inner circle brought about his fall from grace; it must be asked whether his inside knowledge had indeed become a dangerous liability. In fact he had repeatedly warned two journalists that he was in danger of being killed.

One of those who would certainly have been exposed by Bérégovoy was another of Mitterrand's lifelong colleagues from his war years. Though he had died in 1989, at the height of a financial scandal of insider trading called the Péchiney affair, Roger-Patrice Pelat continued to cast a long shadow over Mitterrand's presidency. Accused of having been at the heart of a number of irregular financial dealings involving illegal share trading, secret Swiss bank accounts and shell companies, telephone tapping and payments to people close to the president, Pelat appears to have manipulated, controlled and financed Mitterrand's political career. In September 1993, an extensive article in the popular newspaper *Minute*, was dedicated to investigating the theft of Pelat's papers. Somewhat inconclusive, the article raises a number of complex issues that may never be fully penetrated, but certainly involve the highest level of government; the exact nature of the papers has never been revealed.

But the allegations laid against Pelat were not confined to financial impropriety. During his time as a POW with Mitterrand and the two politicians from the Aude, Pelat also learned of the curious history of Rennes-le-Château. He was to later accompany Mitterrand on his election campaign visits to the village where, on one occasion, in March 1981, they were photographed on top of Saunière's Tour Magdala. Furthermore, in an internal circular of the Priory of Sion it is alleged that Pelat had been its Grand Master and had resigned only one month before his death on 7 March 1989. The letter also refers to Pelat 'as an honest and just man who was tricked by certain American initiates'; this was a direct reference to the Péchiney affair, which involved the New York Securities Exchange Commission investigation of insider trading of shares, by Pelat and others, of an American company called Triangle. This becomes even more plausible in the light of the claim that the Priory of Sion is said to have infiltrated key positions in the financial worlds of New York and London, and that since the early 1980s a split had occurred between the American and European factions of the Priory.

These links between François Mitterrand, Plantard, and Rennes-le-Château, and the claimed affiliation of one of his oldest friends to the Priory of Sion are, at the very least, remarkable coincidences; more probably, they are part of a greater conspiracy. It is hardly credible that someone of the make-up of Roger-Patrice Pelat, having heard of the great secret of the treasure, would not have taken all possible steps to pursue it.

It is possible that among his missing papers were some of the ancient Dagobert/Saunière/Chefdebien documents that referred to the treasure deposits in the Corbières. As Grand Master of the Priory of Sion, he could have acquired these from the other members who had managed to pillage the library of Doctor Paul Courrent, who had died at Embres-le-Castelmaure in 1952. Due to the cloak of secrecy that shrouds these matters, it is not known for certain what actions the Priory has taken since acquiring the archives. However, the enterprises and fortunes of its most prominent member, Pierre Plantard, were to include both the buying up of several significant parcels of land near Rennes-le-Bains and the transfer of a large quantity of gold to Switzerland in 1952. This may well have been just the tip of the iceberg.

Two other Pelat associates, Antoine Gayraud, the old mayor of Carcassonne, and Antoine Courrière were shown, in Chapter 14, to have met Mitterrand during his spell as a POW. Having initiated him into the curious secret history of Rennes-le-Château, both were to be rewarded with successful political careers. But these were not Mitterrand's only contact with the secret of Rennes-le-Château and the Priory of Sion, for at the very centre of his entourage was André Rousselet, who had been the Chef de Cabinet des Prefets de L'Arriège et L'Aude in 1944. That is, he was a chief administrator of the very region in question. Often accompanying Mitterrand on his journeys, Rousselet remained close to his old friend until the end; so it was not unexpected to find him named as the executor of Mitterrand's will. More surprising is his family relationship to Pierre Plantard, a Grand Master of the Priory of Sion. André Rousselet had adopted a daughter named Chantal, who in April 1964 married Jean Maurice Marie (known as Yannick) Plantard, the son of François Plantard, an engineer at Aéro-Spatiale and a cousin of Pierre. Chantal and Jean had a son Christophe Plantard, who works at Canal Plus, the broadcasting company founded in 1984 by his father-in-law, André Rousselet. In 1998 Marcel Plantard, who owns a photographic shop in Nantes, confirmed that his cousin Pierre has remained in regular contact with the rest of his family.

★　★　★

Several financial scandals implicating Mitterrand's inner circle of close friends have surfaced since his death in 1995; some are still subject to judicial enquiry. But there is one particular conspiracy of silence at the highest level of French government that concerns us in this investigation: the true events that led to the destruction of the village of Oradour-sur-Glane, and the massacre of its inhabitants by the Nazis, on 10 June 1944. Though some of the details remain unconfirmed, and many of those alleged to have been involved remain silent, sufficient information has been uncovered to reveal an extraordinary cover-up over this tragic incident.

Oradour-sur-Glane lies 21 km north-west of the town of Limoges, capital of the Haute-Vienne département. Straddling the River Vienne, Limoges is a lively commercial town and a major railway intersection on the mainline from Toulouse, 250 km away in the south, Angoulême and Bordeaux in the west, and from Clermont-Ferrand and Switzerland in the east. The rail network was used extensively by the Nazis for military purposes. But it was also not uncommon for them to use it to transport gold and other valuables, plundered from occupied territories, normally to Germany or Switzerland. Subjected to frequent attacks by résistants – or those who masqueraded as such – these treasure trains contained what could be conveniently considered to be 'spoils of war' of their new owners. Such attacks were known to have taken place in the region of Limoges.

But the trail of events that led to the destruction of Oradour-sur-Glane originated at Montauban, near Toulouse, with the activities of General Lammerding, commander of the 2nd SS Panzer Division *Das Reich*. According to Col Howard Beuchner, the Division was visited in April 1944 by the SS Reichsfuhrer Himmler, and was involved in the transportation of gold and treasure recovered from the mines and caves of Montségur, the Arriège and the Corbières.

Many SS officers are known to have acquired substantial personal wealth through wartime activities, and to have stockpiled their gains in Switzerland or other safe areas. In fact, it was reported in the *Daily Telegraph* that Himmler himself maintained an account (No. 54941) at the Zurich branch of Credit Suisse. It appears that General Lammerding was no exception and had managed to acquire a large quantity of gold for himself during his Division's three-month stay at Montauban.

Within hours of the Allied landing in Normandy on 6 June 1944, General Lammerding and his mighty tank division was ordered to travel north to the Normandy beaches in support of the defence against the Allied invasion. The 750 km journey by rail, expected to take about three days, actually took over three weeks due to highly successful Resistance activity that dogged their progress. As a result of the ingenious sabotage of the flat-bed railway cars, necessary for transporting the tanks, the Division was obliged to travel by road. This necessitated the huge force to be divided into three sections, each taking a different route north. Accompanying the 300 tanks, hundreds of supporting vehicles and 15,000 men, was a small separate convoy consisting of a car carrying the senior officer Lieutenant Walter, an armoured half-track with ten SS soldiers, and a large truck. Ostensibly carrying the regimental records, the truck was later said to have been transporting a treasure that included at least 600 kg in gold ingots.

The activities of General Lammerding and *Das Reich* had been closely monitored by British Intelligence and local agents, who advised SOE operatives, Resistance units, and Maquisards (Resistance activists) as to what actions should be taken to sabotage their movements. It is thus possible that the possession of treasures and gold bullion by Lammerding and his officers was known by at least some local résistants.

On Friday 9 June this part of the convoy arrived at the small town of St Junien, some 30 km west of Limoges along the River Vienne. The town was buzzing with activity since the first battalion of the Regiment *Der Führer* (of the Division *Das Reich*) had already arrived. The regiment was regrouping under the command of Major Dickmann, who had established his HQ at the Hôtel de la Gare having arrived at 10.30am that day. The deaths of two German soldiers, the sabotage of the railway bridge over the Vienne, and the knowledge that there were possibly 1800 Maquisards in the town, added to the general tension. As senior officer, Major Dickmann was responsible for the security of the convoy and its precious cargo, and would quite naturally have ensured it was properly guarded, but without attracting undue attention.

Most of what took place in St Junien during the rest of the day has been pieced together from eyewitness accounts, but with one significant omission; the fate of the truck and its cargo. In stark contrast, the tragic events that took place the next day at Oradour-sur-Glane, have been vividly recorded by M. Robert Hébras, the only surviving resident of the village.

At 2pm, a detachment of about 120 SS soldiers from St Junien, under the direction of Major Dickmann, arrived at the village. A senior officer, Captain Kahn, demanded that all the inhabitants should assemble in the main square. On the pretext of looking for 'prohibited merchandise', Dickmann briefly questioned the Mayor and several individuals. The 648 residents were then divided into groups. The soldiers first led the women and children to the church; then the men, split into six groups, were led to various stone barns within the village. Having ordered his soldiers to shoot the men in the legs, Major Dickmann interrogated each wounded man in turn; obviously without success. He then ordered a complete search of the village, before the systematic demolition of all the buildings. Within two hours the village had been destroyed, all but five men and one woman had been shot, and the church and barns set on fire. The Germans went away empty-handed.

The motive for this atrocity has been generally accepted as a reprisal for local Resistance activity, such as the death of the two soldiers at St Junien. But this explanation doesn't answer at least two questions. Why was the backwater village of Oradour selected by the Nazis? And why did they take so much trouble to search and demolish all the buildings in such a systematic manner?

The first public hint that there may indeed have been an alternative motive came to light in 1988 with the publication of *Oradour: Massacre and Aftermath*. In this book, Robin Mackness describes his extraordinary and dramatic experience while engaged as a freelance investment manager to a bank in Switzerland. In 1982 – the year after Mitterrand's election – Mackness was stopped by French customs officials on the *autoroute* outside Lyon, and arrested for being in possession of twenty 1 kg gold bars; some of these were stamped with the Nazi initials RB – Reichsbank.

He had been asked by the Swiss bank to contact a client in Toulouse, who wished to deposit some gold bars. Due to the client's nervousness, Mackness was requested to transport the gold personally to Evian, from where it would be taken illegally across the lake by another agent, into Switzerland. During a two-hour meeting, the client, whom Mackness renamed Raoul to protect his identity, had related the story of how he came to possess the gold and the events that led to the massacre at Oradour.

Having trained as a Resistance activist, Raoul was ordered to execute acts of sabotage designed to delay the progress of the SS Panzer Division *Das Reich* on its journey north to Normandy. Following the Division from Toulouse, Raoul eventually arrived south-west of Limoges, where he took charge of six young Maquisards. They were ordered to travel as fast as possible to the village of Chaillac, situated on the opposite bank of the river Vienne facing St Junien. He was told that just outside the village of Chaillac they would find a barn, owned by the foreman of a local glove factory, in which they could shelter safely and where they would receive further instructions.

His orders were to sabotage a railway bridge near the village of Nieul, north of Limoges. At nightfall on 9 June, Raoul and his colleagues left the barn to carry out their mission. To avoid the intense Nazi activity at St Junien they crossed the river at St Victurnien, then cycled north on the road leading towards Oradour-sur-Glane. It was at some point along this road that he claimed to have encountered the small convoy that had left St Junien at midnight, travelling under cover of darkness. A fierce fight ensued in which all but Raoul, and a German, who somehow managed to run away, were killed.

It was when he looked into the back of the truck that Raoul discovered the gold ingots, packed in thirty small wooden boxes. Each about the size of a shoe-box, they contained a total of around 600 kg of gold. After some reflection, he decided to bury the gold just inside a field by the side of the road. Having completed the task, he doused the wrecked vehicles and all the corpses, both French and German, in petrol and set them alight. He then cycled away, determined to return to recover the gold once the war was over.

Finding that the gold had been hijacked, Major Dickmann immediately called a crisis meeting with his senior officers. Noting that Oradour-sur-Glane was the nearest village to the place of ambush, they naturally concluded that the gold may well have been concealed somewhere in the vicinity. It was thus that the detachment of SS soldiers arrived at the village on the afternoon of 10 June looking for it.

Research by Mackness for his 1988 book confirmed certain key parts of this account, but all aspects of the gold hijack itself rely totally on Raoul's testimony. For whatever purposes, it appears that Raoul may have been somewhat economical with the truth; there is the matter of his true identity, the name by which he introduced himself to Mackness would obviously have been a pseudonym. But from whom did he wish to remain anonymous?

Roger-René Dagobert recalls that, at the age of fifteen, he had watched the armoured vehicles of *Das Reich* drive past his father's house in Limoges. His father, René, the director of the local undertakers, was given the job of removing and burying the bodies after the massacre at Oradour. In the course of this unpleasant task, he noticed that all the men had been shot in the legs, leading him to conclude that they had been tortured before being killed. But why would they have been?

Despite a reluctance to speak publicly, some locals do acknowledge that theft of gold may be at the heart of the Oradour mystery. But Raoul's version of events is problematic: not one local inhabitant ever found evidence of a burned-out convoy on any road in the area. Certainly, there would have been extensive wreckage; the road surface and verges would have been unmistakably marked and deformed as a result of the heat of the fire. Even a well-equipped clear-up unit would not have been able to remove all traces. Nobody in the area detected the smoke and smell generated by the burning wreckage, tyres, and corpses – and this in a rural area where people habitually rise early, especially in June. One must therefore conclude that a hijack of the gold was executed at a location and in a manner that left no traces. But if a hijack did not take place as Raoul reported, then why did the SS carry out the destruction of Oradour?

Roger-René Dagobert offers another solution. He suggests that the hijack of the lorry and the theft of the gold were far from spontaneous actions, but had instead been carefully planned. There were many independent 'rogue' Maquis units, loosely connected to de Gaulle's Secret Army, whose actions, sometimes motivated more by self-interest than patriotism, were often overlooked provided they continued to harass the Germans. Raoul may well have belonged to one of these. It is likely they stole the gold either in St Junien, or while in transit on the southern approach road that passes by Chaillac, and took it to the barn for safe keeping.

Whichever account one accepts, the theft must have been accomplished without drawing immediate attention from the Germans or their response would have taken a different course. By midday of 9 June, Major Dickmann had ordered the whole population of St Junien to produce their identity papers for inspection at the town hall. Meanwhile, Gestapo officers – assisted by Jean Filiol, head of the Limoges *Milice* – were investigating the Resistance activity of the previous days. The next morning, it appears that two local informers told the Gestapo that they should move their search for partisans to Oradour; evidently to draw attention away from St Junien. Shortly afterwards, Major Dickmann sent a company of specialist sappers to Oradour with orders to look for 'prohibited merchandise'.

Confirmation that others, besides Raoul, knew of the gold comes from Roger-René Dagobert himself. The Gourt brothers, who owned the glove factory at St Junien and the barn at Chaillac, had told him confidentially, in 1962, that the Oradour massacre was connected to the theft of Nazi gold. This was some twenty years before Raoul related his story to Robin Mackness. The manager of the information department of Chaillac's Mairie confirmed, in 1998, that Resistance activists had indeed used the barn in June 1944. Since the Gourt brothers owned the barn, it is most likely that they were fully aware of Raoul's plan, if not actually involved in it. There have even been hints that it was the Gourts who informed the Gestapo about Oradour, no doubt to protect themselves.

Pierre and René Gourt moved from St Junien in 1946, evidently with some new and unexplained wealth. Settling in Nantes, they bought and refurbished two shops (of which Roger-René was the architect) and later became a major outlet for ready-to-wear clothes supplied by the prestigious Yves St Laurent. Intriguingly, the managing director of Yves St Laurent was Pierre Bergé, a close friend of André Rousselet and François Mitterrand.

But there are yet more connections between some of Mitterrand's tight circle of friends and the events that took place in Limoges, St Junien, and Oradour. Prior to their arrival in Limoges in 1943, the Dagobert family had lived in St Nazaire at the mouth of the Loire, until forced to move to avoid the massive Allied bombing of the naval dockyard. As manager of the local undertakers, and as a member of a Masonic lodge, Libre Pensée, Roger-René's father was well acquainted with many other locals, including those who worked in the dockyard. Employed as engineers at St Nazaire were François Plantard and Eugène Deloncle, both members of the Société Anonyme des Chantiers et Ateliers de St Nazaire-Penhoet. François Plantard, as we have seen, was the father of Yannick who married the adopted daughter of Mitterrand's friend, André Rousselet. Eugène Deloncle ran the extremely militant right-wing group La Cagoule, to which Mitterrand is said to have belonged before the war. Furthermore, one of Deloncle's nieces was to marry François Mitterrand's brother, Robert. Another prominent member of La Cagoule was Jean Filiol, the same *Milice* chief implicated in the Oradour affair. Jean Filiol and François Mitterrand, both born at Jarnac, were close friends.

Yet another of Mitterrand's inner circle had connections with Limoges and the Oradour incident. Roland Dumas, alleged to have profited from clandestine Resistance activities, was to become an important government minister (President of the Constitutional Council) and a close confidante of Mitterrand. His father Georges, a financial administrator at the

Limoges town hall, was also responsible for the local Resistance. On 3 March 1944, denounced by a Gestapo collaborator, Georges was arrested and shot for Resistance activities. However, it is suggested in *Les Puissance du Mal* (1996) by Jean-Edern Hallier, that he was actually shot for acts of brigandage in the Haute-Vienne, where trains carrying gold were frequently attacked. Hallier's version may receive some support from an article published in *Le Monde* on 18 June 1998. It reported that during a recent judicial enquiry in which he was a witness, Roland Dumas informed the judge that the five gold ingots, which he had sold in 1992, had previously belonged to his mother. It is difficult not to believe that these were actually part of the 'spoils of war' acquired from the Nazis by his father.

But Jean-Edern Hallier further reveals that during the war the Dumas family gave shelter to the Felderbaums, a Jewish family that had originally fled from Austria. According to former Capitain Paul Barril in his *Guerres Secrètes à l'Elysée* (1996), Joachim Felderbaum formed a lifelong friendship with his contemporary, Roland Dumas. After the war, Joachim adopted the name Jean-Pierre-François, and became a very wealthy financier in Switzerland. It has been reported in the French press that he had been involved in a number of financial scandals, though he has always been quick to refute these accusations. In one lawsuit brought about by two associates of the Bank Romande, he confided his defence to two lawyers Georges Dayan and François Mitterrand. Another lawyer, Roland Dumas, appeared as a character witness. Despite his dubious reputation, Jean-Pierre was later said by investigating journalists to have exerted a strong influence in government circles and to have acted as Mitterrand's personal financial adviser.

With such close links to those directly or indirectly involved with the tragedy of Oradour and the mystery of the missing gold, it is not surprising that Mitterrand should have taken steps to ensure that the truth was never made public. He was a major signatory to an amnesty granted in 1952 to Alsatian conscripted soldiers who had taken part in the Oradour massacre. Despite provoking outrage among those who lost relatives and friends at Oradour, the amnesty decision was ostensibly taken in the interest of French unity. (Alsace had been temporarily annexed by the Germans in 1940, but the Alsatians were always considered to be more French than German.) But it is just as probable that the French authorities did not want to risk any incriminating details about Oradour to be revealed. Mitterrand and his friends were always to maintain a wall of silence about this period, refusing adamantly to respond to requests to reveal the truth.

The arrest of Robin Mackness, in possession of gold ingots, presented the French authorities with a long-awaited opportunity to try to track down Raoul – and of course the whereabouts of the remaining stolen gold. His incarceration and continued interrogation must have been authorized at a high level; the customs contrived to prolong his eighteen-month sentence to twenty-one months. The great interest shown by his interrogators when Mackness revealed that he was en route to Annemasse suggests that they were also aware of the activities of the Priory of Sion and Plantard – who, as we have seen, admitted to having transferred a large quantity of gold to Switzerland.

Raoul's widow, in a later meeting with Mackness, denied the possibility of any alternative version of events to her husband's account – although the reliability of that denial itself is open to debate. But the extent of the cover-up operation following the Oradour incident, whatever provoked it, adds enormously to the probability of a high-level conspiracy. Given the personalities who would seem to be involved in the cover-up, there is the strong possibility that the Germans did indeed find something of rare and exceptional value in the Corbières; of which some could have been hijacked near St Junien.

Despite the evidence to the contrary from both Robin Mackness and Roger-René Dagobert, many Oradour locals deny that the massacre of the village had anything to do with the gold. Their place in this saga is as tragic victims, not participants, and their views must be respected. Others are convinced that the Germans had found something. Confirmation cannot of course be obtained from Nazi records, because they were held at the Reichsbank in Berlin and at the SS headquarters, both of which were totally destroyed by Allied bombing in early 1945. But there is the highly seductive evidence of the American Colonel Howard Buechner, even if some of his assertions appear a little far-fetched. And the visit from the top Allied commanders, generals Eisenhower, Bradley, and Patton, to the mine at Merkers does offer Buechner's account some credibility. However, in view of the continuing conspiratorial activities of members of the late president Mitterrand's administration, the Priory of Sion and other secret societies, it seems that the Germans did not succeed in finding anything significant from the real treasure of the Corbières – that of the ancient Temple of Jerusalem.

THE OCCULT WEB EXPOSED

Order of the Solar Temple · P2
Anti-Communism · Intelligence Services

THE ORADOUR COVER-UP is considerably more than just a conspiracy to conceal the theft of Nazi gold. It is a prime example of the abuse of power for self-interest. Using the influence of their positions, certain French government ministers have contrived to create an impenetrable cloak of secrecy around the incident; somewhat assisted by the laws restricting the investigative power of journalists. Occasionally though, the cloak slips.

Such strategies of secrecy are also regularly employed by groups and societies involved in criminal or politically subversive activities. Of course, not all secret societies have malevolent intentions, but their hierarchical structures and secretive procedures have made them particularly vulnerable to infiltration and manipulation by those with other agendas.

At the heart of the Rennes-le-Château affair is the Priory of Sion; its self-appointed role as guardian of the hidden treasure of the Temple of Jerusalem is intertwined with the goals that can be achieved through association with the world of occult politics. Rejecting the public democratic forum of mainstream politics, the Priory is pursuing a secret right-wing agenda, and has formed affiliations with other similar groups.

Publicly, it promotes a more innocuous and mystical agenda

designed to divert attention away from their true aims. The central claim in their *Dossiers Secrets* is that the Priory of Sion was founded early in the twelfth century to protect a dynasty that carried a specific royal bloodline with biblical associations. A bloodline that included Jesus, and that was shared by the Merovingian kings and their successors, the Counts of Razès. This 1950s fabrication has received considerable promotion through the publication, in 1982, of *The Holy Blood and the Holy Grail* by Lincoln, Baigent, and Leigh.

The Priory, since the early 1980s, has succumbed to division and infiltration, but the main branch still appears to be dedicated to aims that have much in common with the seventeenth-century Compagnie du Saint-Sacrement, and the nineteenth-century Hiéron du Val d'Or. These include the restoration of a popular constitutional monarchy under the religious authority of a French-controlled Catholic Church – in effect the establishment of a French Holy Roman Empire.

Interestingly, the Compagnie du Saint-Sacrement actually worked in opposition to both Louis XIII and XIV, and to the French statesman Cardinal Mazarin, the Vatican's representative in France. Born in Italy, Jules Mazarin was created a cardinal in 1641 on the recommendation of Louis XIII, despite having never been ordained a priest. Appointed Minister of State in 1653, he wielded enormous political power. The hostility of the Compagnie was rooted in two convictions. First, they rejected the legitimacy of the Bourbons to rule France, especially Louis XIV, the Sun King, who was almost certainly not the natural son of Louis XIII, who it was claimed by many at the time (including his personal physician) was impotent. Second, Cardinal Mazarin represented the papacy, which was perceived to be corrupt and not a worthy successor of Christ's mission. There were also close links between the Compagnie and the Jansenist Catholic Church. Championed by Nicolas Pavillon at Alet-les-Bains, French Jansenism appears to have been founded on a mutual desire to reform the Catholic Church in a spirit of traditional strict observance, in which France would supplant Rome as the world's spiritual centre in Christian terms.

Since the days of the Compagnie the political, cultural and economic composition of European countries has obviously changed dramatically. This change has necessitated an evolution in the policies adopted by its political successors. But the underlying philosophy of its heirs has continued to embrace the archetypes and symbols of the so-called chivalric age, largely rooted in the high Middle Ages. This explains why the symbols and references to Knighthood, Templars, and esoteric wisdom are so dominant in the later publications of the Order of Alpha Galates, the immediate precursor of the Priory of Sion. This symbolism, shared also by the Pétainist Vichy government and many of those with leanings towards the political right wing, has proved to have an enormous appeal, evidenced in proliferation of Masonic societies, neo-Templar, and other neo-Chivalric Orders in the nineteenth and twentieth centuries.

Four years before the emergence of the Priory of Sion in 1956, a group of occultists, among which were a famous alchemist, an industrialist and a film director, met at the ancient château of Arginy. They believed that Arginy, situated on the plains between the River Saône and Beaujolais, north of Lyons, had been the secret meeting place of the nine founding members of the Knights Templars. They also believed that part of the Templar treasure had been removed in 1307 from the Paris Temple, for safekeeping. It was taken to Arginy, along with artefacts and documents, and concealed in an underground vault, safe from the avaricious intentions of the French king, Philippe le Bel. This isolated castle became the birthplace, in 1952, of a secret chivalric society that was to experience a much publicized and extraordinary tragedy some forty years later.

French researcher and former architect, André Douzet, having conducted a comprehensive investigation into the strange history and activities surrounding Arginy, has published his findings, which provide a firm basis for this account. Under the leadership of the writer Jacques Breyer, who was residing at the old château owned from 1914 by the noble Marquis d'Uxeloup de Chambrun, Comte de Rosemont, this occult group constituted the new Ordre Souverain du Temple Solaire ('Sovereign Order of the Solar Temple'). In 1950, the Marquis had turned down an offer of 100 million francs, made by an anonymous English colonel, to purchase the château. Perhaps a parallel can be made with the mysterious International League of Antiquarian Booksellers who showed such interest in the château at Rennes-le-Château and its ancient parchments.

Having participated in psychic and occult rituals, the group claimed to have made contact with the spirits of the deceased Templars who then conferred on them the authority to continue their spiritual mission. As at Rennes-le-Château some years later, this heady mix of buried treasure, ancient wisdom and spiritual questing made Arginy the focal point for Freemasons, Rosicrucians and many others drawn to the occult and esoteric. Breyer, continuing his alchemical research for a further seven years, stayed on at the château, of which the oldest part was the circular Tower of the Eight Beatitudes, also known as the Tower of Alchemy due to the alchemical graffiti alleged to have covered its interior walls. Of those attracted to Arginy in 1959 was the head of the French Secret Service, Constantin Melnik, who reportedly participated in night-time ceremonies. Shortly after, reports appeared in the French press associating Melnik with a group of Catholic, monarchist, synarchist anti-Communists that called themselves Templars. Despite denials from Melnik of this involvement, the allegations have persisted and do appear credible when viewed against the overall picture.

What Breyer achieved in the course of his researches, which to the general public would seem to be at best naive, is unknown; though it is reported by André Douzet that psychic contacts enabled Breyer to discover a secret vault, passages and artefacts. Certainly his researches seem to have been more directed to the discovery of the Templar treasure, than any personal spiritual transformation of Breyer himself in the claimed tradition of the medieval alchemists. Despite a certain, possibly inevitable, scepticism from non-believers, the founding of the Sovereign Order of the Solar Temple was a genuine attempt to re-awaken the powerful chivalric archetype of the Templars. Rituals are known to have been practised at Arginy until 1973, though some nine years before, Jacques Breyer and three of his founding colleagues resigned (other evidence suggests, however, that they remained closely connected to the Order). In June 1966, the group elected a new Grand Master entitled 'Jean' – by coincidence the same subtitle applied to the Grand Masters of the Priory of Sion. Publicly launched at the mountain retreat of Sainte-Odile in Alsace, the twin to that at Sion-Vaudemont made famous by Maurice Barrès in *La Colline Inspirée*, the Sovereign Order of the Solar Temple was officially recognized by Prince Rainier of Monaco. The headquarters of the Order became established in the Principality, and came to have a profound and traumatic effect on the oldest ruling dynasty in Europe, the House of Grimaldi.

The founding of the Ordre Temple Solaire ('Order of the Solar Temple', or OTS), in about 1981, was to cause a great deal of confusion with the original Sovereign Order of Jacques Breyer. This confusion was fully exploited by the OTS leadership. The OTS evolved out of several other neo-chivalric and secret societies, all of which have connections with the early nineteenth-century neo-Templar Order, L'Ordre Souverain et Militaire du Temple de Jerusalem ('The Sovereign and Military Order of the Temple of Jerusalem'). This had surfaced under the control of Bernard Raymond Fabré Palaprat in the nineteenth century, as recounted in Chapter 6. For safe-keeping during World War II, the leadership and archives of this Templar Order were entrusted to a Portugese diplomat, the self-styled Count Antonio Campello Pinto Pereira de Sousa Fontes, on the understanding that he would step aside if the membership were to vote for a new Grand Master or Regent.

At a meeting in Paris in September 1970, Count Antonio nominated his son to succeed him as Grand Master. Rejected by the member knights – who elected a French-Pole, General Count Antoine Daniel Zdrojewski – the defeated Princeps Regens Count Fernando withdrew to Portugal and renamed the Order, The Supreme Military Order of the Temple of Jerusalem.

This split allowed the extreme right wing to forge alliances with, and even infiltrate, the Order. This allowed them to operate under the cover of an ostensibly harmless chivalric organization. The Order was covertly linked, from the late 1950s, with the Service d'Action Civique (SAC), a private Intelligence service founded by General de Gaulle, when France was threatened with civil war, and after the General had survived an assassination attempt by Organisation de l'Armée Secrète (OAS) terrorists during the Algerian crisis. The OAS had been formed from dissident soldiers and political extremists who supported the struggle for a French Algeria, and who accused de Gaulle and the politicians of treachery in promoting Algerian Independence. However, the SAC later became an extremist right-wing subversive group that established links with fascist and criminal organizations, including highly profitable drug-trafficking networks. In the 1970s, the Grand Master elect of the Sovereign and Military Order of the Templars, Count Zdrojewski, was in contact with Charly Lascorz, the former head of the SAC – not surprising, since the SAC had gained control of this Templar Order by this time.

Yet another dissident group broke away from the Sovereign and Military Order of the Templars, and established itself as an independent Order in Switzerland. Within a short time a faction led by Anton Zapelli, alleged to have been involved in financial irregularities concerning the Order, broke away from the main branch and formed the new *Grand Prieuré de Suisse*. He directed his recruitment campaign towards Masons, so it is not surprising that he drew some of his new members from the very secretive Masonic *Grand Loge Alpina*, which itself appears to have connections with the Priory of Sion and the Rennes-le-Château affair. Zapelli based his headquarters, perhaps symbolically, at the ancient town of Sion, in Switzerland and in an internal circular for members outlined two principal themes of the Grand Priory. There was a strong emphasis on banking and international finance, in which Zapelli's organization is said to have played an active part. The objective of a united Europe was also high on their agenda, with the assertion that the Grand Priory was dedicated to the fulfilment of an avowed mission of the original Templars – to unify Europe. Attempts to discover direct connections between Anton Zapelli and the other Chivalric Orders, Masonic groups, political parties or criminal organizations have been unsuccessful. However, it is hard to believe that a person of his character, position and interests was not fully aware of the activities of all these other groups, and did not form alliances when expedient to do so.

Meanwhile, a metamorphosis of the Sovereign Order of the Solar Temple was gradually taking place. Though the detail and exact chronology are unclear, certain events and the involvement of certain individuals are indisputable. A key figure was Julien Origas, a French former Nazi sympathizer who, having worked for the SS and the Gestapo in Occupied France, was arrested after the war and sentenced to five years in prison. Originally a Martinist and a member, under the Grand Master Zapelli, of the OSMTJ, Origas joined the Sovereign Order of the Solar Temple in 1965. Seven years later, having become Grand Master of an offshoot, called the *Ordre Renovée Temple* ('Order of the Renovated Temple'), he established links with the European-wide fascist network and other extreme right-wing organizations. At the wedding of Origas' daughter Catherine, in 1977, among the wedding guests were Jacques Breyer, Alfred Zapelli, and Joseph di Mambro who would later become a major influence in the Order of the Solar Temple. Di Mambro and Origas were friends and apparently made frequent and regular visits to Italy, where they maintained contact with the rogue Masonic lodge, P2. Some researchers have suggested that di Mambro had connections with high finance, the international business world and even the Mafia. Both Origas and di Mambro had also belonged to AMORC, the Ancient and Mystical Order of the Rosae Crucis – a Rosicrucian organization that despite offering legitimate 'occult and spiritual' teachings to genuine adherents, has also attracted those with more right-wing views.

In 1979, Joseph di Mambro met the Belgian, Luc Jouret, who was a charismatic figure lecturing on alternative medicine in the New Age circles of Europe and America. Their collaboration was to result in their taking control of the Order of the Solar Temple after the death, in 1981, of Julien Origas.

A British television documentary, screened on 29 December 1997, made the most incredible revelation concerning the Order of the Solar Temple. The Order had already received extensive press coverage three years before due to a series of mass suicides. But the programme revealed that the 'fairytale princess' Grace Kelly, the wife of Prince Rainier III of Monaco since 1956, had been an active but unsuspecting member of the Order.

Born in 1929, Grace Kelly had been a very successful Hollywood film star before her life in Monaco. Yet the experiences of living in the rather detached and unreal worlds of both Hollywood and Monaco may well have had a psychological impact on her; she was alleged to have suffered from depression. Having had a strict Catholic upbringing, she later found herself in conflict with her faith, and looked for new purpose in life. These factors appear to have made her vulnerable and susceptible to the overtures of those offering a new brand of spiritual nourishment.

A close friend and adviser of Prince Rainier, Jean-Louis Marsan, interested in esoteric ideas, was encouraged by Jacques Breyer to set up a branch of the Order of the Solar Temple at his villa in Monaco, and to become Grand Master. Here members could participate in a spiritual quest. Marsan convinced his followers that they were a spiritual elite whose secret know-ledge, gained through the Order, could save the world. From 1981, under the Grand Mastership of Luc Jouret, the members were subjected to subtle and sophisticated techniques, includ-ing the use of holograms, intended to convince them that they were really contacting spirits and seeing sacred objects and symbols – including the Holy Grail.

According to the singer Colette de Réal, an old friend of Princess Grace, she and the Princess attended strange, sexually orientated ceremonies presided over by Luc Jouret at a Solar Temple centre at Villié-Morgon. Situated close to Arginy, this old manor/farmhouse at Villié-Morgon was later bought, in 1983, by a group of Franciscan Friars who discovered a number of artefacts and pieces of unusual furniture there. These were remnants of the rites and rituals of the Order, which appeared to have been a blend of Christian and the occult. In her depressed state, Princess Grace was only one of many vulner-able to exploitation by an amoral and manipulative leadership, whose agenda was far from spiritual. Later, she was asked by Joseph di Mambro to donate 20 million Swiss francs to the Order; whether this was for self-enrichment or to be funnelled into a European fascist underground engaged in subversive activity is not known. What is known is that soon after, on 13 September 1982, the Princess was involved in a fatal car crash on the road leading to Monaco near the point of Cap d'Ail. A cloud of suspicion still hangs over this tragic event, and several details have never been adequately explained.

In 1994, the Order of the Solar Temple achieved world press attention following a series of mass suicides in Canada, France, and Switzerland. Among the dead were successful professionals, businessmen, and businesswomen – including two millionaires – and astonishingly, the two corrupt leaders di Mambro and Jouret. Even more surprisingly, the dead also included two men said to be members of the French Secret Service. Circumstances at the sites and examination of the charred bodies cast many doubts over the suicide theory; at least one 'suicide' victim had suffered several bullet wounds. Without doubt other forces were at work, not least to set the buildings on fire after the deaths. Yet another case where speculation will continue to be prolific but, despite a number of tantalizing details, the actual facts will probably never be known. Some investigators claim that there is no link between the original Sovereign Order of the Solar Temple, founded by Jacques Breyer and his associates in 1952, and the Order of the Solar Temple whose members died such tragic deaths. Outwardly, the objectives and practices of the two groups became quite different. However, it is clear that the OTS leadership was in effect infiltrated over a period of years by those with far right-wing political agendas, as well as those looking for personal financial gain.

It can be no coincidence that the same people crop up in a variety of Orders and neo-Masonic organizations, and that many of these have provable right-wing connections. Furthermore, these people normally attain high grades or positions that give them significant influence. But due to the Orders' administrative structure, they remain largely unaccountable to the membership – a potentially dangerous situation. Furthermore, a closer examination of higher grade personnel of Martinism, Order of the Solar Temple, AMORC, Sovereign and Military Order of the Temple of Jerusalem (Knights Templar), and other neo-Masonic and neo-Chivalric groups, reveals that many of them are connected with – if not actually members of – the 'modern' Priory of Sion. This highly secretive organization seems to attract those who have already proved their enthusiasm and commitment to other societies, and thus it would appear that the Priory invites only carefully selected members to join it.

It cannot be a coincidence that the mystery of Rennes-le-Château is inextricably bound up with the affairs of the Priory of Sion. But what makes Rennes so attractive to the Priory, and how has the Priory achieved such a prestigious position in relation to Rennes?

Although the mystery of Rennes-le-Château springs from the activities and unexplained wealth of parish priest Bérenger Saunière a century ago, it also involves more recent political and financial aspects, that are inter-twined. Many members of the Priory of Sion, and of the other secret societies, have had connections with the financial, business or banking circles, often at an international level. Though the extent and result of these contacts is not fully known, it must be acknowledged that money can buy power and influence, and that political control can be abused to create personal wealth. This combination has attracted many people throughout the centuries with less than honourable intentions; the extraordinary activities of the Italian Masonic lodge, P2 (with which Julien Origas and Joseph di Mambro, leaders of the Solar Temple, maintained regular contact) are no exceptions.

On 17 June 1982, Roberto Calvi, an Italian banker, was found hanging from scaffolding under Blackfriars Bridge, crossing London's River Thames. In the pockets of his suit were found four large stones, a forged Italian passport, and a wallet with £7000 in various currencies. Initially thought to be a suicide, rumours soon circulated that he had been murdered in order to prevent him from revealing the scandal linking the Vatican Bank to international Freemasonry. These rumours were fuelled by the revelation that the manner of Calvi's death displayed elements of Masonic symbolism, and that his briefcase, known to contain sensitive documents concerning the scandalous dealings between the Vatican Bank, lodge P2, and the suspect Banco Ambrosia, had vanished.

In his book *In God's Name* (1984), David Yallop shows that Calvi's death was just the tip of an enormous conspiracy that rocked the political world of Italy and has undermined the integrity of the Catholic Church. Lodge Propaganda Due (P2) was not a Masonic lodge in the strict sense of the word, but a secret group of influential and prominent people formed in order to take power, by a military *coup d'état*, if the Italian government were to be defeated by the Communists. In the face of a perceived threat of Communist expansion, the business and banking sectors, the Roman Catholic Church and right-wing political groups had supported the formation of extreme anti-Communist secret societies. In 1981, a huge amount of secret documents pertaining to P2 were seized by the police; they revealed a membership list of over 1000, but later Italian Military Intelligence investigations put the figure nearer to 2000. Among the members are said to have been 300 of the most influential men in what was dubbed the 'Free World' – some of which were also connected with the Sovereign and Military Order of the Temple.

P2 was one of three specific groups; the P1 lodge was set up in France, P2 in Italy, and P3 in Madrid. The Italian lodge was founded in the late 1960s, allegedly at the instigation of Giordano Gamberini, a Grand Master of the Masonic Grand Orient of Italy, who was a friend of Giulio Andreotti, the Christian Democrat politician. Andreotti headed seven post-war governments since 1972, and was formally charged with corruption and using his position to protect Mafia leaders from justice. Gamberini was also close to Francesco Cosentino who had strong connections with Vatican circles. To set up the lodge, Gamberini chose a successful Tuscan businessman and Master Mason called Licio Gelli, but it was persistently maintained by Roberto Calvi that the true head was Andreotti, despite his denials. However, the real inspiration behind the whole concept was no less than the CIA (itself dedicated to combating Communism), and Opus Dei, an extreme right-wing faction of the Catholic Church which has established itself as the major influence in the Vatican.

Born in 1919, Gelli had acquired a hatred for Communism by the age of seventeen and had fought for Franco in Spain. During World War II, he fought in Albania before serving the Nazi SS in Italy after which he worked as a double agent for the Nazis and partisan Communists. After the war he fled to South America where he became a close friend of the Argentinian dictator General Juan Peron. Following the defeat of

Peron in 1956, he continued to expand his power base throughout much of South America. Having become a Master Mason, Gelli was encouraged by Gamberini to conceive a new lodge of important people, and so the new lodge, Raggruppamento Gelli (popularly known as P2), was born. One of Gelli's most intimate P2 associates was an Italian lawyer, Umberto Ortolani, who, from his military intelligence experiences during World War II, had learned the value of acquiring and storing secret information. As a Catholic he also realized that the true centre of power in his country lay within the walls of the Vatican City, and so he set out to penetrate its long and hidden corridors of power. Manipulating his way into the politics of the election of Cardinal Montini as Pope Paul I, Ortolani soon became the recipient of papal awards and honours and extended his sphere of influence to helping his colleagues in P2. He even managed to get Licio Gelli, a non-Catholic, affiliated to the very Catholic but secretive Knights of Malta, and to obtain unrivalled access to the very heart of the Vatican.

Another prominent figure to join P2 was Michele Sindona. A lawyer who had profited from black-market trading during the war, he had become an expert in Italian tax laws, thus attracting the interest of the Mafia. Employed by the mighty Gambino Mafia family to launder a huge amount of illegally gained income, he was not slow in developing his own interests and became the director of a number of companies. In 1959, he agreed to help the Archbishop of Milan raise money for an old people's home. In raising the full amount of 2.4 million dollars he attracted the attention of Cardinal Montini, to whom he gave advice on a number of investments. What Montini may not have known was that Sindona had raised the money almost exclusively from the Mafia and the CIA. Covert financial support for the social activities of the Catholic Church was often given by the CIA in the hope that this would help deter the Italian electors from voting for Communism.

Within quite a short time, this shady, ambitious, Mafia-connected individual had become a key financial adviser to the Vatican, even acquiring a bank in Switzerland that still had 29 per cent Vatican ownership. Sindona's contacts became prolific and soon ranged from Mafia families, to Pope Paul I, his Cardinals Guerri and Caprio, and the head of Vatican finances Archbishop Marcinkus. Contacts in the political field included heavyweights such as Andreotti and President Nixon, and through his P2 membership, he maintained close links with the dictators that ruled many of the South American countries. Finally, he was able to establish intimate links with some of the world's most powerful financial institutions, Hambros of London, the Vatican Bank, Rothschilds of Paris, and Continental of Chicago. Those involved with P2 turned a blind eye to these and later illegal financial machinations, since the proceeds were thought to be used to support the anti-Communist mission of the lodge. The truth has since been revealed to be somewhat different, and involved the Vatican Bank not only in the loss of millions of dollars but also financial and ethical integrity.

By mid-1973, through an incredibly complex network of financial institutions and banks, Sindona had skilfully managed to swindle, launder and effectively steal vast amounts of money. At the same time he drew praise for his astute commercial enterprises – not least from the Vatican, for which he seemed to be a most accomplished financial adviser. But time was running out as the huge hole in his own banks had reached titanic proportions and was becoming increasingly difficult to conceal.

This massive shortfall was the result of siphoning out funds from his depositors' accounts into those of his associates, among which were P2, the Vatican, the Christian Democrats and right-wing South American governments. A series of financial crises in the USA and Italy exposed the weaknesses of Sindona's empire, and prompted the authorities to begin an investigation. By October 1974, an arrest warrant had been issued. Having taken out Swiss nationality some years before,

Sindona fled to Geneva to be safe from prosecution. Within a year his whole empire had collapsed with many banks owned or connected with him – including the Vatican Bank – either collapsing themselves or at least losing enormous sums; estimated damage totalled around 1.3 billion dollars. Finally, in 1980, Sindona was arrested, charged and despite an attempted suicide, sentenced to twenty-five years in prison.

The removal of Michele Sindona from the scene didn't stop his two P2 colleagues, Gelli and Calvi, from continuing business as usual; though by this time both feared the discovery of their criminal activities and went to great lengths to obtain protection. But the net was tightening and Gelli, lured to Switzerland on secret banking business in September 1982, was arrested and imprisoned awaiting extradition. Much to the embarrassment of the Swiss he escaped almost a year later and was spirited away via Monte Carlo to the relative safety of Uruguay.

A major factor in the collapse of the Sindona-Gelli-Calvi empire was the election in August 1978 of Pope John-Paul I. This apparently simple man was deceptively astute and within days of his election had called for a report into the Vatican finances – a request that sent shock waves through the Vatican Bank and alarmed the three 'investment advisors'. Thirty-three days later John-Paul I was dead, officially of a heart attack, but in the most suspicious of circumstances. The election of Pope John-Paul II, by contrast, effectively brought down the shutters on this scandalous affair, with an official denial by the Vatican of any liability. Sindona's former intermediary Archbishop Marcinkus, responsible for Vatican finances, remains under virtual house arrest within the Vatican; he risks prosecution for irregular financial dealings should he leave the sanctuary of the Holy City.

The astounding and illegal activities perpetrated by Sindona, Gelli, and Calvi within the shelter of P2 reveals a secret society out of control; a perfect example of how the inherent secrecy found in a lodge, and its network of influential people, can be readily exploited. In this instance, certain organizations from whom one would have expected greater integrity, wantonly assisted the three main conspirators. Justification for the suspect enterprises of P2 was the almost paranoid fear of Communist expansion in Europe – the same justification claimed by all those in the Vatican, and by the financial sector which supported Hitler, before and during the war.

An anti-Communist stance was also a mainstay of Vichy politics and as such drew support from the Catholic Church and others, all wishing to advance their own interests. With the war turning in favour of the Allies, many Vichy supporters joined the anti-Nazi Resistance and were sought out by British Intelligence and the Special Operations Executive (SOE) to co-operate in the campaign to disrupt the German occupation of France. Having worked with the Nazis earlier in the war, ex-Vichy résistants were recognized as having specialized knowledge of the German military, administrative and commercial structures. Naturally, these résistants had strong fascist or right-wing leanings, but since a large percentage of the Resistance activists were composed of disaffected Communists hoping to achieve power after the war, British Intelligence was naturally wary in its recruitment. As a result, the more right-wing elements obtained positions of authority in the Resistance and continued to exercise influence after the war. This situation is confirmed in the exposure of the people associated with the Priory of Sion and other neo-Chivalric organizations operating in Europe and America in the Rennes-le-Château affair.

The end of the war and the defeat of Hitler did not bring an end to the British and American Intelligence activities in Europe. In fact, the perceived Communist threat loomed larger than ever with the partitioning of Berlin. Of particular assistance to the Intelligence services was the extensive network of parish priests throughout Europe, with the help of the Vatican through its own Intelligence service.

The Knights of Malta, formerly the Catholic Knights

Hospitaller of St John, today have their headquarters at the Palazzo Malta on the Via Condotti in Rome. Utilizing its worldwide network of over 9000 full Knights and many thousands of lower-grade members, the Order has in effect become the Vatican's Intelligence service. Many prestigious names from other Intelligence agencies known to have had close links with the Vatican – especially from the CIA – have been made Knights. Other prominent individuals from many fields, including politics, the media, and entertainment, have been admitted to the order as a reward for their contribution to supporting and promoting the Catholic faith. Without doubt, the Knight's major role has always been political and until the fall of the Iron Curtain was directed to maintaining a defence against Communism.

British Intelligence (MI6) and the American Office of Strategic Services (OSS), forerunner of the CIA, with the co-operation of the host countries, established so-called 'stay-behind' operations code-named Gladio in Italy and Glaive in France. These were dedicated to a defence against Communism, though not so much an external Communist threat as the possibility of Communist governments being elected in western Europe. As with the Masonic lodges, the cloak of secrecy and the relative anonymity of members were exploited by agents with their own agendas. It was also not unusual for Intelligence operatives living in the twilight world of deception and unreality to be attracted to the occult, unable to properly discriminate between the worlds of fact and fiction. The teasing mystery of Rennes-le-Château and the lure of a fabulous treasure was evidently irresistible to some former résistants and Intelligence agents; their presence lurks in the shadows of this story.

An extensive investigation of the International League of Antiquarian Booksellers and its supposed traffic in ancient French parchments was undertaken by Lincoln, Baigent, and Leigh in their thought-provoking book, *The Messianic Legacy* (1986). Their examination revealed that all the people involved in this unusual incident had connections with the City of London, specifically with the Guardian Assurance company. It was quite normal during the war that many Intelligence operatives were recruited from insurance companies, their professional expertise considered to be invaluable in planning and executing sabotage missions. Furthermore, Lord Selborne, who is stated to be a central figure in the application to export the ancient parchments in 1956, was overall head of the SOE, whose headquarters at 64 Baker Street was only a stone's throw from the secret London headquarters of the Free French operatives. In a personal interview with Lord Selborne's daughter, his passion for maintaining the integrity of the British Empire and interest in the restoration of other European monarchies was revealed. She also mentioned that he had a great interest in genealogies, and had often enjoyed holidays around the Pyrenees.

Several members of the British-based Rennes-le-Château Research Group have been in contact with former members of British Intelligence each of whom had an interest in, and a wide knowledge of, the Rennes mystery. These agents also confirmed that many of their colleagues had been members of various occult, Masonic or chivalric societies. It is significant that the fabrication of the *Dossiers Secrets* and the disclosure of the incident concerning the export of the ancient Rennes-le-Château parchments are typical of almost any Intelligence Service's disinformation techniques. Furthermore, in 1998, a former British Intelligence officer told a Rennes researcher that he had personally seen a room within the Ministry of Defence in the 1970s dedicated to surveillance of the region of Rennes-le-Château. Yet another former Intelligence officer (better known as a highly successful comedian), the late Michael Bentine, warned members of the Rennes Research Group on several occasions that investigation into the affair of Rennes-le-Château could be dangerous. What did he know?

A further fingerprint of Intelligence activity appears in the claim that Pierre Plantard operated under the pseudonym of

'Captain Way' during the Algerian crisis of the mid-1950s. Though detail is sparse, it was inevitable that the stay-behind Intelligence Services would have viewed the deepening crisis with great alarm as France tottered towards civil war. The vacuum left by such political and social upheaval would have provided a great opportunity for both the right wing and the Communists to launch a bid for power. It is therefore not inconceivable that Plantard, with his known right-wing contacts and the political and social zeal displayed during his Vichy affiliation, could have been chosen to assist de Gaulle and the Intelligence agencies in controlling this potentially explosive situation. The selection of Annemasse as the headquarters of the Priory of Sion in 1956, of which Plantard was then General Secretary, appears again remarkably coincidental, since Annemasse is said to have been a centre for the anti-Communist 'stay-behind' operations of European Intelligence.

It is now time to look more closely at the policies and activities of another power player in this world of shadows. This is an organization that over nearly 2000 years has become one of the world's most powerful institutions: the Roman Catholic Church.

15

FAITH, POLITICS,
AND THE CHURCH OF ROME

The Vatican and Politics · Medjugorje Visions · Opus Dei
A Catholic–Jewish Accord

WITH A MEMBERSHIP OF around 900 million, the Roman Catholic Church serves about 90 per cent of all Christians, giving it immense power and influence throughout the world. Claiming inheritance directly from Jesus Christ – 'thou art Peter, and upon this rock I will build my church' reports New Testament Matthew 16: 18, 19 – it has assumed authority and responsibility for the spiritual welfare of all humanity. But apart from this statement, there is no evidence that St Peter did found this Church; or that this institution, evolved over twenty centuries, was ever the intention of Jesus Christ. (In fact, the known successor of Jesus – and the first Bishop of the Christian sect in Jerusalem – was his brother James.) This self-appointed guardian of mankind's spiritual needs has in reality devoted most of its time, effort, and money on political or corporate activities.

Pope Pius X said in 1903: 'We shall offend many people in saying we must of necessity concern ourselves with politics . . . [The Vatican] has not the right to separate political matters from the domain of faith and morals.' This would seem to be a sentiment that has driven Vatican policy for more than 1000 years, establishing the Church as one of the foremost political forces in Europe and many other parts of the world. A specific policy of the Church has been to engage in mutually advantageous relationships with national governments, cemented by the drawing up of concordats (or agreements). A simple expedient for survival, this has, however, made the Church vulnerable to exploitation, and placed it in the position of ending up supporting illegal and unethical regimes.

Thus as a silent partner and the hidden power behind many organizations, the Vatican has covertly provided finance, advice and influence to governments and monarchs alike, some of which have espoused ideologies that are in direct contradiction to the Christian message of Jesus Christ. The Crusades, the Inquisition, forced conversions from other religions, the secretive works of Opus Dei and support for brutal right-wing dictators are just some examples. Secret societies have also operated under the umbrella of the Catholic Church, while other more extremist factions have employed the strategies of such societies. Moreover, the Church, can be seen to be closely associated with some of the various groups involved with the quest for the treasure – not least the forerunners of the Priory of Sion. The interest of the Church however, is less likely to be motivated by the material worth of any gold, than by its symbolic value to itself and its adversaries.

According to the Church's own account, there has been an unbroken succession of 263 popes (and 35 alternative 'anti-popes'), since its founder Saint Peter. As Christ's Vicar on Earth, the pope is both supreme head and spiritual authority. A very frank review of the chequered history of the papacy has been compiled by Peter de Rosa and published as *Vicars of Christ – the Dark Side of the Papacy* (1988). Within this account of very human failings, sinister deeds and conspiracies of some of Christ's earthly agents, episodes that clearly reveal political manipulation of and by the Vatican emerge. In some cases, these have had a direct effect on European history.

The death of Pope Nicholas IV, in 1294, started a most bizarre series of five papal appointments, which ended with a pope who became one of the richest men in the world. In seeking to be elected, a wily lawyer, Cardinal Benedict Gaetani, instigated a ruse that backfired, resulting in the favouring of a hermit, Peter of Morone. Living in a mountain cave in the Abruzzi, Peter had earned a reputation for holiness. Brought to the attention of the cardinals by Gaetani, he became the preferred choice for the Holy Seat. Much to the disbelief of Cardinal Gaetani, who had expected the dirty old hermit to be rejected in favour of himself, Peter of Morone accepted their offer, taking the name of Celestine V.

Disapproving of the decadence of Rome, Celestine took up residence in Naples. There he lived in a wooden cell built within one of the enormous rooms of the Castello Nuovo, overlooking the sea. Continuing to follow his lifestyle of poverty and simplicity, and encouraging others of the Church hierarchy to do the same, he started to give away Church possessions. Alarmed by this turn of events, the cardinals conspired to rid themselves of this liability. Gaetani hatched a more successful scheme, and was duly elected.

Becoming Boniface VIII, Gaetani displayed characteristics of meglomania. He found himself embattled with the powerful Colonna family, against whom he launched a crusade. But a far more threatening adversary was the French king, Philippe le Bel, who matched Boniface in his avariciousness. Together with his chief minister, William Nogaret, Philippe devised a plan to kidnap the pope. The kidnap itself didn't succeed, but the pope was imprisoned for three days in his own filthy dungeon. Boniface never recovered from this traumatic experience, and later died in a miserable state of semi-madness, starvation and neglect.

He was succeeded by Benedict XI who, despite trying to appease Philippe, did not find favour with him and died mysteriously a year later – probably from poisoning. Philippe now took matters in hand and engineered the election of Bertrand de Goth, Archbishop of Bordeaux. Taking the name Clement V, he moved from Rome to Avignon, where he was firmly under the control of Philippe. The magnificent Palais du Pape, built about 1334, can still be seen close to the twelfth-century ruined bridge. The song the bridge has lent its name to, itself highlights the dissolute behaviour found in the Vatican during his reign. The relocation to Avignon was to prove especially useful when Philippe needed help to persecute the Knights Templar, in order to seize their wealth. After seven years of imprisonment and torture, Jacques de Molay, the Grand Master of the Templars, and Geoffroi de Charney, his deputy, were burned to death on a small island in the River Seine on 18 March 1314. Protesting his innocence to the end, Jacques de Molay is also said to have declared a dying curse on Philippe and Clement; both did die within the following year.

At Avignon, Clement was succeeded by Jacques Duese from Cahors. Taking the name John XXII, he was such a disgrace that no pope would take the name John for the next 642 years. Branded a heretic for his wayward views and outrageous behaviour, John attracted intense criticism for the immoral means he used to satisfy his greed. At his death in 1334, he was found to have amassed 25 million gold florins and an equivalent amount in precious gems and objects, making him the richest man in the medieval world.

The relationships between medieval and Renaissance popes and their contemporary monarchs appear to focus mainly on a mutual greed for power and wealth. But in the nineteenth and twentieth centuries, Vatican politics become more sophisticated and often involve internal struggles between competing factions, the two poles of which are liberal modernists and conservative traditionalists. Outside the Vatican, the power blocs of Europe have undergone continual change; papal affiliations continued to be guided only by that which would be best for the Catholic Church.

It was in 1885, some 550 years after the death of John XXII, that Bérenger Saunière became the parish priest of Rennes-le-Château. Aware of the changing political realities in Europe, the reigning pope, Leo XIII, encouraged his bishops to accept the French Republic and to work with it; ironically, he also reaffirmed the superiority of the Catholic faith over all others. However, there remained a powerful drive to restore the monarchy and the status of the Roman Catholic Church in France; this movement used the network of neo-Masonic and Chivalric lodges to influence the democratic process. In democratic countries, intolerance of other faiths was against the growing spirit of freedom of religion, but Leo was prepared to go further and even denied outright any spiritual authority claimed by the Anglican Church. Yet he was still considered a liberal; a perception reinforced when, against tradition, he opened the Vatican archives to inspection. Such inconsistency in the Church's policies and practices can also be found in its often-changing attitude to secret societies.

In 1864, Leo's predecessor Pius IX investigated the neo-Masonic Italian revolutionary organization, the Carbonari, and published his *Syllabus of Errors*. In this he condemned Socialism and secret societies. Yet despite their political activities, the Carbonari were only condemned for the practice of pagan rites and the preaching of religious freedom. Masonry was also singled out as being fundamentally anti-Christian; a view publicly endorsed twenty years later by Leo XIII, who claimed Freemasonry to be one of the secret agencies through which Satan was working to overturn Christianity. But at the very same time, memberships of the neo-Masonic Martinist lodges were comprised mainly of priests – such as Bérenger Saunière of Rennes-le-Château.

The late nineteenth century was the beginning of great social change; throughout Europe, the old empires were struggling for survival, remaining in name but waning in influence. The world was opening up to global trade; the industrial revolution had created new and enormous commercial opportunities, and the distribution of wealth was shifting from the old land-owning families to the bankers, entrepreneurs, industrialists, and speculators. This was a new world that had increasingly less time and need for the monolithic religious institutions of the past.

With so many opportunities for influence presenting themselves in this vacuum, it is not surprising to find among the proliferation of secret societies some which were little more than covers for subversive political activity. But there were also those comprising members who longed for a return to the pre-industrial world based more on the rural and village traditions than the new thrusting and competitive city culture. The occult revival illustrates the uncoordinated attempt by different groups – sometimes in competition – to recreate this 'rural' vision in which it was thought the individual would be more valued. Its adherents considered this to be a spiritual cause. It was against this background that Pope Leo XIII and his cardinals wanted to reassert the power and glory of the Catholic Church.

After twenty-five years as pope, Leo died in 1903 aged 94. The election of his successor was surprisingly eventful. Cardinal Rampolla, the favourite, was ahead after the first two rounds. But as the process for the final round was about to start, the Bishop of Cracow addressed the conclave with a letter from the Emperor Franz-Joseph. The head of the Austro-Hungarian Empire, into which Poland fell, had invoked his ancient privilege of right of veto. Cardinal Rampolla, as Leo XIII's Secretary of State, had been openly critical of the proposed triple alliance between the Austro-Hungarian, German and Italian Empires. He feared this would become too powerful a bloc, disturbing the balance of power in Europe. Though much aggrieved at this secular interference in Church affairs, the cardinals had no option but to withdraw their support for Rampolla, and Cardinal Guiseppe Sarto unexpectedly found himself elected as Pope Pius X.

Although a naturally good and simple man, Pius X was a traditionalist, and led a virtual crusade against modernism. His attitude to the Jews was very much in the same vein as that of most previous pontiffs and is succinctly recalled in Golda Meir's autobiography. She quotes him as saying: 'We cannot prevent the Jews going to Jerusalem, but we would never sanction it . . . The Jews have not recognized Our Lord; we cannot recognize the Jews.' He also gave his blessing, in 1909, to the formation of a society Sodalitium Pianum, also called the Fraternity of Saint Pius V, whose mission was to eliminate anyone suspected of liberalism. Known only by its initials SP or the coded La Sapinière, it was virulently anti-Semitic, anti-Masonic, anti-Republican, and even hostile to the Jesuits and the Scouts. Yet again, the Church was retreating from the modern world, pursuing policies more appropriate to the Middle Ages.

Hard-line traditionalists led by the rebel Archbishop Marcel Lefebvre some seventy years later, were pleased to recognize this bastion of conservatism with the founding of the Priestly Confraternity of Pius X. Threatened with excommunication in 1976, Archbishop Lefebvre continued to support the theological and political right wing. Yet despite his open defiance of Pope Paul VI, Mgr Lefebvre retained his position, leading some to believe that he possessed some secret that lent him protection. Could this secret have been connected to his affiliation – according to Priory documents – with the Priory of Sion?

* * *

The Bolshevik Revolution of 1914, and the subsequent creation of a USSR founded on the ideology of Communism, presented the Church with a new adversary. In the pursuit of state control, Communism denied the principle of individual human rights, included in which was the right to religious freedom and expression. The suppression of religious worship was an anathema to the Catholic Church, which now found itself engaged in a continuing crusade against Communism. This stance has at times cast doubts on the spiritual integrity of the Church, due to some of the dubious and unholy alliances it felt bound to make in pursuit of the 'wider' aim.

252 · Sacred Treasure, Secret Power

Elected in 1939, Pope Pius XII found himself confronted with the results of Nazi expansionism; yet faced with the choice of supporting either Communism or Fascism, the Church considered it to be more expedient to chose the latter. This decision created dilemmas for the Church that have still not been fully resolved more than fifty years later. Having already remained silent over Mussolini's persecution of the Jewish community, Pius astounded many of his own colleagues when he failed to condemn other Nazi atrocities. An underground network of priests and bishops did valuable and sometimes dangerous work to assist Jews and Christians alike to escape persecution, but the Vatican hierarchy, ostensibly to avoid a Nazi attack on the Vatican City, chose publicly to ignore the crimes of Hitler and the Third Reich. Whatever the justification, the lack of official papal condemnation of the Holocaust and other Nazi atrocities, has haunted the Catholic Church ever since, and in the eyes of many Christians and non-Christians has further dented its reputation.

The international standing of the Church did receive a boost from the enlightened papacy of Cardinal Angelo Roncalli, who in 1958 was elected Pope John XXIII. Known as the Good Shepherd, John, a selfless liberal, determined to drag the Church into the twentieth century. He initiated the Second Vatican Council, dedicated to reforming some delicate and thorny issues, such as birth control. But his softening attitude towards Communism drew intense criticism from the more right-wing faction of the Curia and earned him the reputation as a crypto-Communist. But his brief five-year reign is considered by many to have been a ray of light in the dark history of the papacy that was extinguished by his successor Paul VI.

Despite having some leanings towards left-wing elements, demonstrated by his strong anti-Franco stance, Paul VI was essentially a traditionalist and effectively stifled the initiatives being discussed in Vatican II. By reaffirming the traditional Catholic view of the Jews as the rejecters and killers of Christ, he reopened old wounds and divisions within the Church; but he delighted the right wing with his conservative attitude towards birth control, abortion, and other 'moral' social issues. But hidden hands were at work; the pope was by no means his own master.

Founded in Spain in 1928 by Josemaria Escrivá de Balaguer, Opus Dei has become the most powerful influence in the Vatican today. A Roman Catholic organization with an international membership estimated to be about 70,000, Opus Dei has a very formal hierarchy that exercises rigid control. A former Opus Dei member, Oxford University lecturer Dr John Roche has described the organization as, 'sinister, secretive and Orwellian'. Positioned on the right wing of Catholic politics, Opus has engaged in mutual support for the military dictatorships of South America and has been covertly active in the fight against Communism. Massively wealthy, it has established educational institutions through which it can promote its policies, and business and banking enterprises, which have then further contributed to its financial success.

With the fervour of Dominic Guzman, founder of the Dominicans and the feared Inquisition, and of Ignatius Loyolla, founder of the Jesuits, Escrivá pursued his mission with total dedication. His mission for Opus Dei was none other than the role of fundamentalist protector of the Catholic Faith. In effect, he wanted a twentieth-century renewal of the medieval Order of warrior-monks, the Knights Templar. This aspiration was so dear to its founder that the directorate of Opus Dei actually considered attempting to take over the prestigious and ancient Sovereign Military Order of the Knights of St John. Escrivá even managed to resuscitate an old family title, that of the Marquis of Peralta, which had belonged to a distant ancestor, in order to become eligible for the position of Grand Master. Although some members had already infiltrated the Order, the intended take-over never occurred. Opus was nonetheless determined to extend its sphere of influence as wide as possible, a determination that would appear to know no bounds, if the allegations surrounding the death of Pope John-Paul I are correct.

The reforming pope, John XXIII, was a disaster from the point of view of the ultra-conservative Opus Dei, and all attempts to influence his papacy failed; with the election of his successor Paul VI, they were able to regain some of their status at the centre of power. Though not entirely satisfied with the new pope, Opus Dei were generally able to continue with their mission, and to see the Church return to its more traditional stance. However, things were to change dramatically after his death.

The modernizing reforms initiated by John XXIII had struck a deep chord with a large section of the Church, who were disappointed when many of these never came to fulfil-ment. The death of Paul VI offered an opportunity to elect a pope who would continue the reforming work of Vatican II. The election of Albino Luciani, Patriarch of Venice, was a triumph for those opposed to the Conservative-dominated Curia and held out the prospect of a Church more in touch with the needs of its almost 1 billion members – many of whom were poor and underprivileged. Affectionately called 'the smiling pope' for his evident sense of humour and relaxed manner, the truly socialist Luciani took the name John-Paul I and set about transforming the papacy. His more liberal attitude to birth control, abortion, divorce, and homosexuality was sufficient to draw severe opposition from Opus Dei and other right-wing members of the Curia. But it was his determination to confront the corruption, entrenched within the Vatican, that made him an expendable liability.

Evidently suspicious of the activities of P2, and its connec-tion to certain members of the Curia, the new pope ordered a report – which as we have seen included the state of Vatican finances. Such a report would have revealed the criminal acts of Gelli, Sindona, and Calvi, and their involvement with the head of the Vatican Bank, Archbishop Marcinkus; it might also have uncovered the hidden hand of Opus Dei pulling the strings. A mere thirty-three days after his election, this fit, energetic, and smiling pope was dead. Officially, he was said to have died of a heart attack; but the prior revelation of the scandal of the neo-Masonic lodge P2 added much fuel to the rumours of a suspicious death.

There is no direct evidence to connect Opus Dei with the search for the ancient treasure of the Corbières. However, it had certainly established links with P2, the Order of the Solar Temple, the neo-Templars, members of the Priory of Sion, Martinists, the Vichy government, and other groups that operated in the shadowy world of secrecy. It would therefore be hard to believe that Opus was not keeping a close eye on events, positioning itself to take advantage of any future developments on the treasure front.

Following the premature and surprising death of Jean-Paul I, the man chosen to wear the papal crown was the Polish Cardinal, Karol Wojtyla of Cracow, who took the name John-Paul II. It soon became apparent that, for the traditionalists, it would be business as usual with a return to the hard-line stance on social issues and renewed opposition to Freemasonry. But the full extent of Vatican politics was revealed by John-Paul's association with Polish Solidarity – which had emerged out of the Gdansk shipyards – and its stand against Communism. The election of the Archbishop of Cracow to the papacy, at such a critical time in the Cold War, cannot have been a coincidence. This single act of Vatican politics was instrumental in the collapse of the power of the Communist regimes, represented by the fall of the Berlin Wall in 1989, and the fragmentation of the Soviet Union and its satellite countries. But with the demise of this Communist adversary came the birth of a new focus for the Vatican political machine.

As the Mother of God, the Virgin Mary holds a very special place in the Roman Catholic Church and attracts intense devotion from millions of the faithful; a devotion shared particularly by John-Paul II and Opus Dei, who believe she will prepare the way for the second coming of Christ. The assumed return of the Virgin Mary, in the form of apparitions, is thus of major importance to the Church, but as can be seen by the La Salette vision, reviewed in Chapter 8, these may be somewhat less than genuine. There is little doubt that the vision of La Salette was a sham, perpetrated in the cause of Catholic monarchism; similar doubts have also been cast on the authenticity of the famous visions at Lourdes and Fatima. The Church deals with this dilemma by keeping a certain distance, maintaining ambivalence while covertly supporting the elevation of these places to sites of pilgrimage.

In 1981, the Virgin Mary made her first appearance in the Bosnian Croat village of Medjugorje, in the former Yugoslavia. These were troubled times for the Balkan Republic that had been created, from a number of divergent groups, by Marshal Tito, with help from the Soviet Union after the World War II. Situated at the crossroads of Europe and Asia, this confederation of minorities, of ancient heritage, with such different religious, ethnic, and cultural foundations, was potentially unstable, and by 1980, with the rise in Islamic nationalism, the cracks began to appear.

A number of apparitions were subsequently reported, and by 1986, the Vatican began to show an interest, and decided to investigate their authenticity. The messages, allegedly delivered by the Virgin, were that Satan had taken the upper hand, remarkably prophetic in light of Serbian aggression against Catholic Croatia four years later. The site of the visions rapidly developed into a centre of pilgrimage run by a group of Franciscan monks, the fourth largest for all Christians, from which the Catholic Church could derive a huge revenue.

It would appear that Opus Dei, and other factions within the Vatican, could see the opportunities presented by the disintegration of the Yugoslavian Republic and may well have manipulated the civil war to their own advantage. Serbian Intelligence confirmed their suspicions of Vatican influence when they acquired Croatian finance ministry files that showed a 2000 million dollar loan agreement arranged through the Sovereign Military Order of the Knights of Malta. This ten-year interest-free loan, intended to supply the Roman Catholic Croatians with armaments and equipment to continue the fight against the Orthodox Christian Serbs, appears to have been offered almost a year before Croatia declared independence. This certainly suggests some collusion between the Vatican and the Croatian leadership to support and legitimize their war against Serbia.

However, a British C4 television documentary, *Scandal of Medjugorje*, screened on 20 November 1997, uncovered an even deeper involvement between the Catholic Church and the Croatian army, centred round the pilgrimage site of Medjugorje.

According to the programme, with the outbreak of the Croatian-Serbian war, businessman Bernard Ellis set up a charity in England to provide aid for the adults and children affected by the war in the area of Medjugorje. Mr Ellis, who had converted to Catholicism, was the director of Anglo-Steel and through the office of his company arranged convoys of aid worth £20 million per year to the charity's warehouse in the town. The programme alleged that Anglo-Steel profited, by many hundreds of thousands of pounds, in the administration of this charity; the full extent of this was apparently concealed in creative accounting. In addition, a project called 'Mother's Village' was conceived by a Franciscan priest to provide a home for children of the area, allegedly orphaned by the fighting, and a British appeal was set up to raise funds to sponsor the building of new houses.

On the face of it, both appeals were for legitimate and laudable causes, but this exposé implied the hypocrisy of some who claim to be dedicated to serving the needs of the poor, underprivileged, and dispossessed.

The documentary revealed that Medjugorje is actually a prosperous town that had completely escaped the ravages of the war; the local inhabitants, sharing in the huge amount of money being brought into the town by the endless stream of pilgrims, drive around in smart cars and live in desirable houses. The funds raised for an orphanage, for which there is no demand, appear instead to have been used to provide a crèche and nursery school for the children of the town's affluent residents. As for the remainder of the 'Mother's Village' project, only three houses of the proposed village have been built, but £180,000 of the money has been used in building a church instead.

However, the real scandal is found in the nature and purpose of the aid sent to the town. An examination of the aid convoys revealed supplies and equipment more suitable for a small army than refugee aid. Camouflage nets, military-style clothing, footwear, and ex-army surplus equipment found its way, transported by ex-army trucks, to a most surprising destination. Behind the charity warehouse in Medjugorje was a grenade factory and a base for the Croatian Liberation Army. Their commander was the mayor of Medjugorje, a long-time friend of Bernard Ellis. The charity's aid warehouse was in reality nothing less than a supply depot for the Croatian Liberation Army, effectively funded by the Vatican, by the local pilgrims, and by the generosity of an unsuspecting British public.

But the mission of the Croatian army was not just to reclaim the 33 per cent of Croatia that had been occupied by the Orthodox Christian Serbs, and to reinforce the status of the Roman Catholic Church – it was to ensure the permanent removal of the Muslims. Among the aid items were a very large quantity of handcuffs, allegedly to assist the police to maintain law and order in the event of looting; however, it appears that they were used when the Muslims were led out of Mostar. Despite the eventual peace agreement every effort was made to prevent the Muslims from returning to their homes, and over 8000 were evicted. The final triumph of the Catholic Church in Croatia is illustrated by the building of a cathedral in Mostar, allegedly from the proceeds of the pilgrimages and aid donations.

The Medjugorje affair is investigated by Robert Hutchinson in his very readable book *Their Kingdom Come* (1997), in which he also examines the role played by Opus Dei in the Vatican, and their mission for the new millennium. Throughout its history, the Roman Catholic Church has been confronted by adversaries, real and perceived, against whom it felt compelled to take action.

The beginning of the second millennium witnessed the launch of a crusade to 'liberate' Jerusalem from the control of Islam. Successful in 1099, the Christians ruled Jerusalem for nearly 200 years, until they were driven from the Holy Land in 1291. Seven hundred years later, the conditions are different but the perceived threat is the same; the Catholic Church is apparently gearing itself up for a full-scale crusade against the expansion of Islamic fundamentalism in Europe.

The rise of Islamic fundamentalism in the West can be said to have begun in 1973, when the decision was made by the Islamic oil-producing states to quadruple the price of oil. The resulting effect on the world's economy was catastrophic and demonstrated the financial muscle of the oil producers. Within twenty years the worldwide number of adherents to Islam had outstripped that of the Catholic Church by about 250 million. It is estimated that over 5 million Muslims reside in the USA, 5 million in France (which represents approximately 10 per cent of the population), 3.5 and 2 million in Germany and Great Britain respectively. Of course, the majority of these are not fundamentalist, but there is a growing demand for their host countries to recognize and make provision for their cultural and religious differences. This rapid increase in multiracial communities, however inevitable or desirable, has increased social tensions in many European countries.

The Opus Dei and Vatican reaction has been based on theological foundations, namely the attitude of non-Christians to the nature and status of Jesus Christ, and the Church's firm commitment to the conversion of all mankind to the 'true faith'. This follows a certain logic, even if perhaps misguided, since the Church believes that redemption from sin is only possible by the affirmation and practice of the Catholic religion. The evangelizing function is considered to be so important that by avoiding confrontation with the non-Christian religions, especially Islam, the traditionalist sections of the Church believe that they would be failing in their sacred mission.

More disquieting is that multi-racial tensions have been cynically exploited by other groups, some of which masquerade under the general cloak of Christianity. In this case, targets for racial attack extend far beyond the world of Islam and can incorporate almost all non-white and non-Christian cultures. Often motivated by a false sense of nationalism, these aggressive organizations range from far-right political parties, such as the British National Party, to racist and subversive secret societies. Of this latter group, the most sinister and infamous must be the Ku Klux Klan, mainly active in the USA.

Founded in 1866, by American Confederate Brigadier-General Nathan Bedford Forrest, the Ku Klux Klan is a secret society dedicated to white supremacy. Its early membership included many Scottish immigrants who had settled in the southern States, and even today the Klan continues to maintain its links with Scotland. A paramilitary extremist group with loose ties to many other nationalistic and white supremacy groups, the Klan still evokes a powerful image of intimidation – with members clad in white robes and pointed hoods to conceal their identity. One of its most intimidating and recognizable symbols, the fiery cross, has a long and interesting heritage. First used in many northern European countries, but especially in Scotland, the fiery cross (in pre-Christian times a charred stick dipped in blood) was carried around as a signal for a gathering of the clans in times of adversity. Sent from village to village on the command of a Highland chieftain, the cross, called Crean-tarigh or Cross of Shame, was regarded with awe and 'had to be obeyed'. It is said to have been used in the Highland uprising that led to the Jacobite rebellion of 1745. Despite being a very southern American organization, some KKK members were never to forget their Scottish roots.

Restricted by US government legislation, the Klan seemed to have dissolved in 1871, only to re-emerge in 1915 with a renewed racist, anti-Semitic and anti-Communist agenda. Portraying itself as fervently patriotic, the Klan attracted more than 4 million members at its height, preying on old fears and peddling propaganda. In the late 1980s a recruitment drive started in Scotland with KKK members re-inventing their roots. In 1997, Strathclyde police and Special Branch confirmed that they were investigating the KKK threat in Scotland – schools and the Scottish TUC had received their ultra-right-wing propaganda. The main target for this race hate was Glasgow's millionaire Asian businessman, Mohammed Sawar, who was hoping to be elected Britain's first Muslim MP. It is evident that the prospect of an independent Scotland has become a magnet for groups with extreme right-wing agendas.

Many KKK members have also bought themselves into illegitimate Orders of the Scottish Knights Templar, which had already attracted a proportion of militant Scottish nationalists. Once again, as Opus Dei and the Jesuits before, the image of the unfortunate medieval Knights has been hijacked, erroneously, as a powerful archetype of defenders of white Christianity against an array of perceived evil non-white enemies. In 1996, David Duke, former Grand Wizard of the KKK, stood as a Republican candidate for Louisiana. The forty-six-year-old extreme right-winger spoke reverently of his tartan roots (his family came from Edinburgh) and maintained close contact with members of one of the more spurious Templar Orders that claim Scottish heritage.

Dressed up in ultra-patriotic, nationalistic, chivalric, and often Christian, clothes, these groups are proliferating throughout Europe and the United States and are to be feared as much as Islamic fundamentalism. The tragic bombing of the Federal Building in Oklahoma City provides a chilling example. In

April 1995, a 4000 pound bomb devastated the building and killed 150 innocent people. Originally thought to be the work of Islamic extremists or a drug cartel, it became apparent from the arrest of Timothy McVeigh, a disaffected Gulf War veteran, that those responsible were members of a white extremist militia. Further investigation has revealed at least 100 similar groups in eighteen American states that embrace the ethics of the KKK, neo-Nazis, government-hating paramilitaries, New Age millenarians and all shades of the right-wing.

This pattern is also reflected in Europe. Germany witnessed in 1998 a 34 per cent rise in neo-Nazi crimes over the previous year; though there was also a 21 per cent increase in left-wing extremist crimes. In France, the right-wing propaganda of Jean Marie Le Pen's National Front Party has attracted increasing support in his Marseilles constituency and further south-west along the Mediterranean coast, and represents about 14 per cent of the national vote. These seem perfect conditions, not only for anarchical and subversive political groups, organized crime syndicates and legitimate business that trade best in times of unrest, but also for religious fundamentalism. If Robert Hutchinson is to be believed, then the forces of the Roman Catholic Church and those of extremist Islam are positioning themselves for a final confrontation, referred to in the Old Testament as Armageddon.

★ ★ ★

All this seems a long way from the remote area of the Corbières, in the foothills of the Pyrenees, with its ancient past and secret deposits. But as has been revealed in the previous chapters, documentary evidence of the secret treasure has been passed down from generation to generation, guarded by a select number of groups and individuals. Possibly through the theft of ancient archives, the Priory of Sion appears to be party to the secret today. But despite its public appearance only as recently as 1956, it does seem to be the present tip of a long political tradition. This is a tradition that is rooted firmly in the politics of the Right such as Monarchism, Conservatism and many of the policies advocated by the wartime Vichy government.

This stance inevitably brings the Priory into direct opposition not only to the democratic French Republic but also to the general direction taken by the European Union. It is indeed a remarkable coincidence that besides seeing the founding of the Priory, 1956 saw Le Pen become a right-wing National Assembly deputy. Furthermore, he was connected with the extremist OAS in the 1960s, and may well have established contact with members of the Italian lodge P2, the Order of the Solar Temple and members of the Priory of Sion. He certainly shares their political orientation and may well have been able to give them covert support. The nature of the information or evidence the Priory may possess concerning the treasure is not known at the present time, but it is evident that they are actively engaged in gaining control over the region in which they believe it has been deposited. With possession of this fabulous material and symbolic treasure, they will be in a strong position to complete their political agenda; such an agenda would certainly have the approval of Opus Dei and the network of those right-wing secret societies that have proliferated throughout Europe and the Americas.

THE PORTENT AND POWER
OF THE ELUSIVE TREASURE

Looking Forward
A United Europe? · The Fate of the Treasure

THIS MAY BE the final chapter of this book, but by no means is it the end of the story; it merely describes a point in time of the continual evolution of Europe's history. Trying to tease out and present the various strands of this tangled web of deception, political intrigue, and search for treasure has been at times a tortuous task. It is made even more difficult by unavoidable deviations into little-explored areas of occult politics, but telling the story through this process has revealed the extent of influence exercised by religious and political organizations and various secret societies. But other threads are even more alarming. There is the evident increase in all shades of religious fundamentalism on the one hand, and the clandestine activities of self-serving opportunists on the other; both are poised to exploit the temporary vacuums created by the turmoil of conflict. Restricting this investigation to the treasure alone, without considering the many religious, political and occult implications, would have been to miss much of the wider significance and symbolic power of this unique and sensational wealth.

Treasure stories abound throughout the world, but none has attracted as much sustained interest as what remains of the lost treasure of the Temple of Jerusalem, last recorded in the south-west of France nearly 1500 years ago. The evidence collected from all the various sources, including the works of writers and researchers throughout the centuries, indicates that the treasure is probably still deposited in the region of the village of Rennes-le-Château. Though the exact locations of these rich deposits are now probably unknown, some secretive groups and individuals have, in the past, certainly possessed secret and privileged information. And buried deep in ancient mines, subterranean galleries and extensive cave networks, the Jewish treasure has almost certainly also been supplemented by that of others, including the missing wealth of the mysterious Knights Templar – adding yet another dimension to this extraordinary story.

Over the centuries, established and proven facts have added weight to the legends. There have been those, sufficiently convinced of the reality of ancient deposits to become active treasure seekers, who have achieved a small measure of success. But the bulk of the treasure, including that of the Temple, appears never to have been found. In more recent times, treasure-hunters have been seen more openly surveying the region with specialist equipment, including infra-red photography and metal detectors. But by far the greatest number of seekers have operated under a cloak of secrecy, taking the necessary precautions to remain anonymous.

Of course, the sceptics maintain that the whole Rennes-le-Château affair is a fabrication and the existence of the treasure is nothing more than a myth. But they cannot offer any convincing alternative explanation for the overwhelming body of writing, the motives and actions of many different people, over the centuries, that underpin the connections we have illuminated.

Even more remarkable is the number of individuals and groups connected with this remote region who have been involved in the world of occult politics and who in some cases have inexplicably become wealthy. The string of unlikely coincidences, strange events and deaths we have highlighted, continues to reinforce the belief that this otherwise insignificant region conceals a secret of some importance.

Many readers will have had a brief introduction to this story from the publicity arising out of the strange events that occurred a century ago, at the village of Rennes-le-Château. Some have suggested that Bérenger Saunière, the priest of Rennes-le-Château, attained his wealth by the discovery of this particular treasure; it is more likely that he had only discovered the heirlooms that had belonged to the Hautpoul family, who had lived in the château adjacent to the church. But in addition to the family's treasures, hidden a hundred years earlier by Saunière's predecessor Abbé Bigou, were archives and parchments probably confirming the presence of the Temple of Jerusalem treasure in the immediate region and the survival of the symbolic dynasty of French kings, the deposed Merovingians. It was this discovery that enabled Saunière to play a prominent role in the nineteenth-century world of occult politics. The shadowy political arena was used covertly by political and religious institutions and secret societies, especially those that had connections to this ancient region and its noble families, who had at one time been the guardians of the great secret.

The knowledge from which Saunière evidently profited has a value not just in material terms but also on a symbolic level. This can best be appreciated by those with esoteric and occult political interests, initiates for whom symbols can transmit power. Of all the glimpses of events connected to the treasure, some of the most significant are from the dark period of the Nazi occupation of Europe and its aftermath, especially within French and Swiss politics. Obsessed by the alleged power of the Holy Grail, and driven by a vision of a world directed by a modern equivalent of the medieval Teutonic Knights, the Nazi leaders Himmler and Rosenberg initiated a search for the lost treasure. For this they employed the specialist services of Nazi SS officers Otto Rahn, Karl Wolff, and Otto

Skorzeny. The report of Colonel Howard Buechner of the US Army Medical Corps, concerning the actual finds made by the Nazis, cannot be substantiated. But other sources do confirm that they did acquire a certain quantity of gold, of which some was transported through central France in 1944, on the orders of General Lammerding; gold which then fell into the hands of the self-described Resistance activist 'Raoul', in the course of the chance night raid that was to provoke a previously unexplained reaction from the Nazis – the destruction of the village of Oradour and the brutal massacre of its 642 inhabitants. Recent evidence has indicated that the gold theft was actually part of a more widespread web of intrigue than Raoul acting alone. As can be seen from the experiences of Robin Mackness, the Oradour incident has had repercussions that have continued long after the war. Indeed, it can be claimed that François Mitterrand was aware of the actual truth behind the massacre and the theft of the gold, from which those of his 'inner circle' of friends are said to have profited, substantially. These serious and sensitive issues are still under investigation by the French justice system, an investigation that has unearthed corruption at the highest levels of government.

This investigation of the Oradour massacre has also uncovered some very unsavoury activities, arising out of greed and opportunism, which extend to the world of high finance. An inseparable part of European finance is the Swiss banking system. But the role of Swiss banks, especially during and after World War II, has attracted accusations of profiteering and unethical practices. Having acted as repositories for the personal valuables of Jews before the war, and for the looted treasures acquired by Nazi officers during it, the Swiss banks have been reluctant to bow to recent international pressure to reveal the full extent of these deposits. Further criticism has arisen out of the Swiss complicity in the conversion of Nazi plunder into hard currency, vital for the maintenance of the Nazi war machine. Frequently transported by rail through France to and from Switzerland, the plunder, often in the form of gold bullion, also provided rich pickings for some opportunists acting in the name of the Resistance.

An argument has been forcefully advanced, that the Swiss had no option but to comply, since they risked being invaded by the Germans if they did not – and there is some merit in that viewpoint. However, this does not excuse the continuing wall of silence, and begrudging co-operation, met in the attempt to unravel the fate of the pre-war deposits made especially by Jews. To place the blame on the Swiss nation and its citizens would be grossly unfair. As in most other countries, members of the general public are merely innocent bystanders. However, the politicians and financial institutions of the time cannot claim such innocence, and are morally bound to unveil the truth behind their wartime activities. Damning evidence that some Swiss politicians were Nazi sympathizers, and that some banks willingly undertook their role as money-launderers, adds fuel to the charges of impropriety and weight to the demands for public acknowledgement.

The most powerful group lobbying internationally for the truth and subsequent compensation is the World Jewish Congress (WJC). Its president is the Canadian billionaire Edgar Bronfman. With the help of a US senator, Alfonse D'Amato, great pressure is being applied to the Swiss to accede to WJC demands; pressure which includes the threat of a cessation of US trading with Swiss banks, or Swiss banks trading in US markets. If not actually catastrophic to the Swiss economy, discharging this threat would be seriously damaging. The WJC draws its power from networks of politically active Zionists formed within the international pool of about 17 million Jews, largely of European origin with little claim to a truly genetic Jewish heritage. The distinction between being Jewish by religion or race has been so confused that few non-Jews, and even many Jews themselves, are unaware of the reality.

The irony is, however, that some American banks, owned or controlled by Jews, financed industries that were essential to the Nazi war machine. It is hard to believe that commercial interests should have over-ridden such a blatant and brutal abuse of one's own community. But there is a further example of such strange disregard for ethics – the Bank of International Settlements. Established in 1930 from a plan conceived by Hjalmar Schacht (Nazi Minister of Economics from 1933) to handle German reparations settlements from World War I, the bank brought together financial representatives from both the Allied and Axis powers. While the war raged throughout Europe, representatives from the central banks of both sides met, in the most comfortable surroundings of a Swiss castle, to discuss a plan for the economic reconstruction of Europe after the war – irrespective of which side won. Moreover, Montagu Norman, then Governor of the Bank of England, maintained close contact with his old friend Hjalmar Schacht, the man responsible for arranging the financing of Germany's military might. It is quite clear that in the banking world, economic considerations take precedence over human rights.

Anti-Semitism, or more accurately, discrimination against adherents to Judaism, has existed throughout Europe for centuries. There are many possible explanations for it, including jealousy and fear; mainly arising out of their commercial and financial competence. But another probable explanation is Jewish cultural separatism. The tendency for Jews to live in close-knit communities, reinforced by the policy of marriage only within the Jewish community, and the very public display of their culture and religious traditions, has certainly contributed to the perception, by Gentiles, of a Jewish cultural elitism. This perception has been reinforced by the affirmation of Orthodox Jews to be God's chosen people; a claim originating from their own biblical writings, including the Old Testament, and perpetuated in their teachings.

After decades of intense lobbying of the British Establishment by influential Jews sympathetic to Zionism, the dream of a national homeland finally came to fruition in 1948. The State of Israel was founded on the land at one time settled by the twelve Hebrew tribes of the Old Testament. But today, with new objectives, the focus of influence has shifted to the powerful Jewish lobby close to the US administration. While no one can deny the horror of the Holocaust and the treatment of Jews under the Nazi regime, it must also be accepted that the WJC and its offshoots have maximized propaganda potential to attract sympathy for the policies of the State of Israel. These policies, which have at times been aggressively pursued by the Israeli government, continue to provoke antagonism with their Islamic neighbours – most often over the right to occupy and control the land formerly known as Palestine. But while outwardly citing biblical history – and centuries of persecution in other countries – to justify their settlement of this land, there appear to be hidden agendas. The control of Israel by Zionists has not only given their North American cousins a vital strategic foothold in the Middle East but ensures control of the vast, rich mineral resources of the Dead Sea.

But even closer to home, it is possible that the WJC's recent assault on the Swiss also has a hidden agenda. Rather less than a genuine striving for restitution, it may really be directed at destroying the credibility of traditional Swiss banking institutions. If successful, this could shift the focus of world financial power to the Jewish-controlled banks in New York, Chicago, and other major US cities.

It could be argued that the Swiss themselves should indeed accept at least partial blame for this situation. Swiss banking secrecy, while being highly attractive to investors and depositors, has made it especially vulnerable to accusations of unethical, and at times criminal, dealings. This vulnerability was exposed in the scandal involving the pseudo-Masonic P2 lodge and the Vatican Bank. The superiors of P2 were able to milk the Vatican Bank of vast funds, passing them through shell companies and privately owned banks. Swiss banking laws proved to be only too convenient for this gigantic fraud.

The conspiracies and financial irregularities surrounding P2 also revealed the hypocrisy of some of the Vatican hierarchy;

this is, however, not unique to this affair, for the Vatican has indeed a long record of unholy activities. Indeed as one of the world's most powerful political players, the Catholic Church has become embroiled in situations and events in which it has acted in direct opposition to the teachings of its claimed founder, Jesus Christ. The record of individual indiscretions of popes, cardinals, bishops, and priests is both long and appalling, but in many instances only reflects human frailties. But as an institution, the Catholic Church has to carry the burden of guilt for endorsing policies that have put its own position above that of individual human rights. The support given to fascist dictators; the silence and lack of condemnation for Nazi atrocities, especially to the Jews; the active involvement in subversive occult politics, and its established links with organized crime, do not sit well with fundamental Christian principles. The values, such as 'love thy neighbour', 'turning the other cheek' or 'to treat others as you would wish to be treated', that form the basis of Christ's teachings, sit uneasily with some examples set by Rome. But the full involvement of the Vatican in Nazi affairs has extended far beyond a passive, silent acceptance of deplorable activies.

In 1938, Pope Pius XI commissioned an encyclical condemning racism and anti-Semitism, but in 1939, his successor Pope Pius XII refused to publish it – evidently in the hope of appeasing Hitler. Even more damning though was the complicity of the Catholic Church in the plot to establish escape routes for Nazi officers after the war – of which one was Hitler's right-hand man, the infamous Martin Bormann.

Having engineered his way to the very heart of Hitler's inner circle by 1943, Martin Bormann took effective control of the Nazi administration, by which he was able to amass an enormous quantity of wealth. By the middle of 1944, Bormann, with the help of Otto Skorzeny, his most trusted and able acolyte, had established a network of escape routes out of Germany to Italy, Spain, Egypt, and South America; all countries sympathetic to Nazi ambitions. These escape routes, which often utilized Catholic houses and monasteries, were used not only for the transfer of Nazi officers, but also for the huge amount of wealth they had acquired.

Martin Bormann's wife and family took advantage of an escape route that used a network of priests, known as the Vatican Escape Line, which looked after them until after the war. Unable to escape justice, Bormann's wife was eventually arrested by the Allies, at which time she was found to be in possession of a considerable quantity of foreign coins. Some of these were said to be very ancient – possibly of Visigothic provenance. Bormann, who was never caught, had put himself under the protection of a Franciscan monastery in Genoa and sometime late in 1947, met Bishop Alois Hudal who suggested two avenues of escape; either to join Otto Skorzeny in Spain or to follow Adolf Eichmann to Argentina. Eichmann was the Nazi responsible for conceiving the evil Final Solution – the deportation of Jews to death camps.

It cannot surely be just coincidence that Otto Skorzeny, the officer entrusted by Bormann to stockpile wealth and to establish escape routes, was also the officer charged by Himmler in 1944 to find the legendary Holy Grail in the south-west of France. Furthermore, a symbol, variously described as an octopus or a spider (in French, *l'araignée*) found on Priory of Sion documents, was also the name given to the network of Nazi escape routes. The implication could well be that the Priory of Sion was involved with, or at least supportive of, the post-war continuation of Nazi doctrines and politics. This is less surprising when one recalls that the most prominent members of the Priory were either Vichy activists or sympathizers. Furthermore, has the Priory become aware of the fate of the treasure that had been discovered by Skorzeny?

Parallels can certainly be drawn between the ideologies of the fascist dictator-governed countries of South America and the doctrines of the Vichy Écoles Nationales dedicated to a French National Revival. In principle, both subscribed to a firm authoritarian leadership with little regard for citizens' democracy, in direct contravention of republican ideals; and both looked to the military for its sources of leadership.

The Vichy government was a key nodal point in the web of people and events surrounding the search for the lost treasure of the Temple of Jerusalem. Providing a bridge between the pre- and post-war periods, the Vichy episode permitted many varied individuals to follow their own agendas under the cover of wartime activities. It also brought together people who would continue to profit from these activities long after the war. But the full effect of the short Vichy regime on later European politics, notably at a covert level, has been largely underestimated. Friendships formed during the Nazi occupation have profoundly influenced the activities of those at the highest levels of the French government, a major player in the politics of the European Union. Accusations of corruption and financial irregularities can include charges of conspiracy to conceal the fate of missing Nazi gold, and of theft and illegal trading in the ancient archives relating to the remaining treasure lost in the Corbières.

For some, namely the genuine secret society known as the Priory of Sion, the search for the lost treasure is not motivated merely by selfish greed for material gain, but by an ideology manifested in a vision of a new united Europe. Idealistic and romantic, this vision is of a society founded upon the principles of chivalry and governed by an authoritarian but benevolent elite, as characterized in the medieval Grail romances. The ideology has been built on a confusion of Celtic and Teutonic mythology, assumed Templar and chivalric ideals, Atlantean, Arthurian, and Agarthan legend, with a light sprinkling of Platonic philosophy.

This ideology is not far removed from that of the Nazi SS and their desire for a 'super-race', that of the Vichy government and its commitment to a French National Renewal, or from that found expressed in the articles of *Vaincre*, the magazine produced by Pierre Plantard in 1942. This very French version of the Nazi ideology was shared in principle, if not in its practical application, not only by Marshal Pétain, but also by Charles de Gaulle and François Mitterrand. Despite appearing to be in direct opposition, exemplified by the venomous exchanges between them, de Gaulle and Mitterrand were both dedicated to a new vision of France, more akin to the Ancien Régime of Louis XIV than the democratic Republic; and to the restoration of French power in European politics. De Gaulle, very much an idealist, took a stance that was founded on very strong political and ethical principles, whereas his successor François Mitterrand, was a pragmatist, for whom politics were only a means to self-interested ends. This flexible approach to politics made him vulnerable to accusations of lack of political integrity and to persistent claims of involvement with circles of corruption, found within the government itself.

But this French view is only one of several visions of a united Europe, each based on entirely different models and pursuing separate agendas.

Dedicated to a vision of Europe in which the predominant religion is Catholicism, the Vatican has necessarily entered the political arena. Ever since the dissolution of the Holy Roman Empire by Napoleon in 1806, the Roman Catholic Church has employed a range of strategies designed to restore its lost power and influence. Such strategies include those of the 'visions' of the Virgin Mary with the accompanying politico-religious messages encouraging a return to complete obedience to the Catholic Church, and warnings of a catastrophe for Europe if these teachings were disregarded.

To maintain its anti-Communist, anti-Islamic, anti-Protestant, and anti-Masonic stance, the Church of Rome has forged extremely unholy alliances to achieve its aims. Driven by the hard right and fundamentalist sect Opus Dei, the Vatican is actively backing campaigns to counter liberalism and religious compromise, which frequently brings it into conflict with the current trend to uphold individual rights. In fact, on 2 July 1998 it was reported in the *Daily Telegraph* that the

Vatican had taken a tough line on dissenters. The Church was no longer prepared to tolerate any deviations from Catholicism's 'definitive' truths – included in which are rulings on birth control, abortion, divorce, and the non-ordination of women. Head of doctrine, Cardinal Joseph Ratzinger, implied excommunication for those who disobeyed the Church's teaching on faith and morals. Furthermore, he restated the Vatican position on the invalidity of Anglican ordinations, an outright attack on all non-Catholic Christian religions.

In complete contrast, there is a vision of Europe in which religion plays no part. This is the single market, with its single currency the euro, favoured by the huge multinational companies and international financial institutions. Accompanied by uniformity of products and services, and the enforced centralization of political and financial power, the single European market represents a vast economic potential in which citizens are treated as little more than consumers. The market is driven only by financial considerations, with little thought for the quality of life, security and happiness of the people. In March 1999, all the members of the European Commission (a type of European civil service) resigned, some having been accused of fraud and incompetence. Already viewed with scepticism and suspicion, the concept of a politically united Europe suffered a severe blow in the face of these revelations. The common currency is portrayed by its opponents as nothing more than a tool, essential for the creation of more favourable trading conditions for multinationals.

A third vision is that of the anarchist-synarchist; a vision that demands a much reduced and decentralized government with local semi-autonomous regions in which political decisions are guided by 'spiritual' principles. This is not necessarily a religious vision, but one that promotes principles of chivalry, honesty, unselfishness, integrity, honour and charity above any other; placing great emphasis on the freedom of the individual. Despite being viewed as rather idealistic by many people, this vision has strong appeal in this age of materialism and consumerism. There is a growing underground network dedicated to the collapse of the present capitalistic system and the introduction of a new anarchical society. Rejecting the normal democratic political process, the secretive anarchist organizations work through their cellular networks. They are dedicated to destabilizing national and local government by infiltrating key positions. Though not particularly successful yet, they are well placed to benefit from any adverse change in the economy or social order.

Also operating partially under the cloak of secrecy is the Masonic Grand Orient of France, dedicated to a renewed Revolution encompassing secular democratic and social ideals. Unlike the Masonic English Grand Lodge, which since its foundation in 1717 has supported the so-called Establishment from which it had recruited many of its top officers, the Grand Orient of France has been largely in opposition to its government. It has been rumoured that by infiltrating Masonic and neo-Masonic groups in England, the Grand Orient is attempting to establish a parallel to the English Grand Lodge, with the eventual aim of replacing it. One of their key weapons in this aim is the promotion of more esoteric rites and symbolism in contrast to the increasingly pragmatic stance of the English Grand Lodge. Though at first sight this appears to be improbable, it is in fact an actual example of subversive occult politics in action – the unseen force that has shaped and influenced Europe over the centuries.

There is no shortage of other European visions, including those of the Monarchists, Republicans or Social Democrats. There were the imperial ambitions of Charlemagne, the Knights Templar, the Habsburgs, Napoleon Bonaparte, and Hitler, not to forget the expansionist ambitions of the Communist Soviet Union. In the nineteenth century there was a revival in occult and esoteric interests, that promoted diverse social models that integrated Christianity with Gnostic religions and added rather bizarre and indefinable elements of magic and mysticism; a prime example being the original Martinism. The previous century's Occult Revival has to some extent been repeated at the present time, principally by the so-called 'New Age' communities, who often embrace ecological or 'green' issues, and have looked to the pagan religions for inspiration. They generally appear to be attempting to follow a mystical, non-material, and non-technical path.

Of all the occult and secretive groups active in the sphere of European, and especially French, politics, the Priory of Sion has carved out a particularly influential role. Known by different names and serving several masters, the Priory and its forerunners have always been closely connected with people and events, themselves connected with Rennes-le-Château.

Access to the heart of the Priory has proved impossible; master of disinformation and used to operating in the world of shadows, it remains an apparently nebulous organization with little discernible form. Some sources show it to be composed of initiates from the highest ranks of other occult and neo-Masonic groups such as the Martinists, Memphis-Mizraim, Grand Orient, the Benificent Knights of the Holy City, and the Knight Templars. The only information available concerning the Priory comes from their own published sources, augmented by internal letters and circulars, some of which are patently propaganda and not to be taken seriously. However, sufficient information has been uncovered that confirms the facts and claims presented throughout this work. Their primary self-appointed objective has been, and still is, to recover the treasure of the Visigoths, deposited in the region of the Razès, that includes the priceless and symbolic treasure of the Temple of Solomon.

To ensure this function the Priory has adopted the political stance of promoting an extended Catalan independence. This is an echo of the ancient Templar dream of an independent sovereign state, stretching from Narbonne to Barcelona, in which can be found the precious deposits. Having obtained total independence for the region, Priory members would attempt to fill the chief administrative posts, ensuring control over the region, thus safeguarding the treasure.

But guardianship of the treasure is not the only motive for extended Catalan independence; it is part of a much wider separatist movement that is growing, not just in France, but throughout Europe. This movement has developed largely as a reaction against the centralization of governments and, specifically, the pan-European administration of the European parliament, which is considered by many citizens to have resulted in a loss of individual rights and control. The drive for self-determination has fuelled the Balkan conflicts, motivated the aggression of the Basques, and can be seen in the more peaceful local politics of Brittany, Cornwall, Wales, Scotland and many other regions.

The Priory today has adopted the Anarchist-Synarchist model and strategies, but appears to have continued to maintain its links with the traditionalist factions of the Catholic Church – the main force of which is Opus Dei. This gives rise to some ambivalence, in that the legendary heroes of the Languedoc/Catalan region were the Cathars who had been subjected to persecution by the Catholic Church in the thirteenth century. However, most local people justifiably believe that, as in the case of the Templars, the crusade against the Cathars was motivated mainly by the greed of the northern French barons eager to gain control over the rich lands of the Languedoc. These ancient memories are revived in a current anti-Paris feeling, arising out of the current belief that the wealth derived from the extensive vineyards of this fertile region has been exploited by the Paris financiers, considered to be the modern equivalent of northern barons.

The Catholic Church has not been slow to see the potential in supporting the Separatist Catalan movement, since it would give them a foothold in the country whose government had deposed their power, two centuries before. Though only about

15 per cent of French people attend regular masses, the nation is nominally 90 per cent Catholic. It is thus of mutual benefit if the Priory of Sion continues an alliance with the Church of Rome, and it is with this in mind that it is alleged that, at the time of writing, the Priory favours the installation of the Archbishop of Barcelona as the next pope. This claim is given support by the fact that the Priory's headquarters is now established in Barcelona and the current Grand Master is a Catalonian lawyer.

Many writers have maintained that the Priory of Sion, along with many other secret societies, such as the Illuminati, the Solar Temple, The Elders of Sion and the Rosicrucians, form part of a European and possibly worldwide conspiracy. The usual allegation is of a plot to control the world's financial institutions, thereby usurping the democratic processes of most Western governments; effectively enslaving the individual. This rather dramatic scenario does not in any formal sense stand up to closer scrutiny. It does, however, contain grains of truth.

As has been repeatedly illustrated, organizations even from quite different cultural or religious backgrounds but which share a temporary or long-term aim will often forge alliances. It could be argued that such an alliance of interested parties would create, at least in the short term, a conspiracy. Such a situation can occur within the world of capitalism, international finance and commerce. However, far from being a monolithic conspiracy, these flexible alliances are indications of a continuous struggle for market share by separate and competing factions. The unanimous support for Hitler and his Nazi party offered by German industries and banks, and the support by international financial organizations, was motivated less by a desire for mutual co-operation, than by a common fear of Communist expansion, which was an anathema to their capitalist ambitions.

In fact, Europe has always been a battleground for highly predatory political, religious and occult groups. Some of these battles are fought within the democratic arena of open government, but many more are being played out in secret, often involving the use of subversive and occult means.

On the political front, the war against Communism is now but a shadow of the Cold War of the 1960s and '70s, when the world appeared to stand on the brink of Armageddon. But the break-up of the Soviet Union and the re-unification of Germany have done little to allay fears, and the Western democracies are still on their guard. The fear of Communist expansion has been openly exploited by the right-wing National Front parties, parading under a banner of pseudo-patriotism; also by the armaments industry and its financiers for whom conflict or defence always offers lucrative contracts.

There are continual skirmishes within the European Union, as individual governments jockey for position, seeking to obtain political and financial advantages. With increasing integration, most governments are tending towards the middle ground of a Christian Liberal Democratic nature, pushing traditional Socialist and Conservative parties to the fringe. This trend encourages a uniformity favourable to international capitalism. In this respect, it is claimed that the European Union and the single currency have been a triumph for the financial institutions; and, by coincidence, some fulfilment of the Protocols of the Elders of Sion.

Words such as 'convergence' and 'harmonization' are frequently applied to the ongoing evolution of European unity, which, while ostensibly referring to economics, can actually be seen more acutely in the realm of culture. For centuries, Europe has contained an enormous variety of cultures; despite the proximity of countries, the profusion of languages, dress and traditions is remarkable. But this cultural diversity is under threat from the relentless pressure for uniformity driven by the ambitions of multinational companies, of whom many have their origins in the United States of America. These companies have readily embraced the Protestant work ethic and the spirit of capitalism as propounded by the German sociologist Max

Weber. The global expansion of these companies is so astonishingly successful that products, such as Coca Cola, McDonald's hamburgers, and American business methods, have been adopted by almost every country in the world. This US cultural imperialism is a direct result of a free-market capitalism in which the poorer cultures have been exploited and absorbed. Cultural traditions, evolved over many centuries, are rapidly being eroded and replaced by the American Dream of materialistic prosperity.

In the pursuit of their objectives these multinationals have adopted similar strategies and modus operandi to those of many secret societies. The use of propaganda, industrial espionage, and the forming of secret alliances, are all frequently employed by both groups. Furthermore, despite their theoretical accountability to the shareholders, the chairmen and directors can create an almost unassailable position for themselves in much the same way as the hierarchy of a secret society; reinforced by the culture of secret boardroom meetings. Finally, the huge size of global conglomerates can make it extremely difficult to track down those ultimately responsible for the individual companies and their products. These factors have caused some alarm and have helped to create a similar suspicion of conspiracies among multinational corporations as is found among the secret societies in the world of occult politics.

For many people, the American Dream is as dangerous as Communism; they view the European Union not just as a firm bulwark against Communism but also against the Americanization of European culture. This has led to tensions between Britain and the rest of Europe, especially France. As a result of their common Anglo-Saxon roots, and the eagerness of successive British governments to promote very close Anglo-American relationships, Britain's place in the European Union has been the object of suspicion. The French government has introduced legislation to reduce the influence of Anglo-American culture, and continues to guard jealously its own national and regional cultural past. It is this overwhelming desire by the French to retain their national identity that has been so effectively harnessed by the right-wing groups, among which can be found the Priory of Sion.

★ ★ ★

For more than 1500 years, the Roman Catholic Church has been a major force on the political and spiritual battlefield of Europe. From its very beginning, the Church has been beset by enemies within and without – a situation that persists today. By forging alliances with the most successful secular and political powers, the Church of Rome has managed to remain the largest and most influential religious organization in Europe. But dark clouds are looming worryingly on the horizon.

Even atheistic Communism, Orthodox and Protestant Christianity, and the spiritual vacuum found in American materialism are not considered to pose as great a threat to the Church of Rome as its new enemy: Islamic fundamentalism.

This is not really so much a new enemy, but the resurgence of a very old one; Christianity has considered Islam to be a threat ever since its origin, following the death of Mohammed in 632. Both Christianity and Islam have suffered internal schisms, with the formation of sects and factions that vary from liberal tolerance to militant fundamentalism. Conflicts between these two great religious powers reached a head with the Islamic invasion of the Iberian Peninsula in 711 – an occupation that was to last more than 700 years, with continual hostilities. But the biggest clash between them commenced with the launching of the First Crusade in 1095, by which Pope Urban II hoped to regain control of Christianity's holy places in Jerusalem. Successful in 1099, Christendom held onto its precious possessions for the following 192 years, despite the most ferocious confrontations.

It was during this time that the Christian forces first experienced Islamic fundamentalism, through the activities of a fringe Muslim Shi'ite sect called the Assassins. Though methods have changed, modern militants, in the course of killing their enemies, are just as prepared as the ancient assassins to die for their faith. Few people can have failed to be alarmed by the frightening scenes of Islamic militants, apparently in a hypnotic state of ecstasy, eager to die in the service of Allah.

It must be acknowledged, however, that the majority of fundamentalists are not committed to such violent means. The Judaeo-Christian perception of Islam has been formed both from the savage past, and from the current outbreaks of militancy, in countries such as Iran, Iraq, Algeria, and Egypt. There are currently, throughout the world, over thirty points of conflict, most of which have a religious dimension. Content to capitalize on this militant view of Islam, the Catholic Church has no trouble in raising support in the West to embark on a new crusade, to be fought not with military hardware or even economic sanctions, but by latest computer technology and electronic communications. With satellite communications, any place in the world can be swamped by 'Western' propaganda showing undreamed of prosperity, and materialism, as well as an individual freedom unknown in most of the Islamic world. In pursuit of this crusade against Islam, the Vatican appears quite happy to ally itself, if not always openly, then certainly covertly, with the right-wing nationalist groups that are dedicated to racism and ethnic cleansing. Furthermore, it has remained largely uncritical of the most powerful western democracies, that continue to foster and promote a spiritually poor, materialistic culture.

Of even more concern is what will be the response of the Islamic militants, whose traditional methods have embraced international terrorism. A sign that they too have moved into the technological age can be found on the internet. A website entitled Radio Islam promotes Islamic propaganda, much of which is not surprisingly anti-Zionist. However, previous experiences of Islamic insurrection and terrorism should send a dire warning to the West that must not be ignored. The threat of worldwide conflict with Islam and the prophecy of Armageddon could be a reality.

It will probably come as a great surprise to find evidence that the Catholic Church appears to be courting an alliance with one of its most entrenched adversaries in this crusade against a common foe.

For nearly 2000 years, the Church of Rome has blamed the Jews for the death of their Messiah and Son of God, Jesus Christ. This belief in part explains, but does not excuse, the silence of Pope Pius XII during World War II, concerning the Nazi persecution of the Jews and the anti-Semitic policies of Marshal Pétain and his Vichy government. However, suddenly in the last decade of the twentieth century, Vatican spokesmen have publicly apologized to the Jewish community for these reprehensible actions, and lifted the accusation of deicide. Having failed to officially recognize the State of Israel since its founding in 1948, the Vatican has now established full diplomatic relations.

Recently an allegation has been made, by Shimon Samuels, director of the Holocaust Centre, that the Vatican used Jewish plundered gold to help smuggle ex-Nazis to safety in Latin America and the Middle East. The Vatican has yet to make a public response, but what takes place behind the scenes is another matter. Without doubt, the Vatican is attempting to ally itself with this other great adversary of fundamentalist Islam, and it has been seriously suggested that the current Archbishop of Paris, Cardinal Lustiger, could become the successor to Pope John-Paul II. This view is supported by the mainstream Catholic writer Peter Stanford quoted in *The Last Pope* (1998), by John Hogue. Born Jewish but converted to Christianity as a teenager, Cardinal Lustiger has always been a strong defender of Zionism, even maintaining that he is at the same time a Jew and a Christian. Such an appointment would surely cement the relationship between the Vatican and the Jews, thus strengthening the stance against Islamic militancy.

Peter Stanford, however, fears the repercussions following Lustiger's election could herald the end of the world!

It would of course be uncharitable to suggest that this new accord between the Vatican and Israel is motivated by anything other than a mutual recognition of their spiritual missions. The *Daily Telegraph* reported on 14 October 1998 that 5000 Christians marched through Jerusalem in support of the State of Israel. The marchers were fundamentalists, calling themselves Christian Zionists, who believe that the State of Israel is part of God's plan for the world. A growing political force, especially in America, their foundation could well have been a reaction to the appearance of another fundamentalist sect, the Nation of Islam. Under the leadership of Louis Farrakhan (banned from entering Britain for his anti-Semitic speeches), the Nation of Islam has grown to an estimated 1 million supporters, worldwide. According to the media, the Nation of Islam is overtly racist, anti-Semitic, homophobic and is often compared with white supremacy groups. Dedicated to the establishment of an independent Black state, the Nation encourages Blacks to adopt the Islamic faith for solidarity. The rise of all these opposing fundamentalist groups is threatening to lead to major conflicts that were apparently prophesied, some 350 years ago.

In the mid-sixteenth century, a French physician and astrologer, Michel de Notredame, more popularly known as Nostradamus, made a series of cryptic predictions concerning the fate of Europe. His quatrains (four-line, rhymed verses) have been endlessly interpreted, resulting in many different conclusions concerning the details. However, most agree on the general content, much of which alludes to violent conflicts. Some passages are said to contain references to the rise of Hitler and the Nazi party, Communism, and the Arab-Israeli six-day war. His writings also contain prophecies concerning the fate of many historical characters and events, of which an uncanny number have proved remarkably accurate. But will his apparent prediction of a major confrontation between militant factions of Islam, Judaism, and the Christian world be proved right?

It is perhaps less surprising that he placed France at the centre of European events. He was born in 1503, in Provence, and though Roman Catholic, he was of Jewish descent. Given a basic classical education by his grandfathers, he was sent to Avignon and thence to the University of Montpellier to study medicine. After graduation, he exercised his medical knowledge in dealing with an outbreak of plague in Montpellier and Narbonne. Continuing his studies, he earned a reputation for absorbing knowledge in many different disciplines, including astrology, as a result of which he compiled his prodigious divinations. However, living in a France held in the grip of the Inquisition, he was forced to encode his writings and prophesies in order to avoid any charges of heresy.

Being an educated man, of traditional Jewish heritage despite his Catholic upbringing, and with his roots firmly embedded in this ancient region, it is hardly possible that Nostradamus could have travelled throughout the area without becoming aware of its great legends; legends that must, of course, have included the secret of the lost treasure of the Temple of Jerusalem. In fact, there is a persistent local assertion that he stayed at the house of a relative in the village of Alet-les-Bains; a village intimately connected with history of the Corbières, the village of Rennes-le-Château and the lost treasure.

There are at least ten verses that deal specifically with gold, of which Century VIII: 28, 29, 30 refer to gold and treasure from antiquity that one day would be discovered in this region.

Though the prophecies, and especially the numerous interpretations, should only be accepted with some caution, they are legitimate writings within the context of sixteenth-century France. With remarkable foresight, many of the predictions refer to conflicts and upheavals, within his country, that have since occurred; conflicts that have often been centred around power struggles between Catholics, Protestants, Jews, and Muslims. Furthermore, Nostradamus specifically identifies certain cities such as Avignon, Barcelona, Narbonne, Carcassonne, Toulouse, Lyon, and Perpignan. These were cities that were not only renowned centres of learning in his time, but that have also played such a crucial role in the occult history of France.

Throughout the centuries, France has experienced a great number of occult and secret societies and chivalric orders, of which many have played a prominent part, and still do, in both their internal politics and in their relations with other countries. This melting pot of historical events contains some episodes of particular significance – some of which have contributed to the underground politics of the present day. The treasure trail itself can be compared to a golden thread, running through this background of diverse notable episodes and people, that has been woven into a vast tapestry of French and European history. But this ancient treasure has ramifications that extend far beyond the borders of France.

The ancient treasure pillaged from the Temple of Jerusalem has a value far in excess of its material worth. The seven-branched candlestick, the menorah, and its other religious items have enormous symbolic value for all Jews, especially the Orthodox; their value exceeded only by that of the Ark of the Covenant itself. Should any of these items be found and made public, the effect on the Jewish communities in Jerusalem, and elsewhere, would be dramatic, almost certainly resulting in a call from the Orthodox to rebuild the great Temple of Herod from the ruins that can be seen today.

In fact, Rabbi Ariel Bar Tzadok, an expert in the Torah and cabalistic prophecy, reported in 1997 that a cornerstone for the future third temple had already been laid less than 50 metres from the mosque at the centre of the Temple Mount. According to Old Testament prophesy, the rebuilding of the Temple and the return of Jews to Israel will herald the return of the 'true' Messiah. There can be no doubt that many religious Jews are eagerly awaiting a 'divine' signal to commence this rebuilding.

Such a move would reopen one of the biggest wounds perceived and endured by the State of Israel, the presence of the Islamic shrine known as the Dome of the Rock constructed at the very heart of what was the ancient Jewish Temple. Erected in the seventh century, over the rock from which, according to Muslim tradition, Mohammed ascended into heaven, the resplendent golden Dome, one of the holiest Islamic shrines, is visited annually by millions of Muslims. It is inconceivable that the Muslim authorities would permit the removal of their precious and sacred mosque to facilitate the building of a new Temple of Jerusalem. Yet should Cardinal Lustiger be elected to the papal throne, it is tempting to speculate that this mission might receive the support of the Vatican, especially given recent moves to atone for its silence at the time of the Holocaust.

One can only speculate about the scale of the confrontation that would arise if the Jews assumed total access to all parts of the ruined Temple quarters and set about rebuilding. The already fragile and potentially explosive relations between the Muslims and the Jews would surely be pushed to breaking point with unthinkable consequences. Even compared with the impending conflict between the Catholic Church and Islam, a renewed and intensified conflict between the State of Israel and the nations of Islam would be nothing short of cataclysmic.

For the sake of maintaining the fragile status quo in Jerusalem, it would be better if the ancient treasure, lost those 1500 years ago in the foothills of the French Pyrenees, was never to be found, but remained in the realm of legend. Instead, a visitor to this mysterious region can sample the true richness of nature's savage beauty, by sitting on the wall in the sunshine, alongside the Abbé Saunière's tower, and gazing south towards the majesty of the Pyrenees.

APPENDIX

The Myth of the Gold · The Reality of War
The Role of the Swiss Banks

WE HOPE THAT our re-examination of this saga will have opened up some new lines of thought. Not surprisingly, much of the previous work in this field has made links between this 'treasure trail' and parallel agendas. We have attempted to steer clear of pursuing too many alternative agendas, working instead to strip away the disinformative veneers that may have coloured some previous thinking.

Particularly given my personal experience, however, there is one alternative agenda it may be worth examining in further detail. There is a published theory that the Germans did indeed find the treasure on which we have focused in the Corbières, either before or during the War. Were this to be true, it could be that they used it to resolve a few of their financial problems as the War ground on. If initially the treasure was prized by them for its intrinsic, symbolic value, it would have also have been an attraction latterly as a source of funding. The theory is glamorous, partly because of the wealth it would have brought to Germany, and partly because, as we have seen, it involves the panache of Skorzeny, the scholarly researches of Otto Rahn, and the buffoonery of Natt Wolff.

We cannot say conclusively that the Nazis uncovered the gold of the Jews, Templars or Cathars. We have suggested in our last chapter that it would probably be preferable that the treasure itself is left wherever it is, and that the legend lives on. But in some camps the enigma of how Germany financed the War also lives on – and it seems likely that there are quite a few vested interests that would prefer it to stay that way. It is intriguing to ponder whether the Corbières gold could have played a part in this, however. It is quite clear that vast amounts of money were going to be needed to sustain the German war-effort. It is equally clear that such funds did not exist in 1939. This leaves the frightening conundrum of how the Germans did in fact sustain a war that was far more expensive than anything they could have contemplated, and sustain it without any obvious signs of financial stress for a further six years. The only serious shortfalls during this time were manpower and petrol. Shortages of factory manpower were resolved by enslaving the occupied countries of the Reich, thereby freeing German labour for the armed forces. Shortage of petrol, which became very acute towards the end of the War, was not so much a financial stress as a practical one. Petrol had to be imported, and this presented practical difficulties as the Allied blockade began to bite.

The fundamental and perhaps unanswerable question – how did they finance it? – continues to niggle. Time-honoured methods of dealing with financial shortfalls, such as printing money, might have kept the troops happy; but it could not keep essential foreign suppliers happy, for whom hard currency was the only acceptable form of payment.

Under the Schacht strategy, one country at a time was conquered and absorbed into the Reich. Absorbing a country necessarily involved absorbing its treasury, bullion stocks and its entire economy: financial benefits that funded the next conquest. It was a neat strategy and initially it worked perfectly, just as Schacht had outlined in his report to Hitler in September 1934, *Report on the State of Work for War Economic Mobilisation as of September 30, 1934:* 'Thus our armaments are partially financed with the credits of our political enemies'. This strategy came unstuck with the loss of the Battle of Britain, the consequent turning east, and the inevitability of another war of attrition that Germany could neither afford nor win.

It is unlikely that Schacht had envisaged the extremes to which the Nazi Party would go to absorb the economy of conquered nations. As the financial future began to look progressively bleak, the looting of national treasuries and industry was joined by the wholesale looting of individuals. In Germany itself, Jews had long since been considered fair game for looting, and many took apparently prudent steps to protect their belongings, if not themselves. With the coming of the Final Solution, this looting degenerated into full-scale confiscation from all Jews within the Reich, living or dead – even gold teeth were extracted in concentration camps. In France and the other occupied countries, looting of treasures became the officially encouraged norm. Massive convoys returned to the German heartland with paintings and other treasures. Some of the paintings were inevitably diverted to the private collections of those like Goering, for whom they were trophies. Nazi taste- and trend-setters had already decreed that Impressionist paintings (like the music of Mendelssohn) were degenerate. Such paintings were immediately shipped off to Switzerland for sale and conversion into hard currency. As recently as September 1998, the High Court in London was formally advised that as many as 300,000 paintings stolen by the Nazis were still missing. This revelation surfaced during litigation concerning a single painting, currently valued at £700,000, which gives some idea of the sheer extent of this pillage.

Many of these treasures were re-pillaged by the advancing Russians. The collapse of the Soviet Union has revealed and highlighted this, and conflicting ownership claims will most probably keep the courts busy (and the lawyers rich) for years to come.

The pillage of countries overrun by the military is a reality that has been ruthlessly exercised throughout history by most warring nations. Indeed, the treasure of the Temple of Jerusalem, variously pillaged by the Romans, the Visigoths (and maybe the SS) is a prime example of 'to the winner, the spoils'. The sheer scale of the German exercise, and in so short a period of time is, however, unparalleled.

On a very different scale, British Intelligence approached many of the troops returning from Dunkirk, with offers to exchange any foreign currency at the standard rate, with no questions asked. Secrecy still clouds the amounts of foreign currency received in this way, but it is understood that it was sufficient to finance all the activities of Special Operation Executive in Europe throughout the War.

The distinction has been drawn between public and private assets, not because it affects the main saga, but because of the different treatments that have been accorded to both categories since the War. The common factor for both categories seems to be Switzerland (and to a much lesser extent the Vatican, Sweden and Portugal). The reticence of the Swiss has been a severe inhibition, complicating the critical question of just how much was involved in this massive laundering operation, and where it all came from. All that is known is that it sowed the seeds for Swiss banking prosperity for the next fifty years, and assisted Germany in sustaining a ferocious level of fighting, with superb equipment, right up to April 1945, until finally crushed by the military might of the Allied armed forces. This military defeat was in striking contrast to Germany's defeat at the end of World War I, caused primarily by bringing Germany to her knees through blockade.

Many excellent and well-researched books deal with the various aspects of organized wartime pillage. *Blood Money* by Tom Bower gives a first-class account of the tragic ebb and flow of the struggle by Jewish organizations since the War to get financial justice from the Swiss banks. *Hitler's Secret Bankers* by Adam Lebor gives an up-to-the-minute account of the shameful story of how the Swiss banks laundered vast quantities of Nazi loot, exchanging it for the hard currency that enabled

Germany to keep going. *Wall Street and the Rise of Hitler* by Antony Sutton gives a detailed account of the steps taken by Wall Street to finance Hitler's pre-war preparations. Apart from the profit motive, Wall Street no doubt saw these preparations (as did many others) as a lesser evil than the menace of advancing Communism.

There were signs as far back as 1944 that the Allies were already recognizing the enigmas surrounding Nazi Germany's income and expenditure. This awareness appears to have come more from the United States, where perceptions of what was going on in Europe were perhaps clearer and more objective than in blitzed Britain. American perplexity at how the Germans were financing it all were probably compounded by the financial realities they had been forced to face themselves when preparing to enter the War with the Allies. To those with any awareness of international finance, it would not have taken very long to identify the pivotal role being played by Switzerland. Considerations as to what choice Switzerland had had, other than to comply with German demands, only came later, by which time Swiss obduracy had lost her any sympathy there might otherwise have been for her wartime predicaments.

As it was, there was concern about the profits Switzerland (and the other neutrals) might have been making from the War, at the expense of its victims. At a moral level, such profiteering from the misery of others was unjust; at a practical level, the probability of German assets salted away safely in Switzerland was likely to impinge upon the feasibility and enforceability of post-war reparations. Operation Safehaven was instituted in 1944, with the purpose of ensuring that there was a full and proper accounting after the War of the transfers of loot into Switzerland. It was a pious objective, and it would have certainly answered many of the unanswered questions after the War, including the need for part of this book, had those objectives been realized.

Perhaps predictably, the Swiss purported to co-operate, but in fact stonewalled. Their attitude was that Reichsbank gold was Reichsbank gold and that as a neutral country they were not answerable to anybody. When it was pointed out to them what they already knew, namely that the transfers of Reichsbank gold had been staggeringly several hundred times the value of such gold legitimately held by Germany, the Swiss politely requested proof. Their attitude was that they had done nothing wrong, and had merely continued doing what they had always done: trading internationally, for profit.

Operation Safehaven amassed an enormous amount of information between 1944 and 1946, from which a large number of Swiss firms were blacklisted from dealing with American or British firms. It was not only gold that was being chased. We have already seen that paintings and other art treasures were regularly channelled into Switzerland. The same was true for less obvious commodities. There was particular interest in the Swiss Bally Shoe Company, which controlled most of the leather trade in Switzerland. The investigators found a mountain of leather in Switzerland, under Bally's control. Bally had imported vast amounts of leather, using Swiss-controlled intermediary companies. Most of it had in fact originated from Germany or had been looted from occupied countries. Payment had of course been made in hard currency and credits.

Operation Safehaven established that German Nazis, individuals or corporations had participated in no less than 358 Swiss companies. Their purpose was always the same; to assist in the laundering of booty, creating hard currency for the Nazis and profits for the Swiss. In 1945, a Swiss banker estimated that Swiss banks held about SFR 500 million in cash from Germany, and about the same again in gold and other valuables, and rather more in paintings and art. This Swiss estimate, if remotely close, places the value of German assets in Swiss banks at between SFR 1.7 billion and SFR 2.5 billion. Allowing once again for Swiss economies with figures, could this have been enough to back the financing of a six-year war? Unquestionably it could not.

If the above figures are seen as the 'capital account', much useful information was gleaned concerning the 'current account' from a former executive of the Reichsbank. When this executive Dr Landwehr was told that the Swiss had alleged that one billion Reichsmarks (SFR 1.75 billion approximately) had been transferred to Switzerland during the War, he was part staggered, part amused. As merely one executive in the Reichsbank, he had himself transferred fifteen billion Reichsmarks (SFR 26.25 billion) to Switzerland. These are serious figures, and they are getting closer to what must have been needed to wage such a financially expensive war.

It would appear that Switzerland had no intention, then or now, of revealing how much they had received from the Nazis, nor what they had paid for it (in the case of gold). It is fair to assume that the price would have been sharply discounted in the circumstances of the time, and that the profit that was generated was a significant factor in ensuring the manifest prosperity of Swiss banks for the next half-century.

The investigations of Operation Safehaven culminated in the so-called Washington Accord in 1946. With the defeat of Nazi Germany, the Allies insisted on their right of access to German assets, secreted in Switzerland. The Swiss disagreed, proclaiming their neutrality and the irrelevance to them of any further disputes between Germany and the Allies. They modified this stance when the Allies pointed out, quite firmly, that a return to peace in Europe, thanks to the Allies, was unquestionably in Switzerland's best interests.

The Washington Accord was a total disaster, and it reflected no credit on anyone. It was intended to free Swiss assets, frozen in the United States, against release of German assets blocked in Switzerland. The Swiss fell far short of their obligations under this Accord, no doubt aware that the Allies had by now little stomach for enforcing it, their attentions being refocused on the more pressing international problems of the Cold War. The matter then remained shamefully in abeyance for fifty years, during which time the Swiss were left to enjoy the fruits of their association with the Nazis. Even then, the matter would most probably have remained dormant had it not been for the ending of the Cold War, which ironically had been the prime factor in creating and sustaining that dormancy over that fifty-year period.

It is likely that the Allies' zeal in examining the Swiss bank situation in 1945/6 was also motivated by a fear that undisclosed Nazi assets might be used to finance a resurrection of German power – possibly of a Fourth Reich. This fear may well have dwindled in the months after the capitulation of Germany, once the full extent of her defeat and total destruction had been better assessed.

Further, it must not be forgotten that the crescendo of sabre-rattling from Moscow was sending a chill through the West. The wartime alliance with the Soviets had been triggered by the *volte face* by Hitler, when reneging on his former treaty with Moscow. But alliances based solely on such short-term self-interest are at best fragile, and it did not take long after May 1945 for the cracks to start appearing. The euphoria of harmonious victory was very short-lived, and the realities of the Iron Curtain were not long in coming. In the wake of these fears and concerns, the Swiss bank issue paled as the Cold War became the primary international concern.

In considering these realities, it is rather unnerving to realize that, having concluded the Washington Accord as a sovereign treaty obligation, the Swiss government was nevertheless able to relegate it to the 'sometime' tray. Other countries might have felt that, once concluded, there was an international obligation to stick to this Accord.

History will without question leave a heavy burden on the Swiss for their conduct during and after the War, as many eminent Swiss were ruefully conceding as the century drew to a close. One adage has it that the Swiss spent six days a week working with and for the Nazis, and the seventh day praying for an Allied victory. Alongside this of course, one must consider the major humanitarian activities of the Red Cross, and the number of Allied escapees who returned home via Switzerland. But as more and more evidence emerges, these start to pale into insignificance against the preferential mischief in which the Swiss so lucratively indulged, compounded by their refusal in later years to put matters right.

★   ★   ★

We should now turn to the second category of loot that found its way into Switzerland from Germany: that stolen from individuals, and particularly from the Jews. Raoul maintained to me that the gold he asked me to transport was the property of his family, which had become 'invisible' and therefore could not be banked through conventional channels. He was also quite paranoid about being identified as a wartime black marketeer, the usual presumption for unexplained wealth after the War. Raoul's family were far from being the only Jewish family to transfer out of Germany whatever assets they could. Many Jews in Germany in 1930 were only one generation away from the pogroms in Russia and Poland of 1905 and 1906, and they were well aware of the signs.

Similiar to Raoul's story was that of a Polish Jew, Velvel Singer, who had amassed a vast fortune from a sewing-machine refurbishment business. He had no connection with the Singer sewing-machine family, but the coincidence of names was a confusion that did his business no harm. He had prudently salted away a considerable sum in Switzerland before the Nazis marched into Poland, when everything was confiscated and he was incarcerated in the Lodz ghetto. This ghetto was a highly successful commercial undertaking for the Nazis, so much so that they permitted it to continue until 1944 because of the profits it generated for them ($140 million in 1943 alone). Tragically, Singer disappeared into Auschwitz at the end of that year, so close to the end of the War; those of his family who escaped to Canada have been pursuing the Swiss for reimbursement of the funds they knew to have been deposited in his account, but of which there was no sign at the end of the War.

In Germany and other conquered territories, the assets of all Jews were confiscated, and there are horrifying stories of organized torture squads, picking on affluent Jews to persuade them to reveal the whereabouts of assets elsewhere.

In the years after the War, Swiss banks were confronted with a stream of Holocaust survivors, seeking the fortunes lodged there by their murdered parents. In nearly all cases, the Swiss politely declined to recognize them or their demands, even sometimes requesting the death certificates of their deceased parents. A concerted crusade against the Swiss might have yielded results, at a time when the Allies were riding on the high of victory that could have mellowed Swiss intransigence. This would at least have given a degree of material comfort to the remaining years of those who had survived the Nazi hell. As it was, most of these survivors died in abject poverty, a tragedy that can never be undone, but which should never be forgotten.

It is ironic that the bank secrecy laws in Switzerland, on which the Swiss counted when refusing reimbursement to the claimants, had originally been instituted to attract the Jewish deposits in the first place. And these laws were applied equally to both Jewish claimants and to the Allies, when seeking out German deposits for legitimate seizure after the War. It must seem likely from this saga that some of the treasure buried for 1500 years in the Corbières may now be buried under the pavements of Zurich, Geneva, and Lausanne. It is unlikely that the Swiss will ever tell us; it is even less likely that anybody will believe them if they do.

The other factor that has enabled this stalemate to persist for fifty years was the Cold War. This has had a dual effect: firstly, of diverting elsewhere the attentions of the former Allies who might have had the necessary clout to do something about it prior to 1946; and secondly, by trapping the vast majority of

Holocaust survivors behind the Iron Curtain, unable to pursue their claims. It was only after the break-up of the Soviet Union that those Holocaust survivors and their families were able to start to seek out the fortunes that their parents and grandparents had deposited for them in Switzerland.

Estimates of the sums involved cover a pretty broad spectrum. The lowest total figure suggested by the Swiss for amounts held in 'dormant accounts' was $20,000. The highest figure we have come across (not suggested by the Swiss) was $30 billion. In 1962, the figure was encapsulated in a Swiss law at SFR 9.5 million, and by 1973 about three-quarters of that amount had been paid out to claimants, the remainder being distributed to various Jewish organizations. It was never suggested by the Swiss how their own estimates grew from $20,000 to SFR 9.5 million – and nobody with any knowledge or experience of the meticulous Swiss and their meticulous bookkeeping would suggest that there could have been mere oversights.

Under enormous pressure from Edgar Bronfman and the World Jewish Congress, and Senator Alphonse D'Amato, Chairman of the US Senate Banking Committee, the Swiss Bankers Association (which speaks for all Swiss banks) suddenly located a further SFR 38.74 million in 775 dormant accounts. This had apparently slipped their notice in 1962. Later still, there came a 'full and final' offer of $100 million, the designated currency maybe suggesting where the pressure had come from. In August 1998, just two Swiss banks, Credit Suisse and UBS (which had recently absorbed the third giant Swiss Bank Corporation) made an offer in excess of $1 billion. Here was escalation indeed! While this advance from the original $20,000 was welcome to the beneficiaries, the prospect of shooting for the highest estimate was not likely to daunt Edgar Bronfman or Senator D'Amato, for whom this had also become a popular electoral crusade in his largely Jewish New York constituency. One of his aides has affirmed that to D'Amato this is a moral crusade.

Many Swiss citizens are of course also among the first to

condemn the ethics of their own banks and bankers, and there have been many well-reported instances of this. The sheer scale of the campaign by the World Jewish Congress and the US Senate Banking Committee has also been such that repercussions within Switzerland were inevitable. Like the rest of the world, Switzerland has come to feel recession; unlike the rest of the world, this is something the Swiss are not used to. In the search for scapegoats, some Swiss have seen the well-supported resurrection of so many claimants against their banks as nothing less than a witchhunt. The Swiss Press has reported a big rise in anti-Americanism during 1997/98, and there is a rising antipathy against the Jews, whom some Swiss see as having ruthlessly and unjustly exploited even the most minute revelations as bait for worldwide hungry media coverage.

* * *

Endeavouring to trace the movement over some 2000 years of what is probably the greatest treasure the world has ever seen, has been an extraordinary exercise, and remarkable in the way that the patterns and enigmas of history shed light on, and have parallels in, the wartime and contemporary issues raised here. We cannot firmly state that all or part of the ancient treasure has found its way to Switzerland, either in its original or refined form, but such is the nature of the secret Swiss banking network, and the track record of those involved in trying to unearth the gold, that it seems highly likely that some of it has found its way there. Despite the claims of the Priory of Sion, the ownership of this treasure is also at best uncertain. Its provenance is diverse. Yet there can be no justification for Swiss banks continuing to hold it, nor of declining to deny that they are holding any of it.

However, it does not seem impossible that somebody in Switzerland knows part of the answer to our final riddles – just as somebody in France likewise knows the other part.

Robin Mackness

Chronology

  70 Sack of Jerusalem by the Romans – pillage and removal
      to Rome of the sacred Jewish treasure from the Temple
      of Jerusalem.

410 Sack of Rome and the looting of the Roman treasury by
      Alaric the Visigoth.
      Migration of Visigoths to Spain and the Languedoc with
      centres at Toulouse, Carcassonne, Rhedae and Toledo.
      Visigoths' adherence to Arian heresy condemned by
      Church of Rome.
      Franks cross the Rhine and enter Gaul – founding of the
      Merovingian dynasty of Frankish kings.

496 Merovingian king, Clovis, nominally baptized into
      Roman Catholic faith.

507 Defeat of Visigoths by Clovis – Visigoths forced from
      Toulouse to Carcassonne and thence to their fortress
      at Rhedae (now the village of Rennes-le-Château) in
      the Corbières region of the Languedoc. Treasure hidden
      for safekeeping in the ancient mines and caves in the
      area.

632 Death of Mohammed, founder of Islam.

674 Frankish Dagobert II, married to the Visigothic princess,

Gizelle de Razès, becomes King of Austrasia (north-eastern France).

679   Dagobert is assassinated at the instigation of his prime minister; his son, Sigisbert, aged two, is taken secretly to his mother's family at Rennes-le-Château, and later becomes Comte de Razès, Lord of Rennes. Franks now effectively ruled by the embryonic Carolingian dynasty with the approval and support of the Catholic Church.

711   Islamic Berbers enter southern Spain and rapidly expand northwards over the Pyrenees until forced back by the Franks.

800   The Carolingian monarch, Charlemagne, is crowned Holy Roman Emperor.

1095   Pope Urban preaches the First Crusade.

1099   'Liberation' of Jerusalem by the Crusaders.

1118   Founding of the Order of the Knights Templar who are granted the use of the Al Aksa mosque, formerly the Temple of Jerusalem, as their headquarters. Nine years of secret excavations beneath the Temple Mount.
Rapid expansion in the membership and wealth of the Order throughout Europe, especially in the South of France, and the development of an elementary banking system.

1209   Launch of the 'Albigensian Crusade' against the so-called heretical Cathars by Knights and soldiers from northern Europe motivated by the legendary wealth of the region.

1244   The fall of the castle at Montségur, refuge of Cathars and the massacre of 200 Cathars. Cathar treasure smuggled to safety before the fall of the castle.

1291   Fall of the Holy Land to Islam and the expulsion of the Knights. Templars form alliance with James, King of Majorca, to establish a sovereign independent state that would include the Languedoc and its hidden treasure deposits.

1305   Election of the Archbishop of Bordeaux as Pope Clement V; the papacy transferred to Avignon under the control of French king, Philip IV.

1307   Philip issues arrest warrants against all Knights Templars
       alleging heretical practices but in reality to gain control
       of their wealth and the lands containing the treasure.

1314   Death of the last Grand Master of the Templars, Jacques
       de Molay, and the suppression of the Order.

1340   Counterfeiting of gold coins at the former Templar
       commandery at Bézu, near Rennes-le-Château.

Fifteenth and sixteenth centuries – Power and influence of
Rennes-le-Château and the Corbières declines; legends and
local traditions persist, perpetuating belief in the existence of a
fabulous hidden treasure including that of the Temple of
Jerusalem. Firm information relating to the treasure obscure,
and knowledge of exact locations presumed lost.

1732   Marriage of Marie de Negrè d' Ables to François
       d'Hautpoul, first Marquis de Blanchefort and descendant
       of the ancient Lords of Rennes.

1781   Death of Marie de Negrè. Hautpoul archives confided
       to the family chaplain and priest of Rennes-le-Château,
       Abbé Bigou.

1785   Captain Dagobert, descendant of the Merovingian king,
       Dagobert II, obtains permission to reopen the ancient
       mines of the Corbières and to establish a forge. Great
       secrecy surrounds his mining activities.

1788   Abbé Bigou, sensing the forthcoming revolution, hides
       the Hautpoul archives in the crypt of his church at
       Rennes-le-Château. Concealing the entrance to the
       crypt, he leaves a clue in a wooden post near the pulpit.

1789   The French Revolution resulting in the overthrow of
       the Monarchy, the dispossession of the aristocracy and
       the suppression of the Catholic Church.

1790   Captain Dagobert, having no heirs, confides his archives
       concerning the mines and their contents to his Masonic
       brothers of the Grand Orient Freemasonry.

1794   Now promoted to General, Dagobert dies mysteriously,

possibly poisoned during the Peninsular War between the French Revolutionary army and the Spanish Bourbon king. Another General and Freemason, the Marquis de Chefdebien, conspires to acquire the Dagobert archives.

1798   Napoleon embarks on his Egyptian campaign accompanied by members of the Hautpoul and Chefdebien families and others steeped in Scottish Rite Freemasonry.

1799   Napoleon leaves Egypt to return to Paris and takes power in France, establishing a military dictatorship.

1801   Catholic religion recovers some power in France.

1870   First attempt by East European Jews to create Zionism, for the promotion of a national homeland, supported by the Rothschild family.

1885   Bérenger Saunière becomes priest of Rennes-le-Château and employs Marie Dénarnaud as his housekeeper, and later becomes his life-long confidante.

1891   During the renovation of his church, Saunière discovers the Hautpoul archives hiden by the Abbé Bigou.

His brother Alfred, a Jesuit priest, is dismissed from the household of the Marquis de Chefdebien at Narbonne for rifling through their archives.

Over the next twenty years, Saunière spends a huge sum of money, largely unaccounted for, on building projects, entertaining and other activities. Despite later pressure from his new bishop he steadfastly refuses to account for the source of his income.

Involvement with Martinists and other neo-Masonic secret societies at a time of proliferation of secret occult societies, pro- and anti-Republican.

1905   Anti-Semitic *Protocols of the Elders of Sion* published at the Russian Court.

1914   Outbreak of World War I.

1917   Death of Bérenger Saunière. His archives confided to his personal physician, Dr Paul Courrent. Marie Dénarnaud continues to live in Saunière's domain.

1918   End of World War I. Change in the balance of European powers, Russian Revolution and the emergence of anti-clerical Communism. Catholic Church faces suppression throughout most of Eastern Europe.

1919   Formation of the anti-Semitic and anti-Communist German Workers Party, dedicated to racial superiority and German nationalism.

1920   Name changed to National Socialist Party – NAZI – Adolf Hitler playing an increasingly influential role.

Mid 1920s – Social unrest and financial depression in Europe. Low national morale in Germany allowed the Nazi Party to come to power with Hitler elected Chancellor.

1928   Founding of Opus Dei and ultra right-wing Catholic organization.

1929   Dr Courrent retires to Embres-et-Castel, near the ancient mines of General Dagobert. Saunière/Hautpoul archives kept in his library.

1933   Nazi SS Major Otto Rahn sent to the Corbières to search for the legendary Cathar treasure.

1936   Natt Wolf (possibly an SS General) and a British Intelligence Officer, Major Walter Birks, arrive in the region of Montségur.

1939   Mysterious accidental death of Otto Rahn.
         Outbreak of World War II following German invasion of Poland.
         The Marquis de Chefdebien entrusts his family archives, acquired from General Dagobert in 1794, to an archaeological/historical society in Narbonne, which then passes them on to their most erudite member, Dr Paul Courrent, for further study.

1940   François Mitterrand works for Marshal Pétain's Vichy government.

1942   Pierre Plantard emerges as a prominent member of the pro-Vichy chivalric society, 'Alpha Galates'.

1944   Massacre and destruction of Oradour-sur-Glane by SS
        Division Das Reich under the command of General
        Lammerding. 600 kilos of gold bullion apparently
        hijacked from the Nazis by résistants. Roger-René
        Dagobert observes the passage of SS troops through
        Limoges.

1946   Saunière's estate bought by entrepreneur, Noel Corbu,
        from Marie Dénarnaud, who is allowed to remain at the
        villa with the family. Marie frequently refers to a huge
        treasure at Rennes and promises to reveal details before
        her death.

1952   Dr Courrent dies and his archives disappear.
        Plantard claims to have transferred a large quantity of
        gold from France into a Swiss bank.
        Formation of the secret Order of the Solar Temple at
        Arginy.

1953   Marie Dénarnaud dies without revealing the source of
        Saunière's wealth.

1954   First meeting of the secretive political Bilderberg Group
        at the Hotel de Bilderberg, Oosterbeek, Holland.
        Alleged connection to world conspiratorial politics.

1955   Demand for recognition of Merovingian rights made in
        an article in London's *Daily Express*.

1956   Plantard and colleagues deposit statutes of an enigmatic
        society, Priory of Sion, at Annemasse.
        Series of three articles on Saunière's treasure appears in
        a newspaper run by René Bousquet, a former Vichy
        colleague of François Mitterrand.
        Attempt made by Lord Selborne and others, formerly of
        Britain's SOE, to export supposed Saunière parchments
        to England.

1957   Political turmoil in France caused by the Algerian crisis.
        Treaty of Rome formalizes the EEC.

1958   Charles de Gaulle made Prime Minister and, shortly
        after, President of the Fifth Republic.
        Plantard alleged to have played a key role within the

secret 'Committees of Public Safety' that brought de Gaulle to power.

The liberal Cardinal Roncalli elected Pope John XXIII.

1962   Roger-René Dagobert discovers a startling version of events concerning Oradour and the missing gold.

1964   Noel Corbu sells the Abbé Saunière's domain to Henri Buthion.

1965   Julien Origas, a French ex-Nazi, joins the Order of the Solar Temple. All excavations in and around Rennes-le-Château formally prohibited.

Mitterrand given support by René Bousquet, controller of the newspaper *La Dépêche du Midi*, during his election contest against de Gaulle.

1967   Plantard purchases parcels of land around Rennes-le-Château and Rennes-les-Bains near the ancient Blanchefort goldmines.

1968   Noel Corbu dies in a car crash on the road between Castelnaudary and Carcassonne. Less than a month later Abbé Boyer, a keen Rennes investigator, narrowly escapes the same fate.

Robert Charroux's unsuccessful attempt to locate treasure at Rennes-le-Château using metal detectors.

1972   Origas elected Grand Master of the Solar Temple, which now becomes part of a European-wide fascist underground.

1975   Britain's referrendum for entry into the EEC.

1976   Four Israeli 'researchers/archaeologists' visit Rennes-le-Château and region. They return in 1977 and 1978.

1978   Pope John-Paul I elected but dies mysteriously three months later, having initiated an investigation into the Vatican finances.

Exposure of neo-Masonic anti-Communist lodge P2 in Italy and its links with the Vatican bank and organized crime.

Election of Polish cardinal, Karol Wojtyla, as Pope John-Paul II.

1981   First of the sightings of the Virgin Mary at Medjugorje in Croatia. From 1990, area to be exploited for the financial support of the Catholic Croatian army.

François Mitterrand elected President of France; election address made from Saunière's Tour Magdala at Rennes-le-Château.

Plantard elected Grand Master of the Priory of Sion.

1982   Robin Mackness arrested and imprisoned, having been charged with attempting to smuggle gold bars from France to Switzerland.

1984   Robin Mackness released after twenty-one months in prison.

1988   Publication of *Oradour: Massacre and Aftermath* by Robin Mackness. Ensuing controversy in France.

1989   Communist Party in Poland defeated in the first free elections since World War II, presaging the collapse of Communism in Eastern Europe.

Fall of the Berlin Wall.

1990   Opus Dei attains powerful influence in the Vatican.

Catholic Slovenia and Croatia declare independence.

The resulting war leads to old Serbian/Croatian scores being settled and open aggression against Islamic communities.

1993   Assassination of René Bousquet two days before his trial for war crimes.

Muslim fundamentalists murder twelve Croatian engineers in Algeria.

1994   Suspicious deaths of sixty-nine members of the Solar Temple in Canada, France, and Switzerland.

1996   Death of President François Mitterrand.

1999   Resignation of Roland Dumas, President of the Constitutional Council, for corruption. His father was shot by the Germans; it is claimed that he was involved in the theft of gold from the SS at Limoges in 1944.

Sources and Bibliography

Chapter 1

M. Baigent and R. Leigh, *The Dead Sea Scrolls Deception* (London, Jonathan Cape, 1991)

M. Baigent, R. Leigh and H. Lincoln, *The Holy Blood and the Holy Grail* (London, Jonathan Cape, 1982)
The Messianic Legacy (London, Jonathan Cape, 1986)

Claire Corbu and Antoine Captier, *L'Héritage de l'Abbé Saunière* (France, Belisane, 1995)

Encyclopaedia Brittanica

Graham Hancock, *The Sign and the Seal* (London, William Heinemann, 1992)

Christopher Knight and Robert Lomas, *The Hiram Key* (London, Century, 1996)

The Masonic History Company, The Bible – *Masonic Edition* (Chicago, Illinois, W.M. Collins Sons and Co. Ltd., 1947)

Colin McEvedy, *Penguin Atlas of Medieval History* (London, Penguin, 1961)

Alan Millard, *Discoveries from the Time of Jesus* (Great Britain, Lion Publishing, 1990)

Gérard de Sède, *L'Or de Rennes* (Paris, Julliard–Tallandier, 1967)

Chapter 2

Baigent, Leigh and Lincoln, *The Holy Blood and the Holy Grail*
The Messianic Legacy

Dictionary of British Kings and Queens (London, Brockhampton Press, 1995)

Cep d'Or de Pyla, *Lumières Nouvelles sur Rennes-le-Château* (Chene-Bourg, Suisse, Éditions Aquarius, 1995)

Gérard de Sède, *Rennes-le-Château – Le Dossier, les Impostures, les Phantasmes, les Hypothéses* (Paris, Éditions Robert Laffont, 1988)

Margaret Starbird, *The Woman with the Alabaster Jar* (Santa Fe, New Mexico, Bear & Co., 1993)

Ian Wilson, *Jesus: The Evidence* (London, Weidenfeld & Nicolson, 1984)

Prof. Arthur Zuckerman, *A Jewish Princedom in Feudal France* (New York, Columbia University Press, 1972)

Chapter 3

Baigent, Leigh and Lincoln, *The Holy Blood and the Holy Grail*

Richard Barber, *The Knight and Chivalry*, revised edn (New York, Boydell & Brewer, 1995)

Edward Burman, *The Templars, Knights of God* (London, Crucible, 1986)

Louis Fedié, *Le Comté de Razès*, reprint from an 1880 original (Carcassonne, France, Lajoux Fréres, 1979)

Frances Gies, *The Knight in History* (London, HarperCollins, 1987)

L'Histoire Générale de Languedoc, tome 3 (France, Benedictine Monks of St Maur, 1742)

Knight and Lomas, *The Hiram Key*

Franck Marie, *Alet-les-Bains – Les Portes du Temps* (Alet-les-Bains, France, 1984)

Abbé M.R. Maziéres, *Les Templiers du Bézu* (Rennes-le-Château, France, Philippe Schrauben, 1957–9)

Desmond Seward, *The Monks of War* (London, Eyre Methuen, 1974)

Chapter 4

M. Baigent and R. Leigh, *The Elixir and the Stone* (London, Viking, 1997)

W. Birks and R. Gilbert, *The Treasure of Montségur* (London, Crucible, 1987)

Wolfram von Eschenbach, *Parzival*, André Lefebre (ed.) (New York, Continuum, 1991)

Richard Fletcher, *Moorish Spain* (London, Weidenfeld & Nicolson, 1992)

Leonard George, *Encyclopedia of Heresies and Heretics* (London, Robson Books, 1995)

Tania Kletzky-Pradere, *Visitors' Guide to Rennes-le-Château* (France, Bardou Editor, 1985)

Prof. Bernard Lewis, *The Assassins* (Oxford University Press, 1987)

Zoe Oldenburg, *Massacre at Montségur* (London, Weidenfeld & Nicolson, 1997)

Peter de Rosa, *Vicars of Christ – The Dark Side of the Papacy* (London, Bantam Press, 1988)

Andrew Sanger, *Languedoc and Roussillon* (London, Christopher Helm, 1989)

Georges Serrus, *The Land of the Cathars* (Portet-sur-Garonne, France, Editions Loubatières, 1990)

Chapter 5

Baigent, Leigh and Lincoln, *The Holy Blood and the Holy Grail*

Roger-René Dagobert, *Le Roi Dagobert* (Nantes, Cercle Générale Dagobert, 1996)

L. and P. Fanthorpe, *Rennes-le-Château* (Ashford, Middlesex, Bellevue Books, 1991)

Patrick Ferté, *Arsène Lupin – Supérieur Inconnu* (Paris, Guy Trédaniel, 1992)

R. le Forestier, *Franc-Maconnerie, Templière et Occultiste* (Paris, Éditions du CNRS, 1970)

Robert Gildea, *Barricades and Borders, Europe 1800–1914* (Oxford University Press, 1987)

Alistair Horne, *Napoleon – Master of Europe* (London, Weidenfeld & Nicolson, 1979)

Michel Lamy, *Jules Vernes – Initié et Initiateur* (Paris, Payot, 1984)

Philip Mansel, *The Court of France, 1789–1830* (Cambridge University Press, 1988)

The Occult (Edinburgh, Chambers, 1991)

J.M. Roberts, *The Mythologies of Secret Societies* (London, Secker & Warburg, 1972)

Chapter 6

Elizabeth van Buren, *Refuge of the Apocalypse* (Suffolk, Neville Spearman, 1986)

Corbu and Captier, *L'Héritage de l'Abbé Saunière*

Jacques Rivière, *Le Fabuleux Trésor de Rennes-le-Château* (Cazilhac, France, Belisane, 1995)

Gay Roberts, *Mystery of Rennes-le-Château – A Concise Guide* (Llanidloes, Wales, self-published, 1995)

Chapter 7

Baigent, Leigh and Lincoln, *The Messianic Legacy*

Jean-Marie Barette, *The Prophesy of the Apostles of the Later Times* (Quebec, Éditions Magnificat, 1998)

Corbu and Captier, *L'Héritage de l'Abbé Saunière*

J. Deloux and J. Brétigny, *Rennes-le-Château: Capitale Secrète et l'Histoire de France* (Paris, Éditions Atlas, 1982)

André Douzet, *Lumières Nouvelles sur Rennes-le-Château* (Geneva, Éditions Aquarius, 1995)

Michael Howard, *The Occult Conspiracy* (Rochester, Vermont, Destiny Books, 1989)

Matthieu, *Les Dessous d'une Ambition Politique* (Nyon, France, Éditeurs Associés, 1973)

Paul Naudon, *Freemasonry – A European Viewpoint*, translated from the French by Joseph Tang (Great Britain, Freestone Press, 1993)

The Occult (Chambers)

Roger Price, *A Concise History of France* (Cambridge University Press, 1993)

De Sède, *L'Or de Rennes*

James Webb, *The Flight from Reason – Sects of the Late Seventeenth Century* (London, Macdonald & Co. Ltd, 1971)

World History (New Lanark, Scotland, Geddes & Grosset Ltd., 1996)

Chapter 8

David S. Ariel, *What Do Jews Believe?* (New York, Random House, 1995)

Neal Ascheron, *Black Sea* (London, Jonathan Cape, 1995)

Baigent, Leigh and Lincoln, *The Holy Blood and the Holy Grail*

Birks and Gilbert, *The Treasure of Montségur*

Gildea, *Barricades and Borders, Europe 1800–1914*

Joscleyn Godwin, *Arktos: The Polar Myth* (London, Thames & Hudson, 1993)

Howard, *The Occult Conspiracy*

David Icke, *Robots' Rebellion* (Bath, Gateway Books, 1994)

Dr Steve Jones, *In the Blood – God, Genes and Destiny* (London, HarperCollins, 1996)

Lt Col A.H. Lane, *Alien Menace – A Statement of the Case* (London, Boswell Publishing Co. Ltd., 1932)

D.A. Martin, 'Zionist Truths', *On Target* magazine, vol.26

The Occult (Chambers)

Isidore Singer (ed.), *Jewish Encyclopaedia*, 12 vols (New York, KTVA Publishing House, 1925)

World History (Geddes & Grosset)

Chapter 9

Ian and Dieke Begg, *In Search of the Holy Grail and the Precious Blood* (London, Thorson, 1995)

Christian Bernadac, *Le Mystère Otto Rahn – Du Catharisme au Nazisme* (Paris, Éditions France-Empire, 1978)

Birks and Gilbert, *The Treasure of Montségur*

Col Howard Buechner, *Emerald Cup – Ark of Gold* (Los Angeles, Thunderbird Press, 1991)

Carlo D'Este, *A Genius for War – A Life of General George S. Patton* (London, HarperCollins, 1995)

Nigel Graddon, *Otto Rahn – Argonaut or Dupe?* (Penarth, Wales, self-published, 1998)

'The Footprints of Otto Rahn', *Rennes Observer*, March 1998

Hans Jurgen-Lange, *Otto Rahn – Leben und Werk* (Engerda, Germany, Arun-Verlag, 1997)

Otto Rahn, *The Crusade Against the Grail*, translation from the French (Paris, Stock, 1933)

Lucifer's Court, translation from the French (Puiseaux, France, Pardes, 1994)

Gerald Reitlinger, *The SS – Alibi of a Nation, 1922–1945* (London, Arms & Armour Press, 1981)

Ian Sayer and Douglas Botting, *Nazi Gold* (London, Granada, 1984)

Otto Skorzeny, *Skorzeny's Special Mission – Memories of the Most Dangerous Man in Europe* (London, Greenhill Books, 1997)

William Stevenson, *The Bormann Brotherhood* (Great Britain, Arthur Baker Ltd., 1973)

Chapter 10

Christopher Culpin, *Making History – World History From 1914 to the Present Day* (London, Collins, 1984)

Robert Gildea, *France, Since 1945* (Oxford University Press, 1997)

John Hellman, *The Knight-Monks of Vichy France, Uriage 1940–1945*, 2nd edn (Liverpool University Press, 1997)

Howard, *The Occult Conspiracy*

Herbert L. Lottman, *Pétain, Hero or Traitor?* (London, Viking, 1985)

Peter Partner, *The Murdered Magicians – The Templars and Their Myths* (Oxford University Press, 1982)

Price, *A Concise History of France*

Paul Webster, *Pétain's Crime* (London, Macmillan, 1990)

World History (Geddes & Grosset)

Chapter 11

Baigent, Leigh and Lincoln, *The Messianic Legacy*

Nicolas Bonnal, *Mitterrand – Le Grand Initié* (Clamecy, France, Claire Vigne Editrice, 1996)

Martin Gilbert, *The Day the War Ended* (London, HarperCollins, 1995)

Gildea, *France, Since 1945*

Pierre Jarnac, *Les Archives de Rennes-le-Château*, 2 vols (Nice, Éditions Belisane, 1987)

John Laughland, *The Death of Politics: France under Mitterrand* (London, Michael Joseph, 1994)

Price, *A Concise History of France*

Jean Robin, *Rennes-le-Château – La Colline Envoûtée* (Paris, Guy Tredaniel, 1982)

    Opération Orth – L'Incroyable Secret de Rennes-le-Château (Paris, Éditions de la Maisnie, 1989)

Louis L. Snyder, *Hitler's German Enemies* (London, Robert Hale, 1991)

Vaincre Journal, 6 issues held in the Bibliothèque Nationale, Paris, published in 1942

Chapter 12

Baigent, Leigh and Lincoln, *The Holy Blood and the Holy Grail*
    The Messianic Legacy

Jean-Luc Chaumeil, *Table d'Isis* (Paris, Guy Tredaniel, Paris)

Corbu and Captier, *L'Héritage de l'Abbé Saunière*

Deloux and Brétigny, *Rennes-le-Château: Capitale Secrète et l'Histoire de France*

R. Descadeillas, *Mythologie du Trésor de Rennes* (Carcassonne, France, self-published, 1974)

Pierre Jarnac, *L'Histoire du Trésor de Rennes-le-Château* (Cabestany, France, L'Association pour le développement de la lecture, 1985)
Les Archives de Rennes-le-Château

Jean Markale, *Rennes-le-Château et l'Énigme de l'Or* (France, Les Éditions Pygmalion/Gérard Watelet, 1989)

Paoli, *Les Dessous d'une Ambition Politique*

L. Picknett and C. Prince, *Templar Revelation* (London, Bantam Press, 1997)

Price, *A Concise History of France*

Robin, *Rennes-le-Château – La Colline Envoutée*
Opération Orth – L'Incroyable Secret de Rennes-le-Château

De Sède, *L'Or de Rennes*

Webb, *The Flight from Reason – Sects of the Late Seventeenth Century*

Researches of C.M. Scargill, BA (Hons) MA

Chapter 13

Capitaine Paul Barril, *Guerres Secrètes à l'Elysée* (Paris, Éditions Albin Michel, S.A., 1996)

Georges Beau, *Les SS en Limousin, Quercy et Perigord* (Paris, Presses de la Cité, 1969)

Buechner, *Emerald Cup – Ark of Gold*

Jean-Edern Hallier, *Les Puissance du mal* (Monaco, Éditions du Rocher, 1996)

Robert Hébras, *Oradour-sur-Glane – Le Drame, Heure par Heure* (Montreuil-Bellay, Éditions CMD, 1992)

Laughland, *The Death of Politics: France under Mitterand*

Robin Mackness, *Oradour: Massacre and Aftermath* (London, Bloomsbury, 1988)

Webster, *Pétain's Crime*

Le Monde, 18 June 1998

Minute, 22 September 1993

Minute, 25 September 1996

Chapter 14

Baigent, Leigh and Lincoln, *The Messianic Legacy*

Jean-Pierre Bayard, *Le Guide des Societes Secrètes* (France, Philippe Lebaud)

André Douzet, *The Treasure Trove of the Knights Templar*, edited and translated by Filip Coppens (self-published, 1997)

David Guyatt, *Opération Gladio*, reprinted with permission on www.copi.com

Howard, *The Occult Conspiracy*

Robert Hutchinson, *Their Kingdom Come – Inside the World of Opus Dei* (London, Doubleday, 1997)

Alistair Mitchell (ed.), *Secret Lives*, Channel 4 documentary, broadcast 29 December 1997

Naudon, *Freemasonry – A European Viewpoint*

Peronnik, *Pourquoi la Resurgence de l'Ordre du Temple?* (Monte Carlo, Éditions de la Pensée, 1975)

Clive Prince, *Investigation into the Order of the Solar Temple* (London, self-published report, 1997)

Arthur E. Rowse, *Gladio – The Secret US War to Subvert Italian Democracy* (www.worldmedia.com/caq/articles/gladio.html, 1998)

David Yallop, *In God's Name* (London, Poetic Products Ltd., 1984)

Archives of Roger-René Dagobert

Chapter 15

David Grewar, 'The Fiery Cross', *Scottish Notes and Queries*, vol.IX, 3rd series, 1934

Howard, *The Occult Conspiracy*

Hutchinson, *Their Kingdom Come – Inside the World of Opus Dei*

De Rosa, *Vicars of Christ – The Dark Side of the Papacy*

Damian Thompson, *The End of Time – Faith and Fear in the Shadow of the Millennium* (London, Sinclair-Stevenson, 1996)

Wyn Craig Wade, *The Fiery Cross – The Ku Klux Klan in America*, (New York, Simon & Schuster, 1987)

Yallop, *In God's Name*

'Scandal of Medjugorje', Channel 4 documentary, produced by Stephen Bailey, broadcast 20 November 1997

Evening Times, Glasgow, 22 July 1986

Mail on Sunday, 18 August 1996

Chapter 16

Ariel, *What Do Jews Believe?*

Tom Bower, *Blood Money* (London, Pan, 1997)

Olivier Dard, *Les Synarchies – Le Mythe du Complot Permanent* (Paris, Librairie Académique Perrin, 1998)

John Hogue, *The Last Pope* (Dorset, Element, 1998)

Bruce Johnston, 'How Nazi gold scandal taints the Vatican', *Sunday Telegraph*, 27 July 1997

Peter Lorie, *Nostradamus – The Millennium and Beyond* (London, Bloomsbury, 1994)

Partner, *The Murdered Magicians – The Templars and Their Myths*

Georges Passelecq and Bernard Suchecky, *The Hidden Encyclical of Pius* (USA, Harcourt Brace, 1997)

Laurence Rees, 'Banking with Hitler', *Timewatch*, BBC2 documentary, broadcast 1998

Stevenson, *The Bormann Brotherhood*

Prof. Antony C. Sutton, *Wall Street and the Rise of Hitler* (Suffolk, Bloomfield Books, 1976)

Index